Beyond Our Vision

The Journey of a Married Priest

by Michael O'Kane

Tomiko
PUBLICATIONS

Ottawa, 2003

National Library of Canada Cataloguing in Publication

O'Kane, Michael, 1928-

    Beyond our vision : the journey of a married priest / Michael
    O'Kane.

ISBN 0-9692787-6-4

    1. O'Kane, Michael, 1928-. 2. Missionaries – Brazil – Biography.
3. Catholic Church – Clergy – Biography. 4. Catholic Church – Missions
– Brazil – Amazon River Region. 5. Catholic Church – Latin America.
I. Title.

BV2853.B7O53 2003   266'.2'092   C2003-905995-2

To order copies:
    Tomiko Publications
    P.O. Box 39103
    R.P.O. Billings Bridge
    Ottawa, ON K1H 1A1

    Website: www.BeyondOurVision.com

Book design: Greg J. Humbert

Dedicated to
the memory of Jorge Marskell, bishop and friend,
and to the People of God with whom he journeyed
in the Prelacy of Itacoatiara, Amazonas, Brazil

CONTENTS

☙☙

Illustrations

INTRODUCTION
The Other Side

I write these pages in honour of all the 'People of God' who continue to this day, in their small communities of belief, seeking justice and equality. They do so with a hope and faith that inspires me, a pilgrim from a world that prizes more the values of individualism and materialism.

My story is intrinsically woven with the Gospel, and how this Gospel intersects with the conflicting worlds of faith and politics. My story shares how the poor in Latin America changed me, and how the institutional structures of the church and our political systems have failed them.

The world we live in thrives on instant communication. Radio, television, newspapers, and the internet provide people in the most remote corners of the globe instant access to events and information on almost any subject. In the not too distant past, in the tiny isolated villages that dotted the rivers and lakes of the Amazon basin in Brazil, it was much different. Life and its varied experiences were transmitted through the art of storytelling. Night school for the community, especially the young, consisted of sitting and listening to the elders tell their stories. And when a traveler from 'away' visited the community, it was a very special time for all the villagers to learn about what was happening in the world beyond.

I was one of those travelers from 'away'. My journey up the Amazon river became part of my story. The Amazon river is one of the world's largest. Its life-giving waters are a source of sustenance and food for the peoples who live on its shores as it winds its way over half the continent of South America. In its travels from source to ocean, it embodies the mystery, the beauty, the challenges and the tragedies of life. As a living force, the Amazon river gives life and it takes it away.

For a long time our journeys ran parallel, mine and that of the river. In its beautiful panoramas of sunrise and sunset, its teeming abundance of animals and birds, it captured for me the mystery of creation in all its splendour. The fury of its storm-tossed waters forcefully taught me of my fragility and how precious is the gift of life! Embracing those expressions of mystery and of life, and the lessons learned along the Amazon, I have incorporated them into the tale of my own life journey.

By relating my journey as a priest and missionary for forty years, it presents me a unique opportunity to share something of the people I encountered, the colleagues I walked with, and the historical events that affected my life's choices. My journey brought me into conflict with my church, yet set me on a direction that ultimately would enrich both my life and my faith.

As a missionary, my travels on the river of life were symbolically made on a boat, the *bark of Peter* as the Catholic Church is often called. I was born into a traditional Catholic family, and the 'bark of Peter' gave meaning, security and direction to my life. When I grew up I became an officer on that vessel, guiding and embracing all who travelled with us, and gathering together other passengers as we journeyed.

I have a vivid memory of an incident on the Amazon river in the 1960s. In the midst of a violent storm, my larger boat came upon a local fisherman battling the storm in his dugout canoe. The winds and waves were jostling his canoe like a matchstick. I called out to him to come alongside and take refuge aboard our boat. "Thanks Padre", he replied, "but I am going to the other side of the river. Don't worry, the Lord is with me".

In a symbolic way, many years later, I too would find myself in a canoe on stormy waters, moving away from the 'bark of Peter', in a direction different than anything I would have ever imagined. And, like the fisherman, I put my faith in God and He has not failed me.

And so my story begins…

CHAPTER 1

Of Church Bells
and Train Whistles

I was born in 1928 just prior to the Great Depression in North Bay, Ontario, a small town at the time, 350 kilometers north of Toronto. Lumber, mining and the railroad had attracted migrants from the farming communities along the Ottawa River in eastern Ontario, often referred to as 'the Valley.' My parents were Valley people. My mother's parents, Thomas and Margaret (Naughton) Byrnes, had come from the Arnprior-Calabogie area of the valley. My father's parents, Thomas and Catherine (Walsh) O'Kane had their family farm in the Cobden-Eganville area. My dad arrived in North Bay to work as a bookkeeper for a lumber company in 1918. My parents, Annie and Leslie O'Kane, married in 1921. They had five children in the next eight years, a girl and four boys.

They were devout Roman Catholics. Church spires of all denominations dominated the North Bay skyline, just as their doctrines and dogmas were dominant in the lives of its residents. The church was our spiritual mentor, guide and educator. It was central to our lives and formation. The Catholic community in North Bay at this time was emerging as a strong force in the town, and the English, Irish, Scottish, Italian and French families supported their bishop, priests and sisters with a fierce loyalty and pride. The church, in turn, provided devout pastors responsible for the generations of committed Catholics that followed. The priests knew their parishioners by name, and families knew their priests. While all walks of life made up this church community, it was predominantly a church of the middle class and the poor.

Catholic teaching and practice influenced all aspects of our family life. A work ethic of honesty and truthfulness permeated our home. Prayer, both at home and church, attendance at Mass and the sacraments, were part and parcel of our daily lives. It was in this manner that the God of the Old Testament and the Jesus of the Gospels were introduced to us from a very early age.

Although my parents were never overly demonstrative in their expressions of love and affection, their sacrifices, care, and concern were ample evidence of lives based on their love for God, for each other, and for each of their children. I would like to think that their example and love rubbed off on me, my sister Geraldine and my brothers, Tom, Russell and John. The integrity, honesty and quiet dignity exemplified by my father, and the dedication, sacrifice and love of my mother for each of her children and her home, have remained the measure of my own life.

As I grew up, family life was structured and disciplined and we were encouraged at an early age to work together for the family's betterment. Many families in North Bay had large vegetable gardens, and it was the boys' responsibility to weed and water these gardens under the supervision of our parents. Our garden produced large quantities of food that was either preserved and stored for the winter, or sold to neighbours. There were also expeditions to the nearby woods to reap the annual harvest of wild strawberries, raspberries and blueberries. Since most kitchen stoves were wood-burning, the chopping and piling of wood was a common domestic chore. As youngsters we had our paper routes or delivery jobs that taught us to be responsible and productive. Life was certainly not harsh but the economic situation of the times required the resources of all family members. Work, discipline and responsibility marked our young lives.

As a family we had our share of misunderstandings and petty quarrels. Yet love, respect, and affection for one another was always predominant and continues in the families of my brothers, Russell and John, and my sister, Geraldine. The O'Kane and the Byrnes family clan extended to uncles, aunts, and cousins and these strong ties continue to be very much a part of my life.

In the late 1920s my father's employment abruptly ended with the depression and bankruptcy of the lumber company. Shortly afterwards he became a part-time employee with the Canadian Pacific Railroad (CPR) where he eventually moved from the spare list as a brakeman to receiving a steady run. As the only wage earner for his family, my dad suffered the loss of our first home during this turbulent time.

On top of this, family sickness brought on further unexpected debts. My sister Geraldine had a very serious injury as the result of a fall that left her in a body cast for over a year. Her slow recovery required prolonged medical attention. In order to cover all the extra expenses my dad worked the coal trains on Manitoulin Island for over two years to settle his accounts. It was dirty work but assured the family a steady income. In his declining years my dad often spoke to me of his sojourn in Little Current and how difficult it was to be kept from his home and family for lengthy periods.

However, even when a permanent position was secured with the CPR railroad my father's life changed little. His life remained frugal; he indulged in few personal amenities. He belonged to the Knights of Columbus, a Catholic men's organization. He spent many recreational hours at their Clubhouse playing cards with a few close friends and fellow railroaders. Most of his friends were "Valley people" like himself. He loved his vegetable garden as it brought him close to his farm roots. To the end of his life he was a very conservative, cautious person, marked by his experience of the depression. Still he lived that life with quiet dignity, gentle humour and integrity.

My mother was the pusher and the innovator and it was she who made things happen. She wanted the best for her children and so was always the initiator of change for the good of the family. With my father's understandable caution and my mother's determination 'to get ahead', life at home had its moments of suspense and humour. Their relationship with each other was always a battle of mind and wit and an experience for us to witness from the sidelines.

I can remember the festivities of North Bay's first Old Home Week in 1935. Mom dressed my brother John and I up as little urchins. She then dressed herself in the most outlandish outfit she could put together, proceeded to place John in an old baby carriage, took my hand and went off to march in the parade down Main Street. At Halloween she would prance around in her witch costume to frighten the neighbours. At Christmas she dressed as Santa, with one or two of us conscripted as elves. She would rent Bob Bainbridge's sleigh and ponies, and off we would go to deliver Christmas gifts to relatives and friends on Christmas Eve prior to attending midnight Mass. All this was much to the chagrin of my dad.

As adolescents, the girls in most families were busy with their household duties. In their free time they recreated together. The boys hung out with group of friends. In winter, hockey was our major attraction. It started with road hockey in mid-November, and as soon as weather permitted, ice surfaces would appear in back yards. Marten's Lake would be used for weekend hockey games until the heavy snow came. We filled our time with skiing in the hills surrounding the city, and with ice fishing on Lake Nipissing. Snow-shoeing and winter hunting were popular with some of our gang, but hands down, hockey was our all-time favourite winter sport. As I grew older I moved from our bush league to the city leagues and played hockey for Scollard Hall, during my high school years.

My primary education was at St. Joseph's separate school, in the east end of the city about two blocks from home. Favourite teachers introduced us to the world of education, and our circle of friends was extended beyond the city block. As a matter of course, during these years, I received my First Communion, Confirmation, and then I became an altar boy at the Pro-Cathedral of the Assumption.

All of us were sent to the relatively new Catholic high schools in the city. My sister Geraldine went to St. Joseph's College, which was run by the Sisters of St. Joseph. My brothers and I went to Scollard Hall, run by the Fathers of the Resurrection and named after the first bishop of the diocese of Sault Ste. Marie. High school life brought new friends and acquaintances from other parts of the city, even greater links with Catholic organizations, and involvement in sports activities at a city level.

My years at Scollard quite naturally brought me into close contact and friendship with priest teachers and mentors. While discipline was strict and at times physical, the dedication and commitment of these Catholic educators was extraordinary.

Students came from other northern centres to be educated at Scollard Hall. In those years it was one of the very few Catholic high schools available in northern Ontario, so boarding students at Scollard formed close to 70 percent of the student body. To manage such a diverse group, discipline was strict and rules were enforced. Nevertheless, a real bond between students and the priests existed. Students developed a sense of pride in their school. Naturally, a healthy rivalry existed between the public school students at the Collegiate and those at Scollard Hall. The North Bay Collegiate was the largest high school in the area and many of our friends were students there. Whether on the playing field or in the classroom, most Scollard students took seriously their responsibility as Catholic young men to uphold the honour of their alma mater.

Back in the 1920s and 1930s North Bay had a population of 17,000. It was principally a railroad town, a main line for the two major rail companies, the Canadian Pacific and the Canadian National, and also the gateway to the north for the old Temiskimang and Northern Ontario Railway (now the Ontario Northland). The city was also the centre for lumbering enterprises in the area; it was a fur centre for local trappers and a modest amount of mining exterprise existed in the area. Main Street was the focus for family shopping and the social life of the city. One could walk the eight or ten blocks of Main Street on a Saturday afternoon or evening, and know every fourth or fifth person by name.

As in all small communities, families and individuals were identified by the area in which they lived. We lived in the east end of the town in an area called the "Y" – the name originated from the intersection of the main lines of the Canadian National and the Temiskimang and Northern Ontario railroads. It was a close-knit working class neighbourhood for the families of the men employed by the railroad.

Every one knew their neighbours and their business as well. Strong bonds of community built up over the hard times. All were involved in the daily task of making ends meet as family and community; deep ties akin to family took root among the French, Italian, English and Irish immigrants. Protestant and Catholic and three Jewish families made up our neighbourhood. We did not always agree, and there were plenty of misunderstandings and disputes, but a fierce loyalty and pride bonded people together nonetheless.

Except for the two years when my family had to move to a rented house in the Cassells Street area of North Bay after we lost our first home because of the depression, the east end of town was called home. Here was where I grew up and formed my first friendships with the boys of the neighbourhood. With the boys of the Mantha, Bucci, Holmes and Lalonde families we played our games and set out on our childhood adventures. The streets were our fields where games of chase, treasure hunt and tag were played for hours on end. A nearby lumber mill yard became an exciting setting for chase and sword fights. A large wooded area southeast of the city afforded plenty of space to roam, pick berries and hunt for small game. Marten's Lake became our private swimming hole in the summers and our rink for skating and hockey in wintertime.

A large civic park beside Lake Nipissing, nearby the "Y", provided swimming lessons, Sunday night band concerts, and organized ball leagues for the boys. During summer holidays our family received visits from our cousins, the Folkins from Montreal. But the highlight of our summer was always the railroad trip east to Uncle Bill O'Kane's farm in the Valley. Auntie Katie and Uncle Bill, my father's youngest brother and his wife, always welcomed us with open arms to a busy household and a family of six girls and two boys. Their farm was close to the village of Osceola, about twenty miles east of Pembroke, Ontario. We looked forward to our farm adventures, and visits with the Egan cousins on their farms close by. These were special times, and in spite of the confusion and added work, we were always welcomed back.

The northland of Ontario began to open up to the outside world with the construction of highways in the mid-thirties. In May of 1934 the Dionne quintuplets were born on a farm in nearby Corbeil. As the world's only living quintuplets they became instantly famous. People flocked to the area to catch a glimpse of them, their birth being largely responsible for the opening of this section of the northland to tourists.

This area of the province abounded in lakes, rivers and streams with an abundance of fish. Hunters found game aplenty in the surrounding forests. The summer months of July and August were ideal for campers and vacationers. North Bay became a major tourist destination in central Canada. In 1935 the city hosted "Old Home Week", a major celebration for the area and the first of many to promote the north to tourists. Small industries linked to mining and the lumbering business opened up. The economy began to take a turn for the better but we were not aware that world events were about to shatter the peace of our family existence.

CHAPTER 2

A World of Our Own

War came in 1939, and although it was fought in Europe and the Far East, it coloured all aspects of our lives for the next six years. The reality of war came home to us as we watched our older brothers and sisters go off to serve in the air force, the army and the navy. At first the war brought only the discomforts experienced as a result of rationing and the inevitable scarcity of goods and services that followed. However its real anguish, pain and senselessness were soon brought home to us when we began to hear of the deaths of brothers, neighbours and friends.

War brought the outside world crashing in on our protected communal lives. The major theatres of the European conflict, the bombing of London, and the African campaign, became part of our daily conversations. Radio broadcasts and news reports acquainted us with Malta, Stalingrad, and Dieppe. After the Japanese attacked Pearl Harbour in December of 1941, we became familiar with Guadacanal and Iwo Jima. Places in the Far East like Hong Kong, China, and the Philippines came crowding into our kitchens and living rooms.

My oldest brother Tom was killed in an air crash in northern England while returning from a bombing raid over Germany. It was February of 1945, four months prior to the end of the war. In the short space of four years, and before he had reached his twenty-first birthday, Tom had lived his life engaged in the project of war. Four of our neighbours also lost their sons; three others were wounded in action. While the younger generation was able to grieve the loss of brothers and get on with life, parents and the community were indelibly marked by the loss of their offspring.

The horror and tragedy of war were not part of the consciousness of most Canadians at this time. But our country's leaders had roused the nation's patriotism and promoted national unity through both world wars. This Second World War was to end with the Atomic bombing of Hiroshima and Nagasaki in 1945. And of course, it was the War to end all Wars!

ℒℚ

Touched by the events happening in remote and distant lands, my own life took shape during my adolescent years. What a thrill it was to land my first summer job. My teen years were highlighted by the expectations of graduation, of getting ready for my first prom, of going steady with the girl of my dreams! In my high school years I went steady with several young ladies and experienced my first loves. Yet my predominant dream was to become a missionary! Looking back on those years it was evident that my identity was closely linked to the church.

Within the Catholic community I was expected to measure up, to become a young man of character and principle. Our priest mentors both at school and church were very instrumental in forming and developing young men of character. At Scollard Hall, Fathers Norm Weaver, Charlie Brunck, Ted Sobisch, Frank and Leo Dentinger and the Graf brothers were the teachers and mentors who gained my respect and admiration. Although strict disciplinarians they would also go the extra mile to help any of us in the classroom or on the playing field, during school hours or in their spare time.

Several parish organizations such as the altar boys, the Catholic Youth Organization and the Sodality of Mary, brought young Catholics together. The objective of these organizations, quite naturally, was to continue our formation as Catholic young people, deepening our spiritual and church life. The priests and Sisters involved in many of these endeavours were solid role models. I remember my early teachers at primary school, Sisters Sheila and Afra at St. Joseph's, Sister St. Bride at St. Rita's. Fathers Frank Devine, Pat Cavanaugh, Reg Carroll, and Roy Carey, were my priest counsellors and friends at the parish level.

Between my eleventh and sixteenth birthday I lived and breathed scouting, another activity that took place under the umbrella of the parish. Mike Cutsey was our troop leader, who gave of his time and energy to help us grow into young men. George Justice filled the same role with the cubs. Tony Billington, who was with the Royal Air Force as a Ferry Command pilot, and stationed in North Bay at the time, often joined in our scouting activities. How fortunate we of the 5th North Bay Troop were to have men of such great example and character!

The parish church and its calendar of events were central to the life of all families in the Catholic community. While Christmas, Lent and Easter were the major feasts, other church celebrations and devotions made up a good part of every week. We had meetings for altar boys, Confirmation preparation and Sodality meetings. As we entered our teens, the parish Youth Club hosted our dances, corn roasts, sleigh rides and skating parties.

Life during this stage of my journey seemed rather simple and uncomplicated. It centered mostly on family, friends and the church. The church provided us with a religious formation that gave meaning to our lives, outlining our duties and responsibilities as Christians. The rituals and rites nourished our Catholic lives, and church teaching provided simple and clear answers to all of life's questions. Exposure to other ways of thinking was practically nonexistent, and when encountered, was certainly viewed with caution.

This was the world of my beginnings, my sheltered world of religious, cultural and family formation. I was certainly not alone. In many towns and cities across Canada there were hundreds of Catholic youth like myself, educated and formed by dedicated men and women. We all set forth with determination and courage to win the world for Christ and the church, and to ensure that the peace just achieved at the end of World War II would be enduring.

Obviously, life was more complicated than my experience could appreciate. Events were happening in the world and the church that were beyond my capacity to grasp at the time.

The aftermath of World War II saw two factors emerging on the world scene. The first was the battle of the superpowers – the United States and its allies as the defenders of freedom mounted against the spectre of communism. The second factor was the growing discontent of nations and peoples that still lived under their colonial masters. In many instances this second factor played into the hands of communism, which appealed to the discontent of peoples long subjugated as second class citizens by economic and political forces.

Because Latin America still suffered from its colonial past, it became a battleground between the free world and communism. Oligarchies, dictators and the military controlled the lives of the people. Even democracy, as understood by the average Latin American, was also a system of control, one imposed on them by the United States of America. The United States, through its foreign policy and economic power supported the rule of brutal dictatorships and their military. While the Latin American elite benefited, the lives of the marginalized, ordinary citizens were severely disadvantaged and brutally controlled.

In the 1950s and 1960s, the Roman Catholic Church was also a part of this struggle. Though a staunch enemy of communism (and certainly prompted by this fact), the Latin American church was shedding its own colonial past. Prophetic leaders and pastors were moving from a subservient, silent status quo church, to a church that recognized the plight of the indigenous peoples and the marginalized poor. Up to this time the majority of the population had no voice or place in society. The church's plan, which emerged at the Council of Latin American Bishops at Medellin, Colombia in 1968, was to call for radical reform of Latin American society. It was a whole-hearted embrace of the poor and the marginalized in their long struggle for their rights and dignity as human beings, as citizens, and as daughters and sons of a loving Creator.

This crusade was to become not only a war against the evils of communism, but a war against the unjust structures, brutality and corruption of dictators, the military and oligarchies. This crusade carried no arms or weapons, save the Word of God.

Obviously those in power both in Latin America and Washington did not welcome this crusade. It became a threat to the ruling elite domestically, and to the economic interests of the United States. As a result, the war against communism in Latin America became as well a war against the Roman Catholic Church. Her crusade for justice was tarred and feathered. The United States of America, embarrassed by Fidel Castro's overthrow of the Battista regime in Cuba, and facing defeat in the unpopular war in Vietnam, readily joined forces with the political and military powers of Latin America. They were to wage a dirty war against the progressive church, relentlessly smearing it as an ally of communism.

Unbeknownst to me at the time, these struggles and forces would eventually play themselves out in my own hopes and choices.

CHAPTER 3

A Desire to Serve

Gerry Kelly, a Scarboro colleague, often remarked with his tongue in cheek that it was his mother who had the vocation to be a priest and missionary. Yet, as far back as I can remember, I sincerely wanted to give my life as a missionary and priest to the cause of Christ. As a ten-year old at St. Joseph's school, I had listened in awe when a visiting missionary spoke of his life in far off China. His visit made a deep and lasting impression on me.

Why did I want to be a missionary priest? My reasons were as simple and as uncomplicated as this. As a young man, coming from the Catholic community it was a natural and logical choice. Priesthood was seen as a sacred calling, a holy and exalted vocation. The church had become an integral part of my very being. Becoming a priest seemed the epitome of being a follower of Christ. There was no better way of living the Gospel and of bringing Christ to others in distant lands. At the time my motivation was spiritual and single minded.

The priest who had so enthralled me as a grade school student was Father Bill McNabb, a member of Scarboro Missions. So I chose Scarboro Missions as the mission group where I would become a missionary priest. Fr. Damien de Veuster, the leper priest of Molokai and St. Francis Xavier, the Jesuit missionary to the Far East, were Catholic giants that had become models for me. These were the heroes of my adolescent faith; the kind of saints all of us, in the innocence of our youth, wanted to emulate.

As a first step toward achieving my goal I spent a year at the Scarboro Society's Novitiate, a "spiritual year" of formation, and an introduction to the life of a missionary priest. I was pursuing what my faith and family had taught me was a lofty goal. But I was not alone. The call or vocation to priesthood and religious life was answered in those years by thousands of Catholic youth across Canada and the United States. Vocations to priesthood and religious life saw the Catholic Church emerge from the ghettos of immigrants to take its place as a moral force and institution within Canadian and American society.

In comparison with similar religious congregations within the Catholic Church, the Scarboro Foreign Mission Society is a small Canadian organization founded by a maverick Toronto priest by the name of Father John Mary Fraser. Fraser was a maverick precisely because at the turn of the century Canada itself was looked upon as mission territory by Rome. Yet, here was this Canadian priest going off to the mission fields of far off China. In his teens Fraser and his family had emigrated from Scotland. As a seminarian he had studied for the priesthood in Genoa, Italy for the Archdiocese of Toronto. But his life ambition was to work as a missionary in China. Fraser was the first English-speaking priest from North America to work there. His career in China began in 1901, working alongside a French religious order called the Lazarists. He died in Japan in 1962.

Fraser was passionate about the need for a mission society in Canada. When he returned to Canada from his first years in China, he journeyed throughout the country preaching this need to Canadian Catholics. He sought the support of bishops. Although his organizational skills were poor, his perseverance and determination finally paid off. Slowly, he gathered a small group of like-minded men around him in the town of Almonte, Ontario, where he founded the China Mission College in 1917.

In the early 1920s the fledging mission group moved to Scarboro, Ontario, to a property on the shores of Lake Ontario. Known today as the Guild Inn, the move was made in order to be closer to an approved educational institution, St. Augustine's Archdiocesan Seminary. In 1927, a third and final move was made to land leased from the major Seminary. Here, St. Francis Xavier Seminary was built next door to St. Augustine's Seminary.

By the time I began my studies and life with the Scarboro Missions in 1947, the Society had 62 priests and 31 seminarians. John Mary Fraser was a missionary, not an organizer, so he was again back in Lishui, China. In 1935, the bishops of Ontario had asked Monsignor John McCrae of Alexandria, Ontario to take charge of this new missionary enterprise. McCrae, who was an able administrator, gave the needed direction and stability to the fledgling group. The early band of missionaries to China had been forced to flee during the Sino-Japanese War in the mid 1930s. Under McCrae's direction they were regrouping to return to Lishui. In the early 1940s the Society established a second mission in the Dominican Republic.

The new efforts in Lishui, in Checkiang province in southern China were short lived, when Chairman Mao Zedung's Army of Liberation defeated the nationalist Army of Chang Kai-shek in 1949. Many of the priests were imprisoned and finally exiled. With China closed to missionaries by the communist government, another mission was soon established in Japan.

So it was, that at the age of seventeen, with the blessings and full approval of family, I headed off in July 1947 for St. Mary's, (a small town in southwestern Ontario, 40 kilometers north of London). Here I was to begin my training for the missionary priesthood at Nazareth House, the Novitiate of the Scarboro Society. It was my first time away from home. Young men entering the Society followed a spiritual formation program prior to beginning their classical studies. This was a year of spiritual formation as well as a probationary period.

The Scarboro Mission Society had purchased an old estate a few years earlier on the outskirts of the town. Nazareth House was to be my home for the next twelve months. The old stone manor house was surrounded by ancient oak trees, flower beds and a rolling lawn. Within this beautiful setting I was to begin a year of study and prayer. This was my introduction to missionary life.

The manor had a small chapel, a dining room, kitchen, and a large living room, all on the main floor. On the second level there were rooms for priests and several visitors. The third floor had one or two rooms for storage. A classroom had been added to one side of the stone manor. On a small hill set to one side of this main building was the student residence. This was to be my home along with my 16 classmates and our Novice Master, Father Bill Amyot. There was a sports field in a lower area at the rear of the manor that was flanked by several acres of vegetable gardens.

Along with my classmates I began a very strict regimen of discipline and obedience. Each day we were awakened by a bell at 5:30 a.m. This new way of life required our presence in chapel by 6:00 for morning prayers and meditation. Mass and thanksgiving followed this initial period of prayer. At 7:30 we ate a simple breakfast of home-made porridge, bread and jam. Following the short reading from the *Lives of the Saints,* the long overnight silence ceased and we were allowed to talk for the rest of the breakfast period. At 8:00 the bell signalled the end of breakfast and those assigned to kitchen chores and cleaning worked in silence. The remaining novices returned to their rooms for study. From 8:30 until noon we worked on weekly house assignments. These chores included kitchen work, the cleaning of the chapel and sacristy, the maintenance of the grounds, and gardening. We were not bound by silence during this period except in the main building and chapel.

We ate our meals in silence, attentive to the reading of a classic spiritual text offered for our reflection. Study and lecture sessions took place in the afternoon and most evenings, while late afternoon allowed for recreation. Evening prayers followed class or study at nine. Beginning again with night prayers, "grand silence" meant a silence for everyone in the building until breakfast the following day. The final bell at 10:00 p.m. signalled lights out for all. This was to be our daily schedule. We became followers of the bell as it called us to each new assignment. Our disciplined daily schedule was more relaxed on Thursdays and Sundays. On those days we had more private time and recreational sports. On Thursday afternoons we were permitted to go to town for shopping. We were allowed visitors one Sunday a month.

With my fellow novices I had come to Nazareth House to learn to pray, meditate and reflect. This was not meant to be an academic year, but a year that introduced us to the clerical and mission life with its regimen of discipline and obedience. Our little world within the grounds of Nazareth House was far removed from the comings and goings of life out in the world. By choice we were isolated from happenings around us. Our year began with a three-day silent retreat. The first Sunday of every month was a retreat day, and we would end our year with a seven-day retreat. This was a special time of silence, prayer, and spiritual lectures. These special, prayerful times were intended to help us grow spiritually and to build a personal relationship with the Lord of Creation and with his Son, Jesus the Christ.

Class time was an introduction to the spiritual life, to the gospels and prayer. We were introduced to mission life and to a history of the Scarboro Society. We quickly learned the rules that would govern our lives as members of the Society. Each of us chose a spiritual director. This priest became our counsellor and advisor, and the person to whom we made our weekly confessions.

The spiritual discipline we followed determined the daily schedule that became central to our lives for the next seven years. It was adapted from the *Rule of St. Benedict*, and based on the monastic life of the Benedictine Order founded by Benedict, a monk of the 8th century. Our future lives would find us far from any monastery, and so, this spiritual discipline was to fashion a new creation within each of us. We would go out to the world disciplined and committed to our spiritual mission. Based on Augustine's theology that looked upon humankind as inclined to evil, our formation was to help us avoid evil and remain in God's grace. As a student of Christ and as a seminarian of the Scarboro Missions, my task was to conquer my own self and my inclination to sin, so that God could take over my life, my whole being.

This giving of self to a program of self-mastery, obedience and discipline may appear radical to some, even extreme to others, yet it seemed perfectly normal for us, and was hardly questioned. Today, when individualism and the rights of the individual are extolled, many might judge such a process to be a form of brainwashing. Yet in our view, such a regimen was normal for our spiritual growth and well-being. Our goal to become missionaries helped us adapt to such a life. Once we got over our homesickness and settled into a daily routine we grew contented and happy.

My fellow novices and new friends came from all parts of Canada, from backgrounds similar to mine. Our introduction to mission and to Scarboro came exclusively through our Novice Master, Father William Amyot, a veteran of the China mission. His stories and experience introduced us to the Chinese people, and to the life of a Canadian missionary in the enchanted land and strange foreign culture of far away China.

Father 'Big Bill' Amyot was a convincing model for us all. He guided our lives with a firm but fair discipline. He was aloof from his charges, yet he treated each of us with respect, kindness and as persons. He was completely dedicated to the important task to which he had been assigned, and was a model in his personal life of prayer, discipline and commitment to mission life. He was always there to listen to any complaint, or help with any problem. He was also an avid sports enthusiast. His brother Frank had been with the Olympic rowing team and won a gold medal in the 1000 metre canoeing event at the 1936 Olympics. Bill himself was a professional cyclist. He promoted team sport among us, both to build moral character and to use up our youthful energy.

Also assigned to Nazareth House were Fathers Bill Cox and James Leonard. Father Bill was responsible for running the physical plant, and assigned us our various chores and responsibilities. Father Jimmy was the spiritual director who taught and directed us in the celebration of the liturgy for our major celebrations. Both these priests gave lectures on some aspect of the theology of mission and the spiritual life. Priests from the main seminary in Scarboro, as well as from the mission field, would visit with us throughout the year.

By June 1948, eleven of us had successfully completed the first year of training. Only six of this 1947 class at Nazareth House would complete theological studies and be ordained priests.

The post-war years saw a large number of young men and women choosing a religious vocation, entering the church's major seminaries, and religious communities in Canada. These large numbers of candidates would continue until the early 1960s. St. Francis Xavier Seminary for the Scarboro Missions had 47 seminarians while the Archdiocesan seminary across the field had one hundred and thirty theological seminarians in 1949-1950. They came from ten Catholic dioceses across Canada. The future looked so promising that a new million-dollar building was built adjacent to St. Augustine's seminary for philosophy students in 1962.

St. Augustine's had a full complement of priest-professors for both the philosophical and theological programs. St. Francis Xavier seminary had a philosophy course for its students. When Scarboro seminarians completed their philosophy program, we studied theology with our diocesan colleagues across the fields in the classrooms of St. Augustine's.

St. Augustine's seminary was the pride of the Archdiocese of Toronto, Ontario. It was a large institution that had been built in the 1920s, and was the clerical formation centre for the English clergy of Ontario, and dioceses to the east and west. St. Augustine's was large and unwieldy. The student body was from across Canada, and little camaraderie or real community spirit developed there. Large classes did not allow good interchange between professor and students. During free time our smaller seminary became a gathering spot for many students from across the field.

Our seminary, small in comparison with the larger St. Augustine's next door, had an enthusiastic community spirit. Student and priest relationships were excellent, morale was high. The Society was to be our family and so a bonding took place. The seminary was not just another educational institution; it became our family home.

As in any group or organization there were a few who were in the wrong place, but seminary life brought me into contact with some of the finest young men I could ever expect to meet anywhere. This included not just those who went on to ordination, but many who left the seminary to pursue other studies and professions.

Here at the seminary, as at Nazareth House, the spiritual exercises, as well as the disciplined daily routine, would be all important in our formation process. While our first year focused on spiritual development, seminary life introduced me to the academic world of philosophy and theology. As in any educational institute there was a heavy daily program of classes and study. In such a setting, recreation was looked upon by our superiors as an escape valve for all our pent-up energy and vitality. Team sports and activities such as cliff climbing and running became part of our routine and were highly encouraged.

One of the major objectives of our spiritual formation was to help us develop a healthy attitude toward our sexuality. Spiritual lectures extolled the virtues of purity and chastity. Our spiritual directors would counsel us on these matters each week After all, we were adolescent young men living a monastic life apart from the support and ties of family. The celibate life was to be predominant in our priestly lives. By and large I adapted easily to the life and enjoyed the studies. The disciplined monastic style of life I had chosen had a worthy goal, and so it was easy to give it my best.

To this point my life as a seminarian felt well balanced and fulfilling. I lived within a framework of prayer, study and discipline. Although I was not free to come and go as I pleased, I submitted to a daily structure of life that controlled my movements, my recreation and my nourishment. At times it was annoying, inconvenient, and counter to what I wanted to do, but I accepted it as something that would mold my character and contribute to my spiritual growth and development.

I mixed well, developing ties of lasting friendship at both seminaries. There were several close friends from North Bay at St. Augustine's.

Our sports and recreational periods made up for our seclusion from the outside world, and I was an avid participant. We had some great talent on the hockey rink, the football field and the ball diamond. Missionaries, returning home for vacation brought us their stories of drama and adventure in far away lands. I was happily pursuing my goal of priesthood and the life of a missionary.

Academically I was an average student, but not overly zealous in pursuing my studies beyond the prescribed courses. Our curriculum in both philosophy and theology was meant to prepare us for pastoral and missionary work. Looking back on those years from the vantage point of time and experience I can now say that there was limited input. Scripture studies were little more than advanced Bible classes. Moral and dogma theological studies were interesting at times, but presented in the dead language of Latin, and with little debate. Church history was of great interest to me, but it was a history that always showed the church in the best possible light. The shadow side of the church was never really discussed. There was the complete absence of good liturgical formation. This was an area that could have helped prepare us as future pastors, to make our liturgical services more meaningful. Sadly, there was never any attempt to link the Gospel message to the reality of life. My critique of the negative aspects of our study program is much easier to make in hindsight, and from the vantage point of experience, but during those young impressionable student years I was also not exactly on fire in my search for knowledge.

As a future missionary I had no preparation in the understanding of other major religions or cultures. We did have the input and experiences of some of our missionaries, but nothing of any great substance. The library at St. Augustine's seminary was a treasure of books and our own seminary library was adequate. Like many of the students, my studies were limited to what I needed for good grades, so I missed out in fully utilizing the treasure of works that were available.

In our personal growth as Catholic young men destined for the clerical life, the major focus was with how we handled our sexuality. The Ten Commandments were often reduced to those dealing with sexual sins.

Even today the church's major preoccupation deals with sex while the morality of war and other social concerns are marginal topics in comparison. Quite naturally, we were being prepared for celibate lives, and that aspect of our formation seemed of prime importance. Spiritual direction too often dealt only with a healthy sexuality, while healthy relationships, a meaningful prayer life, and intimacy with Christ were often overlooked.

But such problems did not seem to be of major concern to me as a seminarian or as a young priest. The belief system that I held to was that the church had all the answers. It was the chosen instrument of divine revelation and truth. My mission in life, as priest and missionary, was to bring people to an acceptance of church doctrine. Through their acceptance of the church and her teachings, our world would become attuned to God, and His kingdom of love, peace, unity and justice would prevail.

Our course of studies at the seminary was in line with the time schedule of most schools (September-June). During the summer months we returned to our homes to search out summer work to help with our tuition. For three summers I drove a truck delivering bread in the North Bay area. The remaining summers I worked at a drug store in North Bay and at a tourist booth that catered to American tourists at Quintland, the home of the famous Dionne quintuplets. As a seminarian I was expected to conduct myself during the summer holidays in accordance with my calling. I was also encouraged to follow a life of daily prayer.

Each year of studies brought me closer to my goal. I had the support and approval of my family and friends at home. My new life and home was in the seminary. Together with my fellow seminarians and friends I studied and worked toward the goal of missionary priesthood. In December of 1953, six years after entering Nazareth House, I was ordained to the priesthood in my hometown of North Bay. Priesthood was, and is, a revered and sacred calling for the Catholic community. The parishioners of the Cathedral turned out in large numbers for my ordination and first Mass. It was a special and proud moment for my parents and family, as well as relatives and parishioners. My feelings were those of gratitude, honour, humility, but also of pride at finally reaching my goal as a missionary priest.

As a newly ordained missionary priest I set out in all sincerity and commitment to help establish the kingdom of God then and there. I was confident that I had been given all the tools necessary for my future life and that I had been thoroughly prepared for whatever lay ahead. I was soon to learn otherwise.

CHAPTER 4

Testing the Waters

I was ordained into a comfortable middle class church, in a time of peace and prosperity in the western world where there was no thought of ever questioning the democratic, capitalistic way of life.

Elsewhere in the world the situation was quite different. Marxist communism, which had been seen as an enemy of democracy and the church, had spread out from Russia, encircling all of Eastern Europe in its embrace. Mao Zedung and his Red Army had taken power in China, the world's most populous country. Guerrilla groups in Africa and the Far East were rebelling against the colonial powers that had kept their people in dependence and exploited the resources of their countries.

The 1950s and 1960s would see bloody conflicts in all of Africa. Independence would come slowly to fifteen new nations, but at great cost in human blood. Major political deals and alliances were made by the United States to contain these regional conflicts in Africa and the Middle East. Both the United States and Russia propped up and supported regimes all over the world. All this led to America's involvement in the Vietnam War where all the might and power of the American war machine was humbled in defeat by Ho Chi Min and the Northern Vietnamese. It was an unpopular war for the American public, not to mention the terrible death toll exacted on both sides. It also introduced new weaponry and methodology to the profession of war. It intensified the production and proliferation of arms that became an ever more lucrative market for warmongers.

The United States of America during these years became the superpower of the West, and assumed the role of protector and guardian of the free world. The Pentagon became a superpower in its own right, and the Central Intelligence Agency (CIA) took on the task of becoming the eyes and ears of the world, the watchdog of the West.

Communism also continued its advance with chilling abuses against human rights and freedoms. With good reason the Western hemisphere set up its alliances and political partnerships to checkmate and counter the moves of Russia and her satellites. So the Cold War of the 1950s and 1960s saw the superpowers of the East and West carrying on a war of propaganda, espionage and sabre rattling. The countries of the Third World, whose populations and economies had long been subjected to dominance and exploitation by the so-called free world nations, became battlegrounds of the two superpowers.

The churches, too, rallied against the evils of communism. The Catholic Church saw in atheistic communism the greatest evil force since the invasion of Europe by the Saracens. In all of Eastern Europe, Russia, China, Vietnam, Korea, the sad story of persecution was the same. Thousands and thousands of priests, sisters, bishops and laity were imprisoned, tortured, or condemned to labour camps for their opposition to communism. Human beings were systematically eliminated. Thousands of churches and church organizations were closed. People were prohibited, under pain of death, from living their faith.

Catholics in the United States and Canada came to know of these atrocities and the evils of communism. The terrible abuses of this ideology became popular themes in preaching. Our children gained first hand knowledge of the ugly head of communism, through the Catholic school system. Catholics eagerly followed the public, orchestrated trials of prominent church leaders such as Aloysius Stepinac in Yugoslavia, and Josef Mindszenty in Czechoslovakia.

Thousands of exiled missionaries from the Far East brought home first hand accounts of the personification of evil in communism.

A renowned Catholic preacher, Bishop Fulton Sheen, one of the first celebrities of American television, preached this incarnate evil to millions of viewers in Canada and the United States. For the Christian crusade of the Americas, during the 1950s, the number one moral enemy was communism.

This was the world in which I was ordained. I had left an orderly, sheltered upbringing, emerged from the even more sheltered life of the seminary and was now a young missionary priest. Like many of my fellow Canadians I believed in America the good, a superpower that morally and humanely acted for the betterment of humanity. I equally believed that capitalism under North American democracy held the answer to the world's political and economic woes.

At the time of my ordination, the Scarboro Missions was a young, vibrant Mission Society ready to grow. There were 18 missionaries in the Dominican Republic, 12 in Japan, 7 in the Philippines, 6 in Guyana, with mission parishes in Victoria and Vancouver working with the Chinese. The Society administration was considering opening other missions. Paul Kam, a Chinese national was the only remaining priest of the Society in China. Kam had come to Canada as a young man with Monsignor John Mary Fraser in the 1920s. He had begun his studies with the early group at Almonte, Ontario. After ordination in 1925, he returned to work with Fraser in Lishui. In the early 1950s Kam remained in prison, while other Scarboro missionaries had been exiled to their homeland after periods of house arrest and imprisonment. The Society has never received any information about Kam after his imprisonment under the communists.

New missions meant ever greater expenditures; and with a full quota of students the old seminary building was badly in need of major renovations. Since its initial foundation in 1918, the Society had looked to the generosity of Canadian Catholics for financial support to carry on its work. The lifeline between the Society and its donor-subscribers was a monthly magazine. For years it had been called the *China Mission Magazine*. The Society itself came to be popularly known as the China Missions. In the 1940s the Society was officially incorporated as the Scarboro Foreign Mission Society, and the magazine was renamed *Scarboro Missions*. The magazine carried stories of mission work in China and the Dominican Republic. It made appeals both for vocations to mission life and for financial help. Our founder, Monsignor John Mary Fraser, on his return trips to Canada would travel east to west preaching about the missions and the work of the Society. Priests of the Society were regularly assigned to do promotional work in Catholic dioceses across Canada.

Looking toward the future, a Promotion and Public Relations Department was set up in 1952, staffed by missionaries home from China. The objective of the department was to promote the Society and its mission work and to work within the Catholic school system to encourage young men to join the Society. The department complemented the magazine work of raising much needed financial support.

After my ordination I fully expected an appointment to an overseas mission. Decisions about appointments were made by the General Council of the Society in response to the needs of the missions. In those times there was no dialogue or consultation with the members. While my three colleagues received mission appointments, I was appointed to the Promotion Department. So, the first three years of my priesthood were spent travelling throughout Canada, preaching in parishes, speaking to school children, and making the Society and its work known to Catholics nation wide.

The years on Promotion were valuable years for me. I travelled Ontario, did extensive promotion work in the London and southern Ontario regions, and spent an enjoyable six months in Nova Scotia. I also worked in the dioceses of Trenton, New Jersey, the Scranton area of Pennsylvania, parts of New York State and in the mid-west in the diocese of St. Cloud, Minnesota. I was a competent preacher, and an ardent conveyor of the mission message to youth in the primary and secondary schools.

During this time I worked with veteran missionaries and with several colleagues who had been appointed, like myself, to the Promotion

Department. As a team, our morale was very high, and our commitment to Scarboro and to mission was life giving. I was eager to learn from the mission experiences of these veteran missionaries both from China and the Dominican Republic. Along with my younger colleagues I was basking in my first years of priesthood and ministry, and anxiously awaiting my appointment to a mission country. Our promotion residence was in central Toronto. Here we formed a small community that followed a daily program of work and prayer. On special occasions we often joined the seminarians at games out at the seminary. Our daily life was disciplined yet relaxed when compared to seminary life. We had a work pattern; we followed a programed prayer schedule, yet had time for communal recreation and free time. We were working for God and for His kingdom. As with any group we had our personality clashes, but these were usually resolved by talking over the problem. In those times obedience was paramount; there was no room for dialogue over an assigned task. So we did them (perhaps grudgingly) out of deference to our superiors.

In a real sense these years introduced me to the church and its hierarchy, and to the people in the pews. By and large the clergy I met over these years were dedicated people and an example in my youthful life. They were men of prayer, committed to their vocations, yet down to earth with a love for life. We all shared the same ideals, and utilized our gifts and talents for God and the church. We all came from the same mold; we were products of the same programming. Our basic formation was the same and we wore identical uniforms, the white clerical collar and the black suit. Our superiors and the faithful laity constantly reminded us that we were God's clerical army. These were the years when the church was moving from a papist-run religious group of immigrant Irish, Italian, Polish and Ukrainian minorities to a strong, national Catholic Church from coast to coast. The same thing was happening in the church south of the border in the United States. The Catholic school systems and the leadership at the parish and diocesan levels all contributed to the creation of an articulate, educated Catholic population that was beginning to make its mark in the building of a nation. Her churches, hospitals, universities and schools, together with her charitable and social work, contributed significantly to the fabric of the nation.

During those years I met hundreds of the Catholic laity from Cape Breton through to the prairie lands of Manitoba, Saskatchewan and Alberta. Most of them were farmers, fishermen and miners. They were honest, hard working, and God fearing people. Their backgrounds were similar to my own, second or third generation immigrant stock; they were children of parents who had suffered through the depression. Many had served in the Armed Forces during the war, or had lost family members in the war. They had a fierce pride in their Catholic faith, raising their families in the Catholic tradition and devoting their lives to the education and well-being of their families.

For many of these people, the priest was on a pedestal. Most of them came from that tradition that saw the priest as their spiritual mentor, as the one who dealt in God's mysteries. Their faith and their outreach and concern for others made me aware of my frailty and human faults. They inspired me to live up to their expectations and to be worthy of their trust.

Within the clergy I sometimes recognized cliques, professionals climbing the hierarchical ladder, and the few who pursued their ministry with little or no interest in the people. They were in it for themselves, for the prestige and position they held within the church. These were certainly a minority, but they revelled in their position and used it as their divine right to better themselves. I often wondered what kind of priest I would become.

CHAPTER 5

"Which Way Is Proper, Fa?"

In 1957 I was appointed to a new mission that the Society was establishing in the West Indies on the island of St. Vincent. My companion and superior would be Father Leo Curtin an older veteran, who had been ordained for the diocese of Ottawa, then joined the Society and served in China. A colleague of Curtin's China days remarked when he heard of the appointment, "What a pair to send – the rising and the setting sun."

St. Vincent and a smaller island, Bequia, nine miles to the southwest, were beautiful tropical islands with a climate that northern tourists dream about. There was a rainy season from December until June, and a hot season for the remainder of the year. There was lush vegetation, blue skies, and the rolling, blue Caribbean Sea. The isle was mountainous, and its highest peak, Mount Soufriere, was an active volcano. A narrow ribbon of a road ran around the island's coastline. It linked the towns and villages from Rosebank on the leeward north, south to Kingstown and winding north to Georgetown and Sandy Bay on the windward side of the island. Another road ran up into the mountains from Kingstown to the Marriaqua valley, down to Mesopotamia, and on to the seacoast.

St. Vincent was the most southern of the Windward Islands. The Caribs, the original peoples who survived the colonial wars, had long since been exiled to other islands. A tiny remnant of descendants lived on the northeastern tip of the island. Most of the eighty-five thousand population were descendants of slaves brought from Africa to run the sugar mills and cane factories of colonial times. There was a sizeable community of East Indians and some Portuguese, both groups having arrived as indentured labourers to replace the workforce when slavery was abolished. About seven percent of the population were descendants of the English colonists.

Banana crops and the export of arrowroot, nutmeg and coconut had taken over most of the arable land when the sugar industry had collapsed. A few sugar mills were still in operation. A few families owned most of the arable lands; small plots belonging to the general populace dotted the mountainsides. These small plots produced plantains, cassava, peanuts, corn, some coffee and cotton. Fishing was a small industry on only the leeward side of the island.

Kingstown, the capital and major town, was situated in a natural bay on the southwest corner of the island. When I arrived, the island was about to gain its independence from Britain. The Vincentians were a religious people. The major denominations were the Methodists and the Anglicans, and the Catholic community was a distant third, comprising only sixteen percent of the population. There were many other sects and denominations with smaller followings.

Small pockets of Catholicism had been part of the island's history with colonialism from the time of the French in the 17th century. The Catholic community on the island became deeply rooted with the work and influence of a Benedictine monk, Fr. Charles de Verboek who came to the island in 1923. Originally from Holland, Verboek came to St. Vincent from Trinidad where the Dutch Benedictines had a monastery. Father Charles was a tireless worker and over the years built churches all over the island. His brick and mortar creations announced to the Methodists and the Anglicans that the Catholic Church was going to be an important part of Vincentian life. His twenty-four years of dedicated service built-up a small but committed core of Catholics.

Benedictine monks from the same monastery in Trinidad continued Verboek's work until the arrival of the Scarboro Fathers in 1957. Two of these Benedictine colleagues stayed to help us for the first year. They returned to Trinidad when two of Scarboro's China veterans joined us in 1958.

St. Vincent was a Christian country, so not really missionary in the strict sense. But it was my first exposure to another culture and people whose history and tradition and religious expressions were much different than my own. It was a daunting adventure for a young missionary. Almost immediately upon arrival I took over a parish in Mesopotamia in the Marriaqua Valley about forty minutes from Kingstown. For the first months I resided in Kingstown. I then moved to Mesopotamia and lived at the rear of the church. The parish had two mission stations attached to its charge, Gomea and Escape.

British colonialism had rubbed off on the islanders and their lilting English carried the distinct sounds of the King's English. Their government administration, justice system, health and educational departments were based on the English model.

The Vincentian people opened their hearts and their homes to this Canadian invasion. I was received with warmth and a certain shy reserve amongst the parishioners in Mesopotamia, Gomea and Escape. As the initial months went by, these gentle people brought home to me, that while their backgrounds, history and traditions were far different from my own, their sense of God and the Divine was a profound part of their lives. I am sure that this young, brash, white Canadian often acted (either consciously or unconsciously) like the "ugly American." Their patience and their outreach helped me to recognize their values and character as a people. They shared with me who and what they were without apology or reservation. During my few years on the island I tried to be one with them.

The Vincentian people, whose history had been a history of slavery and exploitation, introduced me to a different world perspective about life and things divine. Their understanding and observance of divine and church law was quite different from mine, but their communion with God and their search for spiritual growth was every bit as authentic as my own. My narrow vision of religion and life was flavoured heavily by my Catholic upbringing, strengthened, I'm sure, with a strong dose of "I'm here to save you." But that was soon to change.

Here I was, not yet thirty, the spiritual father of a Catholic community. In one sense, I was in my glory. With dedication and zeal I set about my ministry through preaching, administering the sacraments and celebrating the Sacred Liturgy. I sought to help these people to better know and understand their faith, and hopefully to become more fervent Catholics. This was how I understood my spiritual mission. Charity and reaching out to the poor and the unfortunate were certainly a priority and very much a part of how I saw my mission. In time, my face-to-face encounters with the poverty and deprivation of the people would slowly convince me that justice was also a Gospel prerogative.

During these years I worked at renovating the main church in Mesopotamia and building a new church in Gomea. With the help of several teachers we started Boy Scout and Girl Guide troops. Wilfred Ackers, Theresa Browne and her brother George, became invaluable leaders in this youth formation. Later on, the training and developing of young leaders in the ranks of the altar boys became a priority. The musical gifts of many parishioners gave us first class choirs in Gomea and Mesopotamia. The men of the parish formed a strong unit of the Holy Name Society, and the women became members of the Sacred Heart League. The people responded to all this activity with enthusiasm, and supported me, their young pastor, with their time and commitment. Mission life was good.

Countless incidents come to mind regarding my introduction into the life of the people, but I recount three that have always stayed with me. Two of the incidents were simple and humorous. One day when I was carrying lumber down from the mountains with some of the young people, I paused to get my breath and move the boards off my shoulder. That shoulder was sensitive and bruised from previous trips down the steep incline. Within a short time, one of the boys nicknamed Lion was behind me. Lion had three huge planks balanced on his head. He paused to see what was wrong, and to cover up my lack of energy and bruised shoulder I said to him, "Why do you carry that lumber on your head, why don't you carry it properly?" "Which way is proper Fa?" he asked, "It can't be your way from the look of that shoulder."

On another day, Wilfred the carpenter was doing some repair work on the church windows. He had a heavy board balanced on two strong supports, and was sitting on the board itself. He was using the force of hands, arms and shoulders, to push the saw up and down cutting the hard wood in an effortless way. I said to him, "Wilfred have you ever sawed this way?" and proceeded to demonstrate the Canadian way, the right way. He did it my way with great patience for several minutes, and then said, "Fa, extra effort is needed to push that saw with one hand, give my way a try." Try it I did, and from then on, gave no more demonstrations on the right way.

The third incident was not so humorous. I had been living in Mesopotamia for two years and had become very close to Chippie. Chippie was a local businessman and active in the parish. We were the same age, and shared many evenings together, talking over the meaning of life, religion and world politics. One particular afternoon I dropped into his home. Three business friends from Kingstown were visiting. I knew the three men but not in any close way. I got into conversation with them and felt very much at home. Soon we were into a heated discussion on some political topic. I was not inhibited from speaking my mind, and soon came to odds with one of Chippie's friends. I refused to give in to one of his arguments. He stood up and made the remark, "Oh you're one of those colonial whites, always right." At this point, Chippie quietly intervened, and said, "Charles, the drink is getting to you, you are out of place, you don't insult another friend of mine in my house." "What?" said Charles, "he's white." "Fa's also my friend and friendship has no colour, so sit down, have a drink, and let's get on with our arguments." And that was the end of it. But it was not the end of it for me. This powerful example of what true friendship meant for Chippie has been something I've attempted to make my own.

There were others like Chippie who were my mentors in their service to the parish, in their expression of faith, and in their loyalty. These people helped me to live my Christian beliefs in rubbing shoulders with others. Louise John, Lucy Drayton and Carrie Huggins prepared the children for their First Communion and Confirmation. They were devoted to the young people and accompanied them in all their church activities. Henry Miguel, Ma da Costa, Wilf Acres, and Elfred Wylie were always involved in making parish life a part of the community's life.

My journey among the peoples of St. Vincent was all too short. During furlough in Canada I was asked to take a year at the Coady International Institute in Antigonish, Nova Scotia. I was to live at Scarboro House with several other students from overseas and attend classes at the Coady Institute, located on the campus of St. Francis Xavier University. Antigonish was a small university town and it was easy to settle into the studies and routine. I entered into these studies in social leadership, credit unions and co-operatives with great dreams of bringing such work to the people of St. Vincent and of integrating the Gospel dimension of social justice into my missionary work on the island.

My year of studies at the Coady Institute in Antigonish, Nova Scotia brought me into contact with women and men from Iran, India, Puerto Rico, Trinidad and various countries in Africa. It was an experience that opened my eyes to the many problems facing countries and peoples with newly won independence. As I came to know women and men from various cultures, traditions and history, my religious, political and social horizons were broadened. These new friends, like myself, were at the Coady Institute eager to study and learn new techniques for community and social development in order to better the economic lives of their brothers and sisters back home.

The group consisted of teachers, government workers and priests, as well as co-operative and credit union leaders. Living with this select group and listening to their stories was an education in itself. They spoke about the problems of social and economic development. Most of them were leaders in their home communities and could speak from years of experience. Their stories of dealing with apathy, corruption, and state repression helped me to move from my naive idealism to the harsh reality that people face. Through this interaction I continually asked what my role as missionary might be. How does one go about integrating spiritual and human development?

Our studies at the Coady consisted of courses in economics and developing community leadership. Fathers Moses Coady and Jimmy Tomkins developed the co-operative movement and credit unions in Nova Scotia. These two pioneers and founders of the Antigonish Movement had spent their lives with the fishermen, farmers and miners of Cape Breton, developing a grass roots model for economic development. Our studies included becoming acquainted with their techniques and methodology.

Economic stagnation had plagued most of Eastern Canada even in the years following the great depression of 1929. Lack of employment had forced mass migrations of its people to the job markets in the northern United States, Ontario and the western provinces. Drained of much of their human resources, small fishing and farming communities eked out a subsistence living, subservient to those who controlled the markets and finances.

In response to massive unemployment and widespread poverty, the Antigonish diocese championed the work of Coady and Tompkins. Using the facilities of St. Francis Xavier University, an educational program was implemented for the training of local community leaders. Through the commitment, dedicated work and vision of Coady and Tompkins, local leaders were trained and the people of small communities came together. The farmers and fishermen in their remote communities were connected with one another. The skills of people and community resources were used in a common effort to overcome their economic difficulties. Co-operatives and credit unions were the financial and educational instruments in the movement. The Antigonish Movement was born. Through the years it brought greater financial stability and a degree of prosperity to the lives of united communities in Cape Breton and other areas of Nova Scotia.

My year at the Coady Institute exposed me to this model of grass roots economic and social development. As well as our lectures and studies at the Institute, we made field trips to farming and fishing communities, to marketing co-operatives and credit unions. Such exposure brought us into contact with the leaders of communities and the managers of the co-operatives. These discussions supplemented our formal studies and we were present at meetings at the local level. Men and women at the managerial level shared their insights and experience. Wage earners and their families shared their experiences with the movement and its benefits in their lives.

All in all it was another rich experience for me to be part of a group involved in the work of community development. I shared experiences with new friends from other cultures and countries and learned of their successes and failures. I was exposed to a movement that brought new hope and life to stagnant and dying communities, a movement that gave back to the poor their dignity and pride, and gave them power to build better lives.

My journey took a new turn again. As the spring of 1961 approached and the school year drew to a close at the Coady Institute, my superiors appointed me to a new mission in Brazil, South America. I was to leave my pastoral work and the many new friends I had made on the island of St. Vincent. Now I was heading south to the heart of the Amazon, and to the very heart of my life.

CHAPTER 6

A Decade of Change and Unrest

I was not alone in my changes, my questioning, and my unrest. The world was changing too.

The map of our world in the late 1950s and 1960s could be divided into three distinct geo-political areas. The first would show the "free" world that included the democratic market economies of Western Europe, Britain, North America and Japan. The second would be the "communist bloc" that included Soviet Russia and her satellites in Eastern Europe, as well as China and North Korea. The last group would be the so-called "Third World" countries of the Southern Hemisphere, most of which were seeking independence from a colonial past or freedom from military regimes and despotic dictators.

The Third World was to become the battleground where the ideologies of communism and the democratic market economies struggled to retain or strengthen their influence, economic ties, and military or political alliances.

As part of the "free" world, Canada was only marginally involved in this power struggle. Canadian forces had certainly fought in the Korean War alongside her allies. During the sixties, however, the role of Canada's military was as a peacekeeper in several hot spots on the world scene. It was the United States who became the watchdog and champion of democracy, and who waged "war" on the Soviet bloc by providing armaments, war supplies, political and diplomatic confrontation, propaganda and espionage.

Change was prevalent as well within the United States where the Civil Rights movement, led by the Rev. Martin Luther King, struggled to end legalized discrimination and racism in many of the States of America.

In 1955, Rosa Parks, a black woman, had disobeyed a segregation law by refusing to give up her place on a bus to a white person in Montgomery, Alabama. The arrest of this courageous lady was to initiate a boycott by blacks against this discriminatory law. Martin Luther King, a local Baptist pastor, had founded and become President of the Southern Leadership Conference of American Blacks in 1954. Members of this Conference recognized his leadership qualities and he was invited to lead his fellow blacks in the bus boycott in Montgomery. This sparked the beginning of the Civil Rights Movement that would be led by King for the next 13 years.

King was a gifted orator and his words would inspire a generation of both black and white Americans. King advocated peaceful and non-violent protest, as did Ghandi before him. In August of 1963 his Civil Rights Movement brought 200,000 marchers to Washington, D.C. where King delivered his famous "I have a dream" speech. He won the Nobel Peace prize in 1964. Leading a mass protest march from Selma to Montgomery, Alabama, in 1965, he created national support for federal voting rights legislation. Martin Luther King was assassinated in Memphis, Tennessee in 1968. The Civil Rights Movement under King brought the repeal of segregation laws and greater equality to American blacks. His voice rang out as well against the terrible poverty prevalent in black communities. King was opposed to the Vietnam war. Martin Luther King spoke to the conscience of the white population and changed racist attitudes.

The struggle of America's blacks for equality and the end of legalized discrimination and racism was not without its suffering and terrible cost in bloodshed. After years of being second class citizens in the 'land of the free', the Civil Rights Movement brought greater equality and dignity to the American Black population.

A similar movement in the mid-sixties began among the poor Mexican migrant workers in the California grape industry. This international movement was led by Cesar Chavez, whose boycotting of California grapes in Canadian stores raised public awareness, both in Canada and the United States, of the unjust wages and poor working conditions of these migrant workers.

What was called the "Cold War" between the superpowers of the 'free' world and the Soviet bloc intensified and grew to global proportions. The Berlin Wall that had been erected by the East German communist government in the early fifties came to symbolize the deep divisions between east and west, communism and democracy, and between what was evil in one system and what was good in the other.

History records this era as a period of great turbulence and a time of momentous change. Even the most unchangeable of institutions, the Roman Catholic Church, was affected. Pope John XXIII had been elevated to the papacy on October 27th, 1958 to succeed the austere and aloof Pius XII. Elected at the age of 78, John's pontificate was intended to be a caretaker or transitional papacy. He was not expected to make any significant changes within the walls of the Vatican. Yet, within ninety days of his election this 'old man' announced to the world that he was convoking an Ecumenical Council of the Catholic Church, the first such Council since 1870.

As change has become such a constant element of our modern society, it is difficult to envision or to fully grasp what this meant in the Catholic experience of the sixties. When John was elected pope the Roman Catholic Church was at a level of prestige, power and influence that it had not known since the middle ages. Catholics in Canada and the United States filled their parish churches to overflowing. Committed Catholics took pride in their active parish life and their Catholic schools. Mission activity throughout the world had resulted in thousands of converts. Recruits and vocations were aplenty, filling seminaries, convents and monasteries with future priests, religious sisters and brothers. To the mainstream Catholic the church was a perfect society; it had all the answers, and there seemed little need for change. The church's view on life and its problems was the only one that counted for most Catholics. Catholics, overall, possessed an identity and a deep sense of certainty.

Yet this ancient guardian of religious truth was being directed by this new pope to rediscover its ideals. Pope John was telling Catholics that the church had to approach the world in a more open way. This was the world that had always been looked upon with caution and fear. The Catholic organizations that I belonged to in my youth had sought to protect me from the influences of this world. Yet Pope John was saying the church had to discover new answers for new circumstances and meet the world halfway. One of the Curia's influential cardinals, Alfredo Ottaviani, was strongly opposed to the idea of a Council and rallied the conservative forces of the Vatican bureaucracy to work against it.

John's pontificate was to last five short years, yet within that time period he was to change the face of the Catholic Church forever. His openness, exuberance and sense of humour won the hearts of millions both within the church, and within other denominations and religions. Many historians would judge this Council, convoked by Pope John, the most important religious event of the 20th century.

At the opening ceremony of the Second Vatican Council on October 11, 1962, with 2,381 bishops present from all over the world, the pope's opening remarks were considered by many to be a bombshell, especially coming from the Vicar of Christ. His strong and unexpected message to the Council Fathers would set the pastoral tone for all the Council sessions. He challenged the prophets of doom within the church to be open to the Spirit and to read the signs of the times. He called upon the assembled bishops to withstand the hard liners of the Curia by telling them, "its time to open the windows of the Vatican and allow the Spirit of change and renewal in."

In his opening remarks he went on to say that:

> "It often happens that in our daily exercise of our
> ministry we are shocked to discover what is being said
> by some people who though they may be fired by
> religious zeal are without justice or good judgement,
> or consideration in their way of looking at this matter.
> In the existing state of society they see nothing but
> ruin and calamity. They say our age is much worse
> than past centuries. They behave as if history which
> teaches us about life had nothing to teach them.... it
> seems necessary to us to express our complete
> disagreement with these prophets of doom who give
> news only of catastrophes as if the world were ending.
> In the present state of affairs now that human society
> seems to have reached a turning point it is better to
> recognize the mysterious designs of Divine
> Providence; which ... achieve their purpose and guide
> events wisely for the good of the church, even those
> events which seem to conflict with her message."
> (Edward Stourton, *Absolute Truth*, Penguin Books,
> 1998, pp. 4-5)

This message of John was directed to those within his own Vatican
household, Cardinal Ottaviani and his colleagues, who had been
plotting to undermine the reforming spirit of the Council since the
moment it had been announced in 1958.

pope John's powerful exhortation to the assembled bishops moved
these pastoral leaders to take control of the Council. By his forceful
challenge to the conservatives, John brought forth the leadership
abilities of bishops outside the powerful Curia. These leaders, heeding
the call of John, threw out the prepared agenda and conclusions drawn
up by conservative churchmen within the Curia. In the three sessions
held between 1962 and 1965 their dialogue sessions produced sixteen
documents; four major documents called Constitutions, nine decrees,
and three declarations.

The four major documents or Constitutions dealt with: the Sacred Liturgy; the church as People of God; Divine Revelation and God's manifestation in Scripture and Tradition; and finally, the church's role in the modern world.

Each of these documents had a message for Catholics. They also addressed the church's relationship with other Christian denominations, with Judaism, and with non-Christian religions. The Council Fathers presented a new vision of church not just as the domain of the hierarchy, but as the whole people of God. Bishops shared a common responsibility as shepherds along with the pope. The laity now had a role in the church and served as agents of redemption in the world.

The liturgical life of the church was to be renewed and promoted. The Eucharist was to be celebrated in the vernacular, the language spoken by the congregation. Rites and devotions were to be reformed. The laity were encouraged to make Scripture their own as a distinct presence of God in their prayer life. A new relationship was to be made to the world as an ally in leading people to Christ.

The Council came to recognize Judaism as a relative and as a people of God with their own journey, ending years of religious discrimination against them. Eastern churches were recognized as possessing a distinctive heritage. There was a call for dialogue not just with fellow Christian churches and Judaism, but the great religions of the non-Christian world. Ecumenism was encouraged. Even the secular world offered new possibilities for the church. Religious freedom was endorsed, and the pre-eminence of individual conscience was recognized.

As the teaching church, Vatican II initiated not just reform but an unexpected revolution within itself. Both reform and revolution gave hope to many theologians and laity, but it also caused a loss of identity for many who saw in these changes, not renewal, but the denial of their traditional belief system. The age-old expression of that belief system was being refashioned, and this left them fearful. The aftermath of the Council saw the laity claim ownership of their church in a new way. Self-responsibility and the validation of local churches created a new relationship with the centralized power of the Curia. Responsibility to the world and its citizens in the areas of human rights, racism, discrimination, poverty and injustice became gospel imperatives.

Pope John had remarked, "the deposit of faith, the truths contained in our ancient doctrines is one thing, but the form in which they are presented to the world is another." (Edward Stourton, *Absolute Truth*, Penguin Books, 1998 p. 5) Vatican II had been called by John to initiate both renewal and reform but it went beyond what even the Council Fathers had anticipated. There were revolutionary consequences.

With the validation of local churches and self-responsibility, collegiality took on new vigour in the life of local churches. While mindful of the pope's overall role in the life of the church, local bishops as well as Conferences of Bishops, did not wait for signals from Rome but acted on the needs and the issues of their people. The principle of subsidiarity was evoked on numerous occasions. Although the Council officially ended in Rome in December of 1965 (after three years of formal sessions), most of the Council Fathers returned to their home dioceses with the expressed idea that the real work of the Council had just begun. As Pope Paul VI noted in the final session, "From now on *aggiornamento* (keeping abreast of the times) will signify for us a wisely undertaken quest for a deeper understanding of the spirit of the Council and the faithful application of the norms it has happily and prayerfully provided." *(The Documents of Vatican II*, Walter Abbott, SJ, Guild Press New York, 1966 pp. 738-739) Bishops, theologians and the laity were to understand and interpret the documents as initiatives for a continuing process of change.

The Second Vatican Council revolutionized the Catholic Church. But it has also polarized different approaches to faith and pastoral practice, both within the church structure and how the church presents itself to the world. Some see these approaches as mutually exclusive or in opposition to one another, while others see them as forming a creative (although sometimes unfriendly) tension from which a new church will emerge. The progressives hold that Vatican II was a long overdue and much needed accommodation with the world. Their position is that change within the church would make it a more relevant and effective instrument for the Gospel. The traditionalist hold that the church's long standing suspicion of the world was appropriate and is especially imperative in the modern world. They resisted the reforms of Vatican II and created bureaucratic roadblocks before and after the Council. The final group, the reformists, hold that the Council intended reform but not the revolution that resulted, or the eroding of the church's teaching authority. They would hold for a very literal and conservative interpretation of the Council documents. They would also hold that reforms ended with the Council. No more change was needed afterwards.

In the euphoric days following Vatican II the universal church was astir with new life and energy. The Dutch and German hierarchies and their theologians were in the forefront of the progressive elements within the church. The Canadian and American bishops followed suit. In Latin America, Brazil became the outstanding model of a progressive church. The Conference of Brazilian Bishops was the largest within the universal Catholic Church. Many visionary Brazilian leaders had emerged at the Council sessions, and so when they arrived home from Rome they embarked on a pastoral journey that would attempt to radically renew both church life and the social and political milieu of its 90 million followers.

∽∾

Shortly after his election in 1958, Pope John XXIII had initiated another movement that would directly affect my future life as a missionary. He had invited the churches of Europe and North America to send aid and personnel to the Latin American churches. Scarboro Missions responded to that invitation by taking on the pastoral care of the Itacoatiara church in Brazil. I was a senior member of that first group of Scarboro missionaries that would begin this new mission venture.

In 1961 that first group assigned to the Brazil Mission became focused on our new assignment and all the necessary preparations. In a very real sense Pope John XXIII's vision of church reform would propel me into an uncertain assignment in the "green hell" of the Amazon, and to major changes in all aspects of my life.

CHAPTER 7

Journey to Brazil

After I graduated from the Coady International Institute in May, 1961, I returned to Scarboro headquarters to begin preparations for my new appointment to Brazil. Five of us were appointed to this new mission: Paul McHugh, Vince Daniel, George Marskell, Doug MacKinnon and myself. Paul McHugh, who had been appointed superior of the new mission group, had been ordained in 1955, served in the Dominican Republic for three years and was just completing a three-year term in the Promotion Department. Vince Daniel was looking forward to his first mission appointment after five years as vocation director. George Marskell and Doug MacKinnon had been ordained the previous year. We met with our Superior General, Father Frank Diemert, for briefings on the new mission, and for the details regarding our language school studies.

The language school, located in Annapolis in the state of Goias in central Brazil, was under the direction of the Franciscan Fathers from New York. We were to begin classes in mid-November. Since this was to be a new mission, we set about determing the various tasks that needed attention. Two of us shopped for basic carpentry and machine tools that would not be available in northern Brazil. A Cummins marine engine was the first item on our shopping list because our mission trips to the interior villages would be made by riverboat. Medicinal supplies, some tropical clothing, and personal effects were packed in barrels for shipment to New York. It was agreed that Paul and Vince would travel with our provisions by steamer from New York to Belem, Brazil at the mouth of the Amazon River. I made plans to fly to St. Vincent, pack my personal belongings and get them to Trinidad in time to meet the steamer. Our young colleagues, George and Doug were to fly directly to Brazilia and then bus to Annapolis.

Our mission preparations also included all of the usual requirements for living and working in Brazil. Each of us had to apply for Brazilian visas and work permits. All of our personal documentation, and our medical history had to be translated into Portuguese and officially prepared by a Notary Public, who also had to document a list of all goods we were taking into the country.

As I was making these preparations I completed several preaching assignments during the summer months, spent holiday time with family in North Bay and then returned to headquarters in late September. The ordination class of George Marskell and Doug MacKinnon had been the largest in Scarboro's history, graduating twelve young priests. So, together with other mission appointments, the Brazil contingent participated in a farewell departure ceremony at St. Michael's Cathedral in Toronto. Monsignor John Mary Fraser, Scarboro's founder, was in attendance. The Scarboro Missions was sending missionaries to Japan, the Philippines, Guyana, the Dominican Republic, St. Vincent and the Bahamas as well as Brazil. It was the largest departure ceremony (there were 16 departing missionaries in all), in the history of the Society.

As I prepared to leave for Brazil, my mind was filled with many thoughts. I believed that to be involved in this modern crusade and mission was both a privilege and a challenge. I was in my early thirties, had some mission experience under my belt, and was now selected with four confreres to begin a new mission deep within the Amazon basin. It would have been an understatement to say that I was happy and fulfilled in my profession as a missionary and priest. My Vincentian experience had certainly been a fulfilling one. Yet in my last months there, I had questioned what we as foreigners were doing on a small island that already had a vigorous and local expression of Christianity. Now I was going to the largest Catholic country in the world! With this new and exciting venture about to unfold, and the church in the midst of an Ecumenical Council, questions of mission theory quickly faded into the background.

At the time, my knowledge of Brazil was minimal. Like every Canadian I knew of the famous city of Rio de Janeiro and the beaches of Copacabana. My geography lessons had taught me that the Amazon River was one of the largest rivers in the world, and the jungle along its banks was a source of oxygen for the world. Beyond these facts and a few other generalities I knew little of the country, its history, its peoples, and its form of government. My colleagues were none the wiser. Although we tried to acquaint ourselves as best we could, nevertheless, we set out as innocents to a land of mystery and enchantment. The locale, Itacoatiara, situated in the heart of the Amazon basin, the jungle and the mighty river – all this was the stuff of adventure. And I was to be a part of this thrilling expedition!

As planned, I met my friends as their steamer docked in Port of Spain in mid-October, 1961. We spent two days together, loaded my baggage on board, and then they continued by sea for Belem. I flew ahead to make arrangements for all of us to stay with the Franciscan Friars who were working in Belem. Aside from the usual delays normal for a cargo steamer, my companions soon arrived in Belem. As I awaited the arrival of my companions I had several weeks to acquaint myself with the docks and shipping area, and to get to know a little of this port city. Very quickly I was introduced to what would become my new life. I encountered the blazing sun and sweltering humidity of an equatorial city.

I met American and German missionaries who were working in the Amazon region. Father Jude a Franciscan friar took me along on his twice-weekly visits to a large leprosarium on the outskirts of the city. The complex was like a small town and we would visit the hospital area where the sick and those in the latter stages of the disease were housed. We also spent time in the workshops where patients did woodwork and various other crafts. There was a small school for the children and an apartment area where families lived. It was my first encounter with people afflicted with Hansen's disease, a disease that was prevalent in the Amazon region. Afflicted and stigmatized, these people lived outside the main stream of society.

On other days I walked the streets close to the port of old Belem. The morning fish market was always a hubbub of activity. Hundreds of fish vendors with a myriad variety of fish and sea life competed with each other, displaying their catches and shouting the names and quality of their produce to the jostling crowds of early morning shoppers. From the fish market it was easy to access the large area where fishermen would be washing down their boats, and folding and mending their nets. The flotilla of boats that varied in shape, size and colour was a scene that spoke of a way of life that was both mysterious and exciting. I became a frequent visitor to the area of the docks, captivated by both the boats and the men who sailed them for a living.

Belem's tropical gardens and zoo were also of interest to me. I spent many hours wandering through the lush tropical growth of plants, vines, and huge trees. The zoo had a unique and marvellous array of the creatures that inhabited the Amazonian tropical jungle. For the first time I was to see the howler monkey, the black-spotted ocelot, alligators, sloths, wild pigs, and many different species of snakes, including the anaconda. The zoo aquarium was filled with many of the fish that make the Amazon their home.

My colleagues finally arrived in early November. The next task was to deal with customs and immigration so that our baggage and the prized Cummins engine could be released. This was a much slower process than we had anticipated. Fr. Jude, our Franciscan host, continued to work on the custom's process long after we departed for language school in Annapolis.

While impatient with the delays of Brazilian customs, it was a fitting introduction to the way our new culture and country worked. Our extended time in Belem gave the three of us an opportunity to visit other missionary groups in and around the city. Seasoned missionaries offered us their perspectives, insights and experience on the country, her people and the church that we were coming to work for and to serve. Our personal observations and judgements were based on a North American church, and the limited experience that two of our group (Paul and myself) had experienced with other cultures and traditions.

Leaving the release of our baggage in the capable hands of Father Jude, we flew off to Manaus, the Amazonian State capital. Here we spent ten days in this city known as the "old rubber mecca of the world." We stayed with the Redemptorist Fathers who had a large parish and school in the city. These missionaries from Missouri also had a large pastoral area several hundred miles west of the city on the Amazon River. Our short visit to Manaus allowed us to initiate the process with immigration authorities for permanent work permits as missionaries.

After flying from Manaus to Brazilia, we travelled by bus to Annapolis in the state of Goias, in the mid-west of the country. Here we joined Doug and George and together we spent several months in language studies, and a course of inculturation. These studies would prove to be more than we bargained for.

CHAPTER 8

With Christ in Our Suitcases

The language and culture school was beginning its first year of operation. A similar facility for Spanish students was in Cuernavaca, Mexico. Monsignor Ivan Illich of New York had established both learning centres. Illich, an educator and thinker of international repute, had taken on the task of attempting to make missionaries out of classroom idealists. To accomplish that objective he had brought together an exceptional team of educators in both language and culture.

Our residence and living quarters were part of the Franciscan monastery. Classrooms were in an adjacent high school for the thirty-six missionaries – priests, brothers and sisters from Europe, Canada and United States. Some were from missionary organizations (orders, congregations, societies) and about half were from dioceses in Canada and the United States. These dioceses and many of the missionary organizations were responding to the appeal of Pope John XXIII to come to the aid of the Latin American church.

The director of the school was Father John Vogel, a Franciscan who had worked for many years in Brazil. Both he and Illich recognized that expertise in the language of our host country was of prime importance. Vogel had chosen a group of six local teachers, three women and three men, all trained in linguistics. We followed a language program that had been prepared for personnel of the United States Navy. Our schedule was four hours of intense study each morning from seven until eleven, in groups of six students. Female and male teachers rotated sessions with us. Pronunciation, sound, diction, and grammatical study were the keys to mastering Portuguese. These morning sessions were exercises in concentration that drained our energies. Our afternoons were for language study, alone or in groups. Our evenings were taken up with sessions in inculturation and Brazilian history.

These intensive studies lasted seven weeks. In the following years it would be extended to a three-month period of study for newly arriving missionaries. Because of scheduling, we, as the first participants, were limited to this seven-week period. Upon our return to Manaus, the five of us Scarboro missionaries decided to do a further five-week study program with a private teacher.

To live in another culture and country, and to understand the traditions, history and people, a knowledge of and facility with the language is all important. But to become at home in the language, being able to understand and communicate your ideas and needs, demands total commitment. It requires patience and perseverance, attuning the ear, listening carefully, and making phonetic adaptation. Even with all the study and practice, mastering a language is still a gift.

In order to make the transition from the idealism of our theological and mission studies, to becoming an integrated part of our host country, learning Portuguese was all important. When an educated person experiences a helplessness similar to a child uttering his or her first words, straining to understand the simplest phrase, the situation is humbling to say the least. My language experience which had begun in Annapolis and continues today, still causes me to admire the immigrants who struggles to master English under much more difficult circumstances.

These seven intense weeks of studying Portuguese tempered my romantic and idealistic notion of being a missionary. If I wanted to achieve my goal of being a good missionary in Brazil then nothing short of total commitment was necessary. I asked, "Was I capable of such commitment?" This is how I began the first rocky and torturous steps in becoming Brazilian! Although these weeks were difficult, and the ensuing months even more so in my struggle to master a language not mine by birth, the experience gave me a fighting chance to achieve my goal.

But it was not only language that was a shock. The Brazilian culture also demanded a steep learning curve. In a few short weeks, all my pious and sacred formation, all my accepted ways of thinking about my religious beliefs, and all my cultural biases were put on trial under the scrutiny and cross-examination of Ivan Illich and John Vogel.

Ivan Illich's career as priest and educator had always been an enigma to the establishment. If you have read any of his published works on education, you will readily understand what I mean. His provocative technique of overturning or upsetting the sacred cows of tradition and orthodoxy in religion and education have long scandalized the conservative establishment. Born of a Puerto Rican Catholic mother and a Czechoslovakian Jewish father, Illich converted to Catholicism in his late teens. He was raised in New York. Graduating from Columbia University he decided on the priesthood and became a protege of Cardinal Francis Spellman of New York.

Illich worked with the Puerto Rican population in New York, establishing schools and housing projects for them. He lobbied state and federal officials for financial aid for an immigrant population that had long been disenfranchised and neglected. Illich was equally prominent in educational circles. He challenged the accepted system of education, pointed out its serious deficiencies, and introduced radical alternative pedagogical methods. His interest in the training of missionaries, he often said, was to help prevent more harm than good being done by the influx of North American missionaries into Central and South America.

Illich came from Cuernavaca, Mexico to personally initiate the first students at his newest foundation in Annapolis. A linguistic expert, he studied Brazilian Portuguese with one of the teachers for a few hours each day, and lectured and dialogued with his students from early evening to well beyond midnight. These sessions, where he challenged our "sacred cows," shocked and captivated us all. Some students questioned his Catholicity, while others labelled him a communist out to destroy the church. His stay with us was a brief two weeks but his presence challenged us and made a lasting impression on me.

As I struggled to express myself in Portuguese, Illich's stature took on even greater proportions when he preached in the local cathedral at the Christmas Midnight Mass. Without hesitation and very much at ease, he spoke fluently in his latest acquired language. Knowing I would never be able to master Portuguese with his skill, I also knew that to be articulate I would have to be studious, patient and persevering.

My education from childhood to post-seminary formation, along with my colleagues, had always been in a Catholic setting. I had studied the social encyclicals of Leo XIII on labour, and the ethic of work and capitalism, in a theoretical and abstract manner. In our open forums at the seminary we debated the good and evil of the free enterprise system, of trade unions and the democratic system. The year I spent at the Coady Institute had taught me ways of working to change unjust economic and social systems. In the Catholic primary and secondary education systems of the times we seldom questioned the economic or political systems, or even considered other options. We lived in an ideal world. Our teachers passed on their treasures of knowledge to their student body. Our philosophical and theological studies were in institutions run by the church, the guardian and dispenser of truth. Some teachers and professors may have tolerated questioning at times, but they were the selected human instruments of our guardian and mother, the church, and it was the church that dispensed wisdom and truth to us, without questioning on our part.

Illich and his team gave me a new way of thinking that was both exciting and fearful. For the first time in my adult life it allowed me to move out from that harbour of safe and protected thought. It forced me to think for myself, to challenge what I had accepted without question! Was our safe little Catholic world the best world? Did the church practice what it preached? Was the church itself faithful to the gospel message? What were we, as smug, self-righteous American missionaries, presuming to do in Brazil? We had come, no doubt, with Christ in our suitcases, with all the goodwill in the world to respond to the religious needs of the Brazilian church and people. But within that packaged suitcase, were we also carrying our prejudices, our shadowy view, and our superior American attitude? Did not the Latin American church and people have something to teach us? And what about the good, old, democratic American way of life? Had we ever questioned our own political systems and gods? Were they that much more committed to the betterment of the human condition? How did our civil institutions and our church make use of power and propaganda in their agendas?

In his short time with us Illich took on the role of a devil's advocate *par excellence*. He dared to upset our religious and civil utopias. Illich was like the Old Testament prophet Micah with his piercing black eyes, his sharp nose and his gaunt figure. He rattled us to such a degree that at times we retreated to the safer havens of idyllic myths where we were the products of a perfect church, and lived in an all but perfect civil and political society! At other times we responded in a defensive manner. Illich was tearing down the safe world we had created. Suffice to say that Ivan Illich did not so much teach us what to think, as to how to think. This methodology had the desired effect of upsetting our traditional thought processes, producing a period of confusion, and finally allowing us to see and think differently. It was a process that changed the way I looked at myself, and certainly the way I would continue as a missionary.

During this time our weekends were filled with field trips to the interior of the state of Goias. We were billeted in individual homes and in this way we were introduced to the simple, humble lives of the peasant farmers of interior Brazil where we shared in the communal and church activities of the village. Aside from their subsistence living and working conditions, my most vivid memory is the trusting way the host families and the villagers opened their homes and their lives to complete strangers. We were welcomed as family, and treated with hospitality generated by warm, loving people. Their patience with our faltering Portuguese, their generous sharing of themselves and their home life was spontaneous and genuine. As I learned, it was part of their nature to put their own problems and family preoccupations aside in order to give themselves to the stranger who crossed their threshold as guest.

The seven weeks of language study and inculturation quickly went by, and in mid-January 1962 we ended the first phase of our introduction to Brazil. Bidding farewell to friends and acquaintances, teachers, and fellow missionaries, we all headed toward our various mission areas.

In the last weeks of the course George Marskell had fallen ill with hepatitis. So Doug MacKinnon stayed on with George in Annapolis until George made a complete recovery and was able to travel north to Manaus. Paul McHugh, Vince Daniel and I left Annapolis for Belem. We spent a week in Sao Paulo and Rio de Janeiro visiting some of the tourist attractions on our way. We arrived in Belem to find that Father Jude had completed the necessary custom process for the release of our baggage and equipment. Our next journey would be to travel up the Amazon River by steamer.

CHAPTER 9

Up the Amazon

The opportunity to travel a thousand miles upstream on the Amazon River was a dream come true. We had decided to accompany our baggage and equipment, and the prized Cummins engine. Our scheduled trip was to be on a wood-burning steamer, dubbed the *Barao de Cameta*, an old vessel built in Glasgow, Scotland in 1911. It was principally a small cargo boat with an iron hull, and contained sparse quarters for passengers. A family of four was to share the decks with the captain, his crew and the three of us. After several delayed departures, we left the port of Belem on the eve of *Carnival* in February, 1962.

The trip, while providing the opportunity of a lifetime, was a slow, tedious journey in cramped quarters for three mute missionaries. It was the hot and humid rainy season. The boat had its scheduled stops with cargo shipments, but the captain also bartered and traded as it moved slowly upriver against the current. A constant supply of wood was needed to keep the boilers functioning, and the process of loading the *lenhya* or wood sticks at isolated supply stations was time consuming. At each fuel stop no money ever exchanged hands. The supplier got paid in rice and beans and the loaders were given so many chips or tallies, depending on the number of loads carried and piled aboard. When the wood was all aboard, they exchanged their tallies for yard goods or basic food supplies. Every three or four days at such a stop a cow would be loaded aboard, to be slaughtered en route and served up in stew dishes for crew and passengers.

However slow and tedious the journey may have been for impatient missionaries, I learned that the *Barao de Cameta's* passage was a vital link for isolated communities along the river. For many of these villages its arrival was one of the few contacts with the outside world. And our stops brought us into contact with the people who eked out a livelihood on the land adjacent to the mighty river. They were called *cabocolos*, people of the interior. Most of them lived by hunting, fishing, and planting subsistent food crops. The majority of people in the many communities we encountered were either pioneer migrants or the offspring of successive migrations from the arid northeastern regions of Brazil. They had come in search of a better way of life and the promise of free land, ending up entrenched in a feudal system, subservient to a patron, who for the most part, controlled their economic life.

Our river trip to Itacoatiara took eleven days. Some of the main stops included larger towns such as Obidos and Santarem in the state of Para, and then Parintins, Urucara, Itapiranga and, finally, Itacoatiara in the state of Amazonas. These were all names and places with which we were to become very familiar. The route of the winding river within the states of Para and Amazonas lies two degrees below the equator, while the Amazon basin itself is only a degree above sea level. The scenery was jungle and more jungle, but the sunrises and sunsets were a spectacle of breathtaking colour. The early morning and evening flight of countless flocks of birds was a thrill beyond words.

And the Amazon River! Here we were, three Canadians, travelling upstream against the force and the power of one of the world's mightiest rivers. We were to witness the force of its current as our steamer inched its way ever so slowly upstream. The river had a life of its own that gave life and sustenance to thousands of creatures. In its journey down to the sea the river varied in width from a mile to almost three hundred miles around Belem. Its mighty force expelled its muddy, fresh waters three hundred miles into the Atlantic Ocean.

This river would become central in our mission life and work in the future. We would learn to respect its force and power, and try to understand its powerful personality.

In the early hours of the morning of the twelfth day aboard the *Barao de Cameta*, we disembarked and bade our farewell to the crew. We had arrived in Itacoatiara. Many of the townsfolk welcomed us as we made our way to the parish house of the incumbent pastor Father Alcides Peixoto. We had informed him of our approximate arrival date by telegram sent from Parintins.

We spent two days in Itacoatiara in the little home of Father Alcides Peixoto. His residence, adjacent to the river, was in the main plaza not far from the church. His two maiden sisters Maria and Teresa who cared for the household, were also the parish secretaries. They taught catechism as well. Alcides introduced us to many faithful parishioners, the mayor, some local politicians as well as navy and airforce personnel. As *gringos* coming to take over the pastoral charge of the area, we were on display.

Alcides also took us on a tour of the town, acting as our interpreter. The people received us with that warm and embracing hospitality that is uniquely Brazilian and that we would come to know so well. Our few halting expressions responded inadequately to the poetic, charming and lengthy words of welcome offered by the townspeople.

At the time of our arrival Itacoatiara was a small town with a population of around eleven thousand inhabitants. Over the course of the next few years we would get to know Itacoatiara well. Its history went back several hundred years. The town was the seat of the municipal area that extended close to one hundred miles up river, and about seventy miles down river. It was situated on the northern banks of the Amazon approximately one hundred and eighty miles east of the Amazonian capital of Manaus. It was a port city as the river was the principal communication route that linked the innumerable villages and communities east and west of the town. A highway was under construction to link up with Manaus. There was a small airport on the outskirts of the town that served the Brazilian airforce. Air travel was limited to weekly flights on an amphibious aircraft that landed on the river close to the port itself. Several passenger boats served the

South America

VENEZUELA

COLOMBIA

ECUADOR

PERU

Manaus •

X
*Prelacy of
Itacoatiara*

BOLIVIA

BRAZIL

CHILE

PARAGUAY

URAGUAY

ARGENTINA

N

W ←→ E

S

Prelacy of Itacoatiara
92,000 square kilometres

population, making three trips a week to and from Manaus and down river as far as Parintins.

The main *praca* or city plaza was situated on a high embankment adjacent to the main port. The plaza was open to the river at its south end and was flanked with the *Matriz* or mother church at the north end, several businesses (the telegraph and post office, and the local pub) on the west side, and the main high school and several residences on the east side. Huge mango trees dominated the central plaza. The business section was located within a two block radius immediately west of the plaza and flowed down to the port. There were small detachments of the Brazilian navy and airforce on either side of the church. The main avenue of the town ran north from the plaza. The town itself spread to the east and west along the river. The courthouse was on the main avenue one block from the church. The municipal offices and the town hall were on a street that linked the main avenue with the town market. Opposite the town hall there was an electrical generating plant powered by an old diesel engine. Electricity was usually quite dependable, although there were blackouts when the town coffers were empty or the diesel supply had not arrived.

The town consisted of three principal areas at the time of our arrival in 1962; the central quarter that I have just described, the *barrio* quarter of *Espirito Santo* that was west and north of the main market, and another *barrio* called *Juary*, that sprawled in a swampy area along the river east of the plaza.

There was one bank in the town, several jute plants, a rubber factory and a sawmill. The town was the major commercial and trading centre for both the municipality of Itacoatiara, and four neighbouring municipalities. There were several other small denominational churches in the town, a private girls school, a school run by the Baptists, several elementary schools, a public health centre and a small maternity hospital under construction. Medical assistance was minimal although there was a public health doctor and several nurses connected to the health centre. There were two or three self-trained dentists in town, and many drugstores with an abundance of prescription drugs and injections sold over the counter. The town boasted of four vehicles that were something of a novelty. Most of the townsfolk walked to their destinations about town, but a good number of the younger generation travelled by bicycle.

Depending on the season there was a constant flow of farmers and traders. Local fishermen were always out on the river in the early hours of the morning and late afternoon. The river supplied an abundant variety of fish for the townspeople, their main diet. The large market, and a smaller one in the barrio of Juary were always a hub of activity. Farmers came to town mostly by canoe, or in small-powered boats to pay their taxes. They would buy supplies, arrange or pay a loan with their *patrao* or patron. They would also come to the parish house for baptisms and marriages.

The name *Itacoatiara* originated from an indigenous word meaning *painted rock*. There were two seasons, the rainy extending from December until June, and the dry season for the rest of the months. The temperature would drop in the rainy season to around 30°C (86°F). During the dry season it would hover close to 40°C (104°F), rising to 45°C (113°F) in a very hot year. During the month of June there was always a breeze that carried colder air down from the Andes. We usually referred to this as our winter when the temperature would drop to 18°C (65°F), and we would all suffer from the 'cold spell.'

Obviously the river dominated the lives of the people. It was their main supply and communication route. In a normal year it rose and fell between 40 and 60 feet, inundating huge areas of the adjacent jungle, and linking interior villages through a series of small rivers and streams with inland lakes. The river was about a mile and a half wide in front of the town and its current was strong. An evening breeze could always be counted on to cool things off in the day's evening hours. Travelling upstream to Manaus was a trip of twenty-two hours, but only fourteen hours downstream from Manaus to Itacoatiara.

After our short visit with Father Alcides Peixoto and our introduction to Itacoatiara, our future hometown, we made our way to Manaus aboard the *motor da linhya* or line boat, one of the vessels that traversed the river route to the capital. Along with seventy or eighty Brazilians and their hammocks and belongings, we travelled upstream making innumerable stops to discharge passengers, small livestock and supplies en route. The meals aboard were usually boiled fish, rice, beans and *farinha* (a type of flour meal). At night we hung up our hammocks on the main deck with the other passengers and slept in the open air. We quickly learned that the *rede* or hammock was always a part of river travel. You carried your bed, and the hammock was strung wherever there was space with many willing hands to tightly secure it.

Manaus, the capital of Amazonas State was to be our temporary home for the next five months. It was situated at the mouth of the *Rio Negro* or Black River. It was famous for its Opera House built during the rubber boom, and its floating docks built by the British. While we visited these historical attractions, our time in Manaus was taken up with more important tasks. Upon arrival from Itacoatiara, Paul, Vince and I took up residence with the Redemptorist Fathers. Here we reunited with George and Doug. George had finally recovered from his bout with hepatitis. Our language studies continued with a private teacher. We helped out in a limited way at some of the city parishes that were under the care of the Redemptorists.

Mary, the mother of Christ, plays a very prominent role in Latin American Catholicism. The Redemptorists had introduced devotion to Our Lady of Perpetual Help at their parishes in both Belem and Manaus. Tuesday was novena day and the novena celebrations were scheduled from early morning until late evening. These novenas were special prayers and devotional services dedicated to Mary. These services attracted nine thousand devotees each week to the Manaus church and over fourteen thousand to the church in Belem. So the next few months introduced the five of us to parish work while we began to use our newly acquired language. We also spent time upriver in the prelacy of Coari on the river Purus, where we were introduced to life in an interior parish.

Manaus was the home of Archbishop Dom Joao de Sousa Lima, and Itacoatiara was under his church jurisdiction. Father Mario Anglim the Redemptorist superior arranged a visit with Dom Joao and the five of us met with him at his residence for the first time in March of 1962. He welcomed us to his Archdiocese, and over several visits during our remaining months in Manaus, we came to know him well. He arranged visits with the police and the immigration department. He also prepared the church documents and letters that would allow us to work as foreign priests within the country. The official date for assuming the pastoral care of Itacoatiara was set for August 1, 1962.

The Archbishop requested that Paul McHugh and I spend Holy Week in Itacoatiara. It would be an opportunity not just to help with the liturgical celebrations, but also an opportunity to get to know Fr. Alcides, the pastor and his assistant, Francisco Pinto, as well as the leaders of the various Catholic organizations. These visits acquainted us with the general workings of the parish. During Easter time it also provided us an opportunity to visit, along with Fr. Alcides Miguel Monteiro, the village of Sao Sebastiao on the river Uatuma. Miguel Monteiro had been contracted by Fr. Alcides to build a cargo boat for us.

Soon we would officially assume the responsibility of the church in Itacoatiara. In the evening hours of July 31, 1962 the five of us Scarboro missionaries boarded a Redemptorist boat and pulled out of the port of Manaus. Our destination was Itacoatiara, the community of the "painted rock." We were launching out on our own to begin the pastoral care of the municipality of Itacoatiara and the four other municipalities that were linked to it, an area of 92,000 square kilometres.

Mario Anglim, the Redemptorist Superior accompanied us on this fourteen hour trip down the Amazon River. As we made our way past the floating city that had built up on the edge of the port, the mood was exhilarating yet pensive. In a very real way we felt we were journeying toward our destiny, as a team, motivated by the same ideals, the same hope and faith. Yet each of us was so different and distinct from one another, looking out over the Amazon River with our own thoughts and dreams and doubts. The greatest adventure of our lives and the most provocative challenge to our faith had just begun to unfold.

CHAPTER 10

Gently Putting Things in Place

The setting off of powerful fireworks always heralded formal visits to towns and villages from government and church officials. According to custom, as our boat approached the town of Itacoatiara on August 1, 1962, we signalled our arrival by firing several firecrackers. In response, the crowds awaiting our arrival on shore, ignited an avalanche of colourful skyrockets, while church bells rang out and anchored vessels joined in with their sirens and bells. As well as being a welcoming salute to us onboard the approaching boat, it gave notice to the townsfolk of our imminent arrival and was a signal for them to gather to meet us at the town dock.

Our arrival and our subsequent beginning of pastoral work as missionaries was an historical event in the long history of Itacoatiara, both from a church perspective, as well as socially and politically. Historically there had always been ties with the Portuguese church. Now five Anglo-Saxon Canadians were coming to live among them. We would be doing pastoral work in the municipality of Itacoatiara, and the four other municipalities that were linked with the town of Itacoatiara – Uricurituba, Silves, Itapiranga and Urucara.

Hundreds of townsfolk singing hymns lined the shores and stood on the docks as lines were thrown out, and our boat was safely secured. The two resident clergy, Padres Alcides Peixoto and Francisco Pinto, and the town officials welcomed us Crowds jostled to greet us and a procession led us from the docks up the small hill to the main plaza situated in front of the church. An eloquent spokesman for the church and the town, Mr. Sebastian Vasconcellos Dias, welcomed us with a masterpiece of oratory, telling us that the hearts of all the townspeople were open to receive us. Mr. Dias, a fervent Catholic, was manager of the Bank of Brazil and was a leader in the town's economic and social life.

One of the great gifts of all Brazilians is their openness and warmth to the stranger. This welcoming of strangers and hospitality is natural, honest, and all embracing. They truly and sincerely hold out their hand and heart to the newcomer. As foreigners, coming into the town of Itacoatiara to serve the townspeople as their pastors, we were made to feel as brothers who had come home. The warm enthusiasm and genuine reception of the people that surrounded us matched Mr. Dias's words of welcome.

The resident pastor, Alcides Peixoto, welcomed us and offered his full co-operation in the pastoral transfer. On behalf of the Archbishop of Manaus, Padre Mario Anglim introduced each of us, and gave a brief outline of the work of our Mission Society. Following this official welcome in the town park, the crowds moved to the church where prayers were offered that our work would be fruitful.

After a brief church ceremony the five of us were engaged by well-wishers in the town park. Our limited vocabulary was tested to the limit as we answered questions regarding our families left behind and about Canada. Was it close to Portugal? Did we like Brazil? How did we like the town of Itacoatiara? Our well-wishers were genuinely interested in us as persons and were intent on making us feel welcome. Everyone who greeted us was spontaneous in offering us an invitation to come to their homes. Many offered to show us the town once we got settled.

Our home was to be with Alcides Peixoto and his sisters for the first few months. His sisters, Teresa and Maria, assigned us our rooms and helped us to settle in. Mario Anglim stayed on with us for a few days, so as visitors we took over the Peixoto household. Our first evening meal introduced us to a typical Itacoatiara menu: fish soup, broiled *tambaqui* (a delicious local fish) served with rice, beans, and small amounts of hot pepper sauce. Dessert was a small piece of fresh fruit, a portion of preserved fruit and goat's cheese. The meal ended with a small cup of Brazilian coffee.

For the first six weeks we lived out of our suitcases, shared rooms, and although somewhat cramped for space, managed quite well. By this time we were comfortable sleeping in the hammocks we strung-up each evening on convenient posts around the house, and then rolled up again each morning.

Alcides Peixoto and his family were native to Itacoatiara. He had succeeded Monsignor Joaquim Pereira as pastor of the area. Alcides had grown up under the tutelage of the old Portuguese pastor. Following high school in Itacoatiara, Peixoto studied at the seminary in Manaus and in southern Brazil. After ordination he had returned to his hometown to work alongside the ageing Pereira. Small in stature like many Brazilians, Alcides was in his mid-forties. He had been pastor for ten years and was serious about his pastoral responsibilities. His young assistant Francisco Pinto, had been with Alcides since his ordination three years previous. As was the custom, Pinto lived alone, taught in the local high school to support himself, and shared pastoral responsibilities with Alcides.

There were three or four small devotional churches in the town. Services, however were held only in the main church, Our Lady of the Rosary (*Nossa Senhora do Rosario*), and in a church situated in the *barrio* called the Colony of the Holy Spirit, on the western end of the town. There was a daily Mass each morning both at the main church, and at the local convent school that was under the direction of the Sisters of St. Dorothy. There was a schedule for daily baptisms and marriages to accommodate people who journeyed from the interior.

Alcides did all the interior pastoral visitations. He had a small houseboat called the *Carmecita*, about twenty-four feet in length and powered by a small Lister engine. He travelled with his older brother on these trips. His brother was the motorman and handled the wheel. With such a huge pastoral area to be covered, Alcides spent many months throughout the year visiting the interior towns and villages. During his absence, Francisco Pinto carried on with the pastoral work in the town and his work as a teacher.

The Dorothean Sisters ran a convent school for around one hundred and fifty girls. The sisters were well qualified, competent, and dedicated educators. Their curriculum ranged from the primary grades through high school. Their school was a private institution maintained by tuition fees. Applicants submitted to an entrance exam for the higher grades. Many of the students were from the interior towns and lived at the convent during the school year. The school and its religious educators had a reputation for excellence in learning and youth formation.

The sisters were also very active in the catechetical program for the children of the town. On Saturdays and Sundays a full schedule of classes introduced the Catholic faith to the town's children and prepared them for their First Communion and Confirmation. The senior students in the convent school formed a voluntary brigade of 'catechism teachers.' These youthful catechists held classes in all of the barrios of the town for the religious instruction and formation of the children.

The mainstay of Alcides' parish organization was the *Liga do Sagrado Coracao de Jesu*, the Sacred Heart League, one for the men and another for the women of the parish. Alcides was the chaplain for both groups, but an elected lay group headed these organizations. To be a member of the League meant a serious commitment to the life of the parish community.

In the pre-Vatican II church, a devotion of piety prevalent in Europe and most of the Americas was to the person of Christ under the form of his Sacred Heart. This devotion involved a personal commitment to frequent confession and communion on a monthly basis. Observing the first Friday of each month fulfilled the commitment.

This devotion began in France following a series of apparitions of Christ to a French contemplative sister, Margaret Mary Alacoque in the 18th century. It was a devotion that asked for atonement to the Sacred Heart for the sins of the world. On Good Friday, Christ as Saviour had died for our sins, so the first Friday of each month was marked as the day when the committed Catholic atoned for personal and communal sin by going to confession, receiving communion and assisting at Mass. The apparitions had been sanctioned by the church, and so devotion to the Sacred Heart became a prominent practice in most parishes.

In the parish life of Itacoatiara this devotion to the Sacred Heart became an important instrument in evangelizing the Catholic population. It served as a unifying force in the life of the parish community, and strengthened individual commitments. There were scheduled confessions leading up to the First Friday and on the day itself. Confession was considered a sacred duty in preparation for the Mass of the Sacred Heart. The priests would spend hours hearing the confessions of parishioners not just from the town itself, but from neighbouring communities. Many League members in small villages along the Amazon River would leave their homes at midnight and paddle all the way to Itacoatiara in time for confession and the first Mass at six in the morning on First Fridays.

An incident that took place on one of these Fridays has always remained with me. It occurred during our first months in Itacoatiara. I was hearing confessions in the early morning hours, and as usual, there was a huge line-up of penitents waiting. The person confessing was a man from the interior. He hesitantly made his confession, and so I proceeded to give him counsel and to question him as part of my role, to ensure that he made a worthy confession. "Had he confessed all his sins?" I asked. There was a long silence. Then in a very gentle voice, he said, "Father, you do not know me, but God knows me and completely understands me. I am a man."(*O Senhor nao me sabe, mas Deus me compreende.*) The gentle voice had used the verb *saber* that limited my knowledge of the penitent, and the verb *compreender* that was the fullness of knowledge for his Creator. That was a lesson in humility that has never left me. I remain grateful to that unknown man from the interior, who ever so gently spoke of God's love and gently, put me in my place.

The parish was a frenzy of activity on First Fridays, with the church overflowing at both the morning and evening Masses. Special Eucharistic devotions were held throughout the day, facilitated by the League presidents and their committees. At these solemn events League members would wear their insignia, a red scapular, and their banners would adorn the Sanctuary of the church. Monthly meetings of League members would plan and co-ordinate activities for each month, and encourage the enrolment of new members.

There were also two smaller church groups active in the life of the parish. The Legion of Mary followed a spirituality based on the ideals of Mary, and promoted a high ideal of morality for the youth of the parish, especially young women. Father Francisco Pinto had also formed a nucleus of high school students in the Young Christian Student movement. Vince Daniel and I took over the chaplaincy of the League, and George Marskell worked with the youth. Doug MacKinnon became co-ordinator of the catechetical program.

These were the principal activities that fostered an active and vigorous Christian input in the lives of the townspeople. Alcides followed a similar practice in his pastoral work in the interior towns and villages. In fact, this pastoral practice was the norm in most parishes and churches in North America at this time. Considering the limited resources both in clerical and religious personnel, and in finances, it worked quite effectively in Itacoatiara.

In addressing the Catholic religious history of Itacoatiara and the surrounding area, it must be borne in mind that Brazil was, and is the largest "Catholic" country in the world. In our area within the state of Amazonas, the Jesuits had begun work in Urucara, and had mission bases along the Uatuma and Jatapu Rivers in 1750, but they were expelled in 1754. Another group of missionaries from Portugal, the

Mercedarios, also did extensive work along the Urubu River. In the mid-1800s when the capital of the state was Saraca, later named Silves, a Portugese priest, Daniel de Oliveira, became pastor of Saraca and worked there until his death in 1893.

Father Joaquim Pereira had begun his pastoral work in Itacoatiara and surrounding area in 1911. He worked as pastor of the town and the surrounding area until 1955 when Alcides Peixoto took over. Joaquim Pereira's forty years of pastoral work, that Peixoto had inherited and built upon, had resulted in a strong core of active Catholics in the whole area. Joaquim Pereira had come from Portugal as a young priest, and worked alone in this vast area, the size of many dioceses in Canada. For many years he travelled to the interior villages in a large eight-man canoe, a trip to the outer boundaries of the area taking weeks.

In his later years Pereira completely lost his sight. Local folklore attributed this loss of vision to the constant glare of the tropical sun on the river waters. Pereira died in 1958 but had become something of a legend. He oversaw the construction of the new church in Itacoatiara in the early 1950s, and it is said he climbed the scaffolding, blind and clad in his dark cassock, to examine the ceiling and pillar moldings with his hands.

Scarboro's mission to Itacoatiara had come in response to an urgent plea of Pope John XXIII. The churches of Latin America were in need of clerical personnel. As we began our pastoral missionary work in Itacoatiara, this was the church institution and faith community that we took over from Alcides Peixoto and Francisco Pinto.

Both Peixoto and Pinto, after guiding us through our first weeks, went on to pastoral assignments in Manaus. Our manpower allowed us to schedule Sunday Masses in two of the larger chapels in Itacoatiara, and our pastoral visits to the larger towns of Silves, Itapiranga, Urucara, and Uricurituba became more frequent.

Adapting to functioning within this pastoral system was not difficult for any of us. After all, we were ordained as priests, trained to celebrate Mass and to administer the sacraments. Celebration of Mass and many of the sacraments was still conducted in Latin. Our Portuguese 'church' vocabulary was slowly built up, and the Sunday Scripture readings gave us material for the composition of our sermons and reflective spiritual talks. Slowly but surely our Portuguese improved and we came to feel at home in our role as pastors.

As a missionary I was gently putting things in place, and as I learned, on some occasions, I was being put in my place as well.

CHAPTER 11

A New Way of Life

Inculturation was quite another matter. Adapting to another climate and foreign way of life is one thing, but to inculturate means to take on another people's history, traditions, value systems, thought patterns and perspective that evolve from that history, those traditions and those values. Most of us mastered the language with a good degree of efficiency and even expertise within a couple of years. Others had the enviable gift of being able to speak and understand like a Brazilian. Inculturation, on the other hand, was a consciousness that took a lifetime, and came only by personally striving for it.

As our first weeks and months quickly went by, we established a good rapport with many of the townspeople. The majority of the people were "Catholic" in name, but not all attended church. There were also several small Baptist and Pentecostal churches in the town. Gradually we became accepted as persons and friends, and not solely because we were priests.

Another pastoral event that helped in this process was the planning and staging of a Mission throughout our whole area. The Redemptorist Fathers, with whom we had stayed in Manaus, were invited to send a team to preach the parish Missions. Their religious congregation was famous for its preachers. A parish Mission was an instrument of evangelizing, not unlike a religious revival. It was held approximately every two years, and had as its objective the renewal of the faith and practise of the lay Catholic. Again, it was common in parish life in Canada and the States during the 1940s and 1950s.

We had been in Itacoatiara for a year when we began preparations for a Mission that would be held in all of the major towns. Scheduling and preparatory work took place on our visits into the interior. It was to be a major religious event in the lives of the people. Three Redemptorist Fathers, each aided by a Scarboro priest, formed three teams to conduct the week-long Mission in each of the nine towns, culminating with a two-week long Mission in Itacoatiara.

There was a tremendous response on the part of the people. Their strong religious sense and natural spirituality ensured capacity crowds in every town for each of the seven days. Men, women and children enthusiastically took part in this religious revival that strengthened the faith communities of the area. As members of the Mission team, this religious event helped us as missionaries to gain a deeper insight and respect for the religious values and expression of the parishioners. As new pastors, the event provided us with another opportunity to integrate into the lives of the people, and further adapt to mission life in our Amazon surroundings.

While our new boat was being built, Alcides loaned us a smaller version of the *Santa Teresinha*. The *Carmecita* was used for pastoral visits to the other municipalities. Teams of two priests began regular trips to these interior municipalities, and became the contact persons for the people of that area when they came to town. Our pastoral area extended over a 92,000 square kilometre area that extended east and west from Itacoatiara along the Amazon River. Three of the municipalities east of Itacoatiara were north of the Amazon along river tributaries.

Each town or village had at least one *festa* a year to celebrate its patron saint, and so pastoral visits were scheduled in order to coincide with these major events. These river trips to the interior towns and villages were called *desobrigas* from the Portuguese verb meaning to fulfil one's obligation. On these pastoral visitations, villagers made their confession and received the Holy Eucharist. But as well as being a religious celebration these *festas* were also community celebrations that became a time for people to socialize and get together.

The major *festas* went on for a period of eight days. On these days there were scheduled celebrations in the village chapel. Confessions, baptisms, morning Mass, evening prayers in honour of the patron saint, and the celebration of marriage were on the religious agenda. These religious festivities would end with a large procession and solemn Mass on the saint's feast day. A carnival-like atmosphere surrounded the community celebrations. Vendors would come to sell dry goods and home utensils. Small kiosks for eating and drinking were set up. Evening would see the universal game of bingo being played after the church services. Finally, there would be the selling-off by barter of gifts or baked goods. The final evening of the *festa* would be filled with music, merrymaking and dancing.

These celebrations were major events in the lives of the people, and had been traditionally celebrated each year. It was one of the few yearly opportunities for people to come together from their isolated villages to visit and to celebrate. One of the negative factors that accompanied these celebrations was the over indulgence of alcohol, hardly conducive for a religious celebration yet understandable when you considered the austere lives of the people.

Outside of the villages and towns, people lived very isolated lives. There were no telephones or television. Travel was difficult, and almost always involved a canoe and a paddle. There were few radios to speak of. Subsistence farming and fishing under difficult conditions made life severe for the majority of these people. Their lifestyle was primitive, and there were few of the luxuries that our North American standards would consider basic.

People who lived in the interior were called *cabocolos*, that is, a person from the jungle. They were truly pioneers, eking out a life for themselves under the most difficult of circumstances as subsistent farmers working a small plot of land. Jute was the principal money crop. Coffee, cocoa, bananas, oranges, limes, brazil nuts were also cultivated. Where the soil was suitable, rice and beans were also harvested. In some areas rubber trees were tapped.

The average small farm would consist of a half-acre hacked out of the jungle surroundings, close to the water's edge. Jute would be planted and then when harvested it could readily be submerged in the water to begin the curing process. There would always be a few chickens, ducks and some pigs to supplement their diet. Cattle were scarce in the area upon our arrival, but some farmers owned a goat or milk cow.

Most farmers owned their land by right of tenure or outright purchase. Tenure meant that they had lived and worked on the land for seven years. Others were *posseiros*, working the land with intent to own. Few possessed actual deeds to their land, but would retain their receipts after they paid their yearly tax. The system in practice for the registration of land title was deplorable. The local Land Title and Registration offices in most of the municipalities were terribly inefficient in keeping up-to-date files. Often this was because of corruption and bribery. Deeds of ownership or possession and other legal documents were often misplaced or disappeared.

Our pastoral visits to the interior regions, both in the dry and the wet season, brought us closer to the people. It helped us understand their way of life, and the many difficulties they faced. Meeting them at church or on a festive occasion was one thing; witnessing their day-to-day struggle was quite another.

For example, the harvesting of the jute, which reached five or six feet at maturity, was a particularly onerous task. The farmer cut the stocks by hand with his machete. The stocks were then submerged in water for 36 hours to allow the unravelling process to begin. Working in water up to his waist the farmer thrashed armfuls of stocks and then placed the product on makeshift racks to dry. Snakebites, arthritis and rheumatism were the health hazards suffered by the farmer who worked long hours in the water, exposed to the hot sun.

Just as their social life depended so much on the extended family and community celebrations, so too did their economic life. Very few were ever financially independent. Instead they were tied to their boss or *patrao*, who was usually the owner of the nearest country store. They also depended on him for food staples, for the sale of their crops and for small loans.

As we became more and more involved in the pastoral life of Itacoatiara, a number of major problems became obvious. Access to education was not available for the greater number of people, namely the poor. The convent school, administered by the Dorothean Sisters, was private, accessible only to those who could pay a tuition fee. It provided an excellent education but for the privileged few. A further problem was seen in the fact that the high school was only for girls. The one public high school, the five elementary public schools and the private Baptist school were all over extended.

Negotiations with the major superiors of the Dorothean Sisters to enlarge facilities, and open a co-educational facility had no chance of success because their congregation did not allow the sisters to teach in a co-educational setting. Their Convent schools allowed for young boys at the elementary level only. Discussions at the parish level were long and divided. A majority of the parishioners saw the greater benefits and opportunities for more children in a larger co-educational school, but the sisters had an influential group of loyal supporters among the elite. And with good reason, they were educators *par excellence*. After exploring all possibilities, it became evident that further discussion was futile. By mutual agreement the Dorothean Sisters decided not to continue in Itacoatiara.

Negotiations and talks took place with the State Educational Department. They were open to more classrooms for children of the greater populace. A contract was agreed upon whereby the church would provide and maintain larger facilities, and would organize and supply the supervisory staff and teachers. The state would pay the teachers' salaries.

We then made contact with the Precious Blood Sisters, a newly-founded local Congregation in Manaus. They were willing to staff the school and establish a Convent in Itacoatiara. The majority of parishioners voted in favour. The decision was a major change in the workings of the parish, and came about fourteen months after our arrival. We were losing the services and the presence of a group of sisters, the Dorotheans, who had made an invaluable contribution to the life of the church and to the people of Itacoatiara. Their departure was a serious loss for many in the town. They had been the mentors for the children of the town's leading families for many years.

Eight Precious Blood Sisters arrived in late 1963 and immediately began to prepare for the new school year. The convent facilities had been expanded to accommodate them. The parish centre, which was under construction even prior to our arrival, was finally completed. The new school increased enrolment by one hundred and fifty children. Looking toward the future, a teachers' college in the new facility began classes for student teachers. In the ensuing years George, Vince and I taught religion and English in the schools.

But this was not the only problem we had to face when we took over the mission in Itacoatiara. Illich was right. Although we came as missionaries and teachers, we were also students. Our introduction to life in the Amazon continued each time we interacted with the people along the mighty river.

CHAPTER 12

The Santa Teresinha

Our pastoral area in the Amazon rain forest was dominated by the river. The waters of this great river were a major factor in the lives of the people. In a normal year the river rose and fell between forty and sixty feet, but sometimes the rainy season was heavy and long, or a dry season brought months of intense heat and drought.

Both extremes would seriously affect both the crops and the lives of the people. In flood times, the river would become a raging torrent inundating crop and pasture lands, destroying all in its wake. During an extremely dry season the interior lakes and streams would dry up, making travel difficult. Both flooding and drought also affected the fish patterns, and fish was their prime source of food.

Until recently the river, its tributaries, streams and lakes were the only means of travel. All sizes of ships and boats, from super tankers and ocean vessels to the lowly canoe, were a common sight on the river. Consequently, without a boat we could not have accomplished our missionary activities.

Our boat builder, Miguel Monteiro, was ten months overdue in the construction of our boat, but, when completed, it was a beautiful craft and worth the long wait. The hull and ribs were constructed out of *itauba*, an Amazonian hardwood, as were the roof and main supports of the upper structure. The wheel house, kitchen, toilet and shower sections were finished off in Amazonian cedar. When the Cummins engine was installed, the hull caulked and painted, the boat was christened the *Santa Teresinha*. It was sixty-three feet in length with a 24 hp. diesel engine. The style of construction was typically Amazonian, built for durability and for carrying heavy cargo.

The *Santa Teresinha* served us well for many years. As well as being used for pastoral trips to the interior, the *Santa Teresinha* carried building material from Manaus to Itacoatiara and to the interior towns and villages for construction purposes. In our first years it also transported tons of *Alliance for Progress* foodstuffs that were distributed to the sick, the elderly, expectant mothers and the poor.

We had brought the Cummins marine engine that powered the *Santa Teresinha* from Canada. This proved to be a mistake since there were no Cummins dealers in the State. There was nothing wrong with the engine *per se*, but as the service hours mounted we began needing to import from Canada various parts for an overhaul. In our early years the Booth Shipping Lines had regular runs from Montreal and New York to Belem at the mouth of the Amazon and up to Manaus. The Scarboro headquarters would prepare barrels of medicines and other equipment needed at the mission. These barrels, along with the engine parts, would be shipped once a year with arriving missionaries.

Eventually a major overhaul of the Cummins engine was required, so an inventory of parts was drawn up and mailed to Scarboro. One of our more inventive missionaries in Canada felt that for such a rebuilding job, a top rate mechanic should come from Canada to do the work. He placed a classified ad in the *Toronto Star* that ran something like this:

Wanted

Mission group in the Amazon, Brazil requires marine diesel mechanic to overhaul Cummins engine. Mission group will pay airfare and provide two weeks of great fishing. For more information call Scarboro Missions.

The first response to the ad was the newspaper itself; they wanted to know if the ad was for real. Once Scarboro assured them of its authenticity, it ran for several days and many inquiries were received at Scarboro. As staff at Scarboro began to investigate the mechanical expertise of those who responded, people at the *Star* sensed an opportunity for a human interest story. On their own, the *Star* made contact with the Cummins Marine agent, and in short order Cummins phoned Scarboro with an offer of one of their top marine mechanics, Bernie Lesage. The *Star* then assigned a reporter, Jim Foster, to accompany him down to Itacoatiara. Bernie was a young man who knew engines and had recently been promoted to plant supervisor in the Cummins plant in Whitby, Ontario. Jim Foster was a veteran newspaper reporter.

When we were informed of what was happening at home we began preparations for the arrival of Bernie and Jim. Padre Doug MacKinnon, our trouble-shooter and mechanic, checked our supply of new parts. A short list of small parts was ordered via Scarboro and arrangements were made to ship them with Bernie and Jim. While some of the missionaries were very much opposed to importing a mechanic from Canada to overhaul the engine, others saw the favourable public relations as important for the Society at home, and as a source for financial help for our mission work. Once we got word of the arrival date of Jim and Bernie excitement filled the air. We began to debate just how long the overhaul job would take, and of course bets were wagered.

I was assigned the task of meeting Bernie and Jim. At the time two Varig Airline flights from the north arrived in Manaus each week. I travelled to Manaus by Line Boat from Itacoatiara to make arrangements so that Customs would not detain the parts that were coming in with Bernie. We also had to present a list of tools that Bernie was bringing into the country in order to work on the boat engine. A friend, Lucymar Barreto, who worked with the Caritas program of the Archdiocese, and was familiar with the process involving Customs accompanied me to the airport.

As usual, Bernie and Jim were held up at customs for a few hours processing the tools and the parts, but we were on our way from the airport by mid-morning. We were scheduled to leave for Itacoatiara from the port area at four in the afternoon. We were in the middle of the hot season and our two visitors felt the humidity and the heat immediately. Their flight had been a long and tiring overnight trip to the heart of the Amazon. In an unknown culture, surrounded by strange sights and smells, baffled by a strange language, our two bedraggled guests were quickly fading. We boarded the Line Boat in the hope of gaining an offshore breeze and a little space. The throng of fellow passengers all claiming their hammock space met us instead.

I'm sure that both Jim and Bernie wondered what they had got themselves into, and what lay in store for them down river. As our boat moved out of the crowded port on the Rio Negro, they gained some relief with the stirring of an evening breeze. Their energies were renewed by the adventure they were now embarking upon. Their fellow passengers were anxious to meet these strangers from abroad. But the majestic river, the floating city adjacent to the port, the sights and signs of the shoreline held their attention as we moved out into the middle of the river.

They were treated to the incomparable beauty of an Amazonian sunset and the sudden arrival of a tropical night filled with legions of stars that one could almost reach out and grasp. Life onboard took on its own rythmn. Tables were set up and dinner was served in several sittings. A typical Amazonian meal of fish, rice, beans and *mandioca* was served. The presence of Bernie and Jim, as the greenhorn *gringos* in the company of Padre Miguel, turned a rather commonplace river trip home into an exciting time for the passengers. Eager hands filled their plates with food as they attempted to show their warm hospitality to the new arrivals. People introduced themselves and wanted to know the background of their new friends.

Following their first exposure to Amazonian hospitality and their first local meal, we secured a bench where we enjoyed the cool breeze and tropical sky. As the Line Boat made stops at little villages or isolated farms along the Amazon, Jim and Bernie got their first glimpses of life along the Amazon. About 11:00 p.m. they were in for another surprise as we strung out their hammocks, while fellow passengers joked and smiled, so that a weary Jim and Bernie could settle in for a much needed sleep. Like most first timers, they were leery of the hammocks, wondering whether the ropes would hold, but in no time sleep overtook them.

We arrived in Itacoatiara in early morning and made our way to the parish house with all our baggage. We were greeted by my Scarboro confreres, and after introductions and a wash up sat down for breakfast. After a good breakfast visit our visitors were put to bed. Later on in the day they were given a brief tour of the town, and taken down to the boat where they would be spending much of their time.

Both Bernie Lesage and Jim Foster had their respective assignments. Bernie wanted to get at the job of rebuilding the motor as soon as possible. Jim was to write daily articles for the *Toronto Star*. At the time our communication with the outside world was limited to a telegraph machine. So we called in Miguel Menezes the local telegraph operator and made arrangements with him to send out Jim's stories to the *Star*. Padre Douglas was our mechanic and he had volunteered his services to work with Bernie. We cautioned Bernie to begin his work slowly, and only to put in a half day initially until he adjusted a little to the heat and his surroundings.

But Bernie wanted to tackle the job and finish it as soon as possible. So after taking only a couple of days of rest, Bernie and Doug set up their schedule for working on the boat. And of course, as they began the initial work of tearing down the motor, the rest of us began wagering just how long it would take. Under normal circumstances, with all the necessary tools and equipment, Bernie had rebuilt similar motors in three to five days. He calculated that under these less than ideal conditions, he and Doug could do the job in a week to ten days.

Their work progressed on schedule as they quickly stripped down the motor. Each day they would leave the parish house at seven, return for lunch at mid-day, then return to the boat until nightfall. Jim would accompany them and usually sit on the boat and write his articles.

Most evenings he would spend a few hours on the typewriter. Benjamin, our boat captain, offered to be onboard and available to help out the two mechanics. We had a young student from the school who delivered cold drinks and some fruit down to the boat workers each mid-morning and mid-afternoon.

Within a few short days it became evident that Bernie was not going to rebuild the motor in either a week or ten days. He found the heat unbearable down in the hold of the boat. Sleeping in a hammock was not his cup of tea; to make things worse, the pesky mosquitoes got through his net and tortured him. One night a rat fell from the ceiling plump into his hammock. Bernie was far from amused. Newly married, Bernie also missed his wife and soon discovered he could only phone her from Manaus. All of the mechanical work had to be done by hand. Bernie also realized that some small but essential parts were missing.

So, after twelve days on the job Doug and Bernie decided to take a few days rest in Manaus. Bernie could phone his wife and the missing parts could be purchased. Arriving back in Itacoatiara they set about with renewed vigour to tackle the rebuilding job. Working in strange surroundings, with little of the equipment he was accustomed to, Bernie began to feel the pressure as time was passing.

Jim, in the meantime, was getting his stories out, and for the first week the *Star* printed the story on its front pages. Jim's stories focused on Bernie and his committed task of rebuilding the Cummins engine so that the missionary Fathers could carry on their pastoral work with the boat. His stories brought into play life in the Amazon, and the difficulties of adapting to a new culture and language. They focused as well on the difficult climatic conditions, the strange foods, the mosquitoes and bugs that a newcomer encountered. As Jim faithfully produced his perspective of life's difficulties on the Amazon, we as missionaries watched the unfolding drama of life for these two visiting Canadians.

One particular day, when Bernie and Doug came up from their work on the engine, it was evident that things had not gone well. The atmosphere was heavy as we sat down to lunch. Attempting to lighten the mood, I jokingly enquired as to when we could expect the engine overhaul to be finished. Poor frustrated Bernie exploded! "Why was I not down at the boat giving them a hand. That just might help the situation." Tim Ryan and myself promptly volunteered. So, that afternoon, down we went. We were given the task of washing down some of the parts in gasoline. Tim would haul up engine parts from the engine room and I would wash them down on deck.

An hour or so into the work I picked up a piston rod, held it up for a look, and remarked, "Look at this piston Tim, I think it's bent!" Poor Bernie shot onto the deck from below, grabbed the piston, examined it, shook his head in dejection, and threw it overboard with a few exclamatory remarks agreeing that the piston was indeed bent. "How will we ever get this damn job done," he muttered, completely frustrated and at the end of his rope.

With a major part missing it now looked as if the job could never be completed. He was into his 18th day of repairs. The highway between Manaus and Itacoatiara had recently been opened. Although it was a dirt road and the trip was an endurance test that took ten or twelve hours, it was still much less time than by boat. So Bernie and I set out for Manaus to scour the boat repair shops in search of a Cummins piston. Bernie, with good reason was both frustrated and tired out. A job that he normally expedited in a few days had become a major operation. I'm sure he felt his expertise as a mechanic was also in question.

We set out for Manaus in the early evening hoping to arrive in the city by early morning. The trip involved crossing two rivers by hand operated ferries. The first few hours went well but then we ran into a terrible stretch of road. We ended up with a flat tire, and after repairing that, travelled for a few more miles only to discover the road blocked by a fallen tree. Forewarned, I had stashed an axe in the jeep. After fighting off hordes of mosquitoes we set to work to clear a path for the jeep. Then on we went again, but the condition of the road would only allow us to proceed at a snail's pace. Dawn found us still almost

A young missionary, Michael O'Kane
with one of his younger parishioners

Procession of Our Lady's image in Itacoatiara

Teachers College, Itacoatiara.
The Amazon River is seen in the background

The *Santa Teresinha*

A young vendor
making a living

High water on the Amazon during the rainy season

Michael O'Kane celebrating mass during the
festa in Itapiranga, Amazon, 1982

Off to work by canoe

a hundred kilometres from Manaus, but at least we were close to the last eighty kilometres which was a paved highway. We reached the outskirts of Manaus around seven in the morning, a journey of 340 kilometers that took twelve hours. As we came into the city, Bernie remarked, "Oh hell, when I agreed to come down here to fix a measly motor, I never imagined I'd have to take on the jungle as well." We both had a good laugh.

We ate a good breakfast at our parish house in Manaus, and I suggested to Bernie that we both should get some sleep. But no, Bernie insisted we were here to look for an all important piston and we better start. Two days of searching and enquiring produced only leads, but no piston. Frustrated and worn out we finally hit pay dirt and found our piston in a small repair shop a distance from the main port. We had visited at least forty marine mechanic shops before we had success. On this trip we were able to get through by phone to Canada and Bernie was able to talk with his wife. We celebrated our good fortune of finding the piston by indulging in a fancy dinner. That night Bernie slept like a baby and the next day we began our journey back home.

Once back in Itacoatiara, the team of Bernie and Doug immediately set to work. Doug had already begun the rebuilding and the situation was beginning to look brighter. But now Jim was faced with a dilemma; he had run out of writing ideas, and to make matters worse, the local telegraph office had ceased operations because their generator had quit. Even though we made arrangements to send Jim's stories to Manaus and then onto Canada, Jim felt it was time for him to go home. The place had started to get to him. So Jim booked a flight on a small plane for Manaus the following day.

Down at the river, work on the boat continued to progress; the end of the road seemed in sight. However, just as the last few parts were assembled and checked, Bernie discovered that there was no gasket for the head of the motor. But there was a solution. Jim was going to Manaus and then to Miami where there were Cummins dealers. We contacted Manaus and through a friend made arrangements for Jim to pick up the precious gasket and send it back to Manaus in the hands of the pilot.

As it turned out our gasket set came back from Miami with none other than Jim. He had arrived in Miami, picked up the gasket set, and then phoned the *Star* to inform them that he was returning to Toronto. But his editors told him to return and see it through to the end of the saga. Shortly after he returned to Itacoatiara we used a set of borrowed batteries to turn over the rebuilt motor. A short run on the Amazon assured us that the motor was once again in tip-top shape.

Renewed by their success against such great odds, Jim and Bernie agreed with Padre Douglas that everyone should journey down river to Urucara (a journey of eight hours) to fish for a day. It would also serve as a test run for the engine.

Thirty-three days after their arrival in Itacoatiara, with the *Santa Teresinha* as good as new, Bernie Lesage and Jim Foster bid their goodbyes and headed for home. Jim Foster produced some excellent articles for the *Toronto Star*, which carried his *Mission Adventure on the Amazon* for several weeks in September and October of 1968.

The *Santa Teresinha* sailed on for another ten years as a mission boat. Without doubt that Cummins engine was the most unique in the history of Cummins' engines, and most certainly had the most expensive main gasket.

However, as the years passed and we entered more into the lives of the people, we did begin to feel that the size of the boat was a countersign to our work. The *Santa Teresinha* was finally sold. Subsequently when new parishes were established in the interior towns and pastoral regions, we began to use smaller boats for pastoral visits. I was a boating enthusiast and, during my time in Brazil, had several small craft equipped with outboard engines that I used for visiting the many interior villages and communities. But not without adventure and misadventure.

CHAPTER 13

Life on the River

Within a short time most of us adjusted quite well to life on the river. However, river travel and the spartan lifestyle in the interior villages was not for all of us. Trips were long and tedious and storms could build up suddenly, scaring the living daylights out of even the most hardy. Yet all things being considered, our river voyages were quite safe providing us plenty of time for relaxation and reading.

Our pastoral mission activities to the interior towns and villages along the river were as important as our work in Itacoatiara. A schedule was set up for the river teams to visit the towns of Uricurituba, Silves, Itapiranga, Urucara and Sao Sebastiao. These visits, outside of *festa* celebrations, would acquaint us with the needs of each area. It was also an opportunity to get to know the civic and church leaders and for them to get to know their new pastors. These towns were the seats of government from which many, far more remote interior villages, were governed.

These historical municipalities were well-established areas with smaller populations than Itacoatiara, but with long traditions of their own. Naturally, they wanted their own resident pastor who would care for their spiritual needs, and for the needs of the interior villages attached to them. Those of us who adapted to river travel, wanted to become familiar with the whole territory, so in the beginning our pastoral river teams did not focus exclusively on any one particular area.

Our ministry in the Amazon and its river basin took up a great deal of our time. It is worth recounting some of the stories that unfolded as we travelled the main river and its many tributaries as missionaries. These stories will give you a flavour of the conditions under which we worked, and provide a snapshot of the lives of the people that lived along the shores and in the interior of the Amazon region.

$$\mathscr{O}\mathscr{Q}$$

Antonio was the captain of the *Sant'Ana II* on one of its first trips to Itacoatiara when one of the padres went overboard. The boat had just been completed without the railing on the poop deck installed. The padre had stopped for a brief pastoral meeting in Itapiranga in the early afternoon. Leaving Itapiranga around 5:00 p.m., the padre and Antonio were the only ones aboard. It was customary to have a shower and wash up as the heat of the day gave way to early evening breezes. The padre took over the wheel while Antonio showered on the poop deck. To accomplish this, you threw out a pail into the river, allowed it to fill with water, and then soaped and showered on the rear deck. When Antonio had finished he returned to the wheelhouse so the padre could take his shower and then prepare a light evening meal.

After an hour or so, when the padre had not returned, Antonio rang the signal bell but still no padre appeared. Moving slightly out into the current, Antonio left the wheel and scurried to the back of the boat, but still there was no sign of the padre. By this time darkness had fallen, and Antonio, slowing the boat down, quickly came to the realization that the padre had slipped on the smooth and wet surface of the deck and tumbled into the river. He turned the craft around and began moving down river with his searchlight on.

After about forty minutes he spotted the padre clinging to a fallen tree. A possible tragedy ended happily, and within a few days the padre made sure that the railing for the poop deck was installed.

On another memorable river trip I set out for the mission of Uricurituba from Urucara. It was about a six-hour run downstream on the Urucara River and then across the Amazon and upstream to Uricurituba. Francisco Assis, a young fellow in the parish was accompanying me;

he was handling the wheel and I was serving as the motorist. As we moved out onto the Amazon storm clouds began to form upriver and quickly very strong winds assaulted us. We were confident since the boat was in good shape and the motor was performing well. Rainstorms were not infrequent, so there seemed to be no cause for alarm as we began our crossing of the Amazon. The opposite shoreline was probably two kilometres away. Battling the side current, the boat could make that distance in about forty minutes.

As the storm bear down on us, the river took became quite unsettled. The waves grew in strength and raged at us in a criss-cross fashion. As they beat against the hull, water came in through the side portals causing the boat to rock heavily. Assis was steady on the wheel but he rang for me to come to the front. He pointed to the dark clouds that were rushing downstream. The rains came first in sheets that made it difficult to see, and then torrential rains hit us with a fury. We knew we were nearing mid-river. Assis looked at me as if for confirmation to continue our crossing. I rushed back to the engine room. The engine hummed its steady beat but water was still coming over the sides. I worked the bilge pump, and was about to advise Assis to turn back when through the side portal I glimpsed the figure of a lone fisherman in a dugout canoe battling the waves to avoid being swamped. He was less than forty feet away, heading for the shore from which we had come. I ran to Assis and motioned for him to turn toward the canoe.

As we approached the canoe, I shouted to the fisherman through the wind to come alongside and take refuge from the raging storm. "Thanks, padre," he shouted, "It's okay, I'm going home and God is with me. Don't idle the engine." The sudden onslaught of the storm had me petrified with fear, and yet the calm assurance of this lone figure in his dugout canoe, battling the forces of nature brought me a sense of calm. I rechecked the motor and then told Assis to turn toward our destined shore. Assuring Assis that all was well I gave him a slap on the back, and went back to the pump. We rode out the storm and the winds, and the heavy lashing of rain gradually gave way to a tropical downpour. As we approached the shoreline and headed upstream, Assis gave a shout of relief and triumph. We both looked far across the waters for any sign of our valiant fisherman, and silently thanked him for his raw courage and trust in God.

In the ensuing years when I ran into heavy waters and storms on the lakes and rivers of the region (and in my life's journey as well), I always remembered my fisherman friend. Then I could face the storm with renewed courage and determination.

Another time, I was heading home from Silves on a beautiful Sunday afternoon. Once a month I used to head down to Silves early Saturday morning and spend the weekend in the parish there. On this particular Sunday I had taken off a few minutes before four. My steering system was not functioning all that well at the time so I was handling the boat from the engine. The lake was like a mirror, the tank was full, and I was looking forward to arriving at the lagoon just after nightfall. Each time I made this trip I was anxious to reach the upper end of the lake before nightfall in order to enter the right channel that would take me to the lagoon where I docked the boat. On this occasion I was to be met by Sister Helen between 6:30 and 7:00 in the evening.

At the time, my boat was a fourteen-foot aluminium craft with a thirty-five horsepower engine. About forty minutes out of Silves a breeze started up and the lake became choppy. I had shoved my duffel bag under the front end of the boat, but my jacket lay over the front seat. I noticed the wind was starting to catch my jacket so I decided to retrieve it before it blew overboard. Now the smart thing to do would have been to cut the motor, stand up and grab the jacket, and then continue on. But not me, it became a game as I took my hand off the steering column and attempted a balancing act, my body arching toward the front of the boat trying to grab the jacket.

The boat was travelling full speed, and I made several tentative passes, always reaching back for the steering column to steady the boat if it swayed. Confident that my balancing act would work, I arched forward one final time and made my pass for the jacket. Just as I got a hold of the jacket the boat swung violently to the left, and I was flung overboard. When I hit the water, I grabbed the side of the boat as it briefly went below the waterline. Then when it surfaced it jammed against my jaw and gave me quite a gash on my chin. Although stunned I was somehow able to summon the strength to pull myself back into the boat. Immediately I grabbed the steering column and slowed the boat down. I washed my bloody face and bailed the water out of the boat. A few minutes later the evening breeze help to clot my wound that I held tightly together with a wet handkerchief.

Needless to say, I did not make the channel prior to nightfall. I was lucky though! That evening was bright with a full moon, so I was able to find the right channels to the lagoon landing. Sister Helen and a lay volunteer Lucia were awaiting my arrival. I was safely on land again, and my faithful greeters hustled me off to the hospital for some repair stitches. We were late but we did make Sunday evening supper, and a good night's sleep found me ready to begin another week.

♋♋

From my first years in Itacoatiara, I loved the river, the intertwining side rivers and streams, and lakes that made up the mosaic of the Amazonian water system. With the first outboard boat that I had built for working out of Urucara, I was introduced to the many channels and tributaries that a person could use to journey from Urucara to Itacoatiara. With two 25hp engines we had fairly easy access to our home base in Itacoatiara. A trip of five hours by outboard took twelve or thirteen hours by regular boat.

I also enjoyed using the boat for duck hunting in the dry months of November and December. And I believe that I introduced water-skiing to the region. For me, being on the water was an adventure. It became a challenge to take on the great Amazon, and to battle through whatever winds or rain blew my way.

Isolation, long hours of river travel, and lack of the most basic necessities were part of life for everyone in the Amazon region. So our small outboard boat was often used to make emergency trips with the sick to Itacoatiara.

In our first years in Urucara there was no medical clinic. The people relied on the expertise of their elders and on home remedies. Clinton Thomas, a Church of Christ minister, ran a small clinic out of his house. He was knowledgeable in medicine and was an expert in first aid. Padre Justino also operated out of our house, and Justino's expertise came from experience. I often remarked that Justino knew the Merck manual (a medical dictionary that gave a rundown on diseases, their symptoms, and treatment), by heart. Both men were generous with their time, and tended the sick with compassion and diligence as best they could.

One evening a young couple brought their young son into Clinton's home. His stomach had been torn open by a gunpowder explosion. The father, Antonio, had left home early to tend his mandioca patch. His wife, Maria, had gone down to the river's edge to wash; the youngest child Fatima was with her. The two young boys, Antonio Jr. and Francisco were playing in and around their small home.

The eldest, Antonio, age seven, had discovered a large can suspended by a wire from the thatched roof. Getting it down the boys discovered their father's material for loading his shotgun shells. Evidently they had watched their father making his shells. Little Chico had also discovered some matches. Antonio Jr. found a bottle that contained the gunpowder. He took a match from Chico, ignited it and dropped the match into the bottle. It immediately exploded against his stomach. As he lay screaming, Chico ran to the river for his mother. She ran to the house and found young Antonio writhing in pain. She tried to stop the flow of blood and to clean the shattered glass from the child's exposed entrails. Antonio was writhing in agony until shock set in. Helpless to do anything, she carried the child to the river's edge where she placed him in their canoe and paddled to the mandioca patch, shouting for Antonio her husband.

Hearing her cries the father ran to the riverbank and down into the river as she approached. She explained what had happened to the young Antonio as she cradled him in her arms, the boy sobbing in a state of shock. The father paddled the canoe home and told Maria to stay in the canoe. Hastily he gathered a few necessities and had the other children take their places in the canoe. He covered Maria and young Antonio with a blanket. Then they set off for Urucara, two hours away by canoe. They arrived at nightfall and made their way up the bank to Clinton's home. But Clinton was away, so Phyllis his wife sent for Justino. Justino was also away, so I hastened down to Clinton's.

Phyllis and I tried to calm the poor parents and set about examining the wound. We gave the youngster an injection for pain, and then attempted to clean up the exposed organs. I had to cut part of young Antonio's stomach wall to allow the organs to be enclosed. Both Phyllis and I knew that we had to take the child to Itacoatiara, and to medical help there.

I returned home to prepare the outboard for the trip and to get a supply of gas. Unfortunately, then the rains came. Worried about travelling during a storm and the added danger of young Antonio catching pneumonia, I knew we had to get another boat. Justino was visiting downriver in the *Sant'Ana* and would not return for another day. By this time many of the townspeople had got word of the accident and one of the merchants, Jose Falabella, offered us his boat. Again preparations were made, and the situation was explained to the parents, Antonio and Maria.

By the time the boat had been fuelled and the boat's crew alerted, it was close to dawn. We had some bread and coffee, the child was carried aboard with his family, and we set off for Itacoatiara, thirteen hours away. It was a long and tiresome trip. Time was of the essence. I carried enough injections to administer for pain control, but each hour lessened the child's chances for life.

When we finally arrived in Itacoatiara at 7:00 p.m. we sent word ahead to the sisters at the clinic. I hurried to the padres' house to get the jeep. We bundled the family aboard with little Antonio and drove to the clinic. There the sisters took over; the doctor had been alerted, and the child was prepared for an emergency operation. But the doctor had scarcely begun, when poor Antonio's respiratory system failed, and the child died. We had come all that way on a wing and many prayers, but it was far too long for the poor child's system. Young Antonio had been close to fifty hours in that condition.

Within four hours of arriving, we set out once again for the sad, long journey back with Maria and Antonio, little Fatima and Chico, carrying Antonio's body home to Urucara for burial.

⌀⌀

Another one of my adventures further demonstrates the extreme isolation from adequate medical facilities. This one, however, had a happier ending.

The village of Sao Sebastian was located upriver at the mouth of the Uatuma river, about two hours from Urucara. One morning three young men arrived by canoe to get help. One of the men of the village, Jose Manuel, a woodcutter, was in serious condition back in Sao Sebastiao. Jose Manuel had been cutting timber a day's journey from Sao Sebastiao. A tree had fallen on him, pinning him to the ground, breaking his leg, and gouging his hip severely. Miraculously he had slowly been able to free himself, and crawl to the shoreline. He managed to get into his canoe, get out into the current, and painstakingly head for home. He had lost consciousness many times en route, but a fisherman had noticed the apparently empty canoe, and came to his rescue. Now Jose Manuel was in Sao Sebastiao and needed emergency help.

After consulting with the young men, Clinton and I felt that it was imperative that we get Jose Manuel to Itacoatiara. Accordingly, we prepared the outboard for the journey, and with medical supplies, headed for Sao Sebastiao. We arrived there around noon hour, and went to Jose Manuel's home. Family and neighbours had cleaned the gaping hole in his hip, and had tried to make him comfortable. His leg was broken in two places. Clinton gave him several injections for pain and a tetanus shot. We had brought several old mattresses from the maternity unit in Urucara; these were placed at the front of the boat. Some of the men made a stretcher, and Manuel was carried down to the boat, and placed in the front end on the mattresses.

We left Sao Sebastiao for Itacoatiara around four in the afternoon. In order to avoid storms and dangerous logs on the open Amazon, our journey was to take us up to Itapiranga, on to Silves, and there meet up with the Urubu river. The journey would be slightly longer, but we felt we could arrive at the highway crossing on the Urubu river before midnight.

We had placed Jose Manuel on the mattresses under the front end of the boat, to protect him from the winds and rain, yet he was subjected to the grinding bumps of the rough waters. Several times we slowed the boat to give him some relief and administer injections for pain. We had to stop three or four times because of the blinding rain. But the boat performed well, and we finally made our destination. The tenseness of the journey had exhausted myself and Clinton.

Our hope was to catch a truck or jeep at the highway crossing, and proceed to Itacoatiara. The owner of a small store generously made a makeshift bed for Manuel Jose and served us coffee and bread. Clinton and I strung up our hammocks, and awaited any vehicle that happened along. Manuel Jose slept fitfully. Clinton and I got little sleep because of the gnats that were doing a job on us; we had picked them up from the old mattress. Finally at dawn a truck drove up to the ferry. Explaining our emergency situation to the truck driver, he and his co-workers made space on the truck for Manuel Jose's makeshift bed. We all climbed aboard and drove into the town, arriving at nine in the morning.

Manuel Jose was unloaded at the clinic, and the sisters prepared him for the doctor. We had feared that gangrene might have set in; his hip and leg were swollen and bluish. But after examination, more injections and suturing, the doctor reset his fractures and put on a cast. Manuel Jose stayed in the clinic for several days. Clinton and I rested up at the padres' house. Two days later Clinton and I returned to Sao Sebastiao. We came with the good news that Manuel Jose was on the mend, then we continued onto Urucara. A week later Manuel Jose returned home by line boat to his family. After six weeks on crutches, he was as good as new.

ॐ

My experience with the waters of the Amazon helped me to understand the everyday reality of those who lived and worked along this great body of water. And there was always danger lurking below the surface of these waters, even for the most experienced. This was so true for Antonio Pereira da Silva, a fisherman who lived on the river on the Ilhya da Cumaru, several miles upstream from Itacoatiara.

As a son of the river, Antonio was well aware of its dangers – its treacherous currents and sudden storms that could sweep down the river making it a crashing wall of water. He was a seasoned fisherman with powerful arms and an expertise in handling his canoe that could carry him to Itacoatiara in short order.

One day Antonio went to his daily task of fishing. The piraibu were biting. He let out his baited line into the current, made it secure on shore and settled his canoe close to shore. He played the line, waiting for a strike.

Two colleagues found Antonio's overturned canoe several hours later. Righting the canoe they found his line still made fast to the bow of the canoe. They began to reel in his line only to discover that it was heavily weighted. Probably caught on bottom, they thought. Both of them worked the line, pulling it into their canoe. Antonio's body gradually came to the surface and then, to their surprise a huge piraibu. As they brought Antonio's body to shore they found that a fishing hook was imbedded in one of his hands. Antonio had made a strike, the piraibu had taken his bait-line. His friends quickly understood what had happened. In playing the fish Antonio had brought him to the surface close to his canoe, but as he reached for his club to stun the fish the line slipped just as the powerful fish plunged back into the deep. As the fish did so the line was pulled through Antonio's hands, a second hook tore into his hand and he was carried to the bottom by the big fish.

At Antonio's funeral his family and friends grieved the loss of the 29 year old fisherman. His friends spoke of his love and reverence for the river and his expertise as a fisherman. The murky waters of the Amazon claimed another victim.

I was a slow learner, but over many years my respect and admiration for the relentless flow of the Amazon, and the people who lived on its shores, became a deep and lasting one.

CHAPTER 14

A Life Jacket
to a Drowning Person

These were only a few of the situations that made the mission team realize how inadequate the health facilities were in Itacoatiara, despite the gargantuan efforts of a few. There was only one health clinic, administered by the state, which served the needs of the whole population. The closest hospital was in Manaus, 280 kilometers away. The trained personnel attached to this local clinic included a doctor and eight nurses. There was also a department attached to the clinic with specially trained personnel who worked to eradicate malaria that was prevalent in the area. The health personnel tended to the sick of Itacoatiara as well as the five interior municipalities. It was an impossible task. Hansen's disease (leprosy), malaria, tuberculosis, and pneumonia were prevalent. Manaus at this time had the largest leprosarium in the world. The state health clinic provided excellent preventative and educational programs to attack these sicknesses, but they lacked the adequate resources (trained personnel, funding, and sufficient medicines) to do more.

No facilities or personnel existed for emergency cases that arrived daily from the interior. The unattended sick were left to fend for themselves. Out of ignorance and as a result of the lack of health education programs, people flocked to *curandeiros* or shamans, who were no more than witch doctors that made use of home remedies and religious omens in an effort to effect a cure.

Many pharmacists also acted as pseudo medical professionals. Pharmacies abounded and drugs were sold over the counter. Regulations with respect to the sale and the administration of drugs were not enforced. Even among Brazilians it was a common joke to refer to Brazil as the largest drugstore in the world. American drug companies dumped their products on a populace where health care was minimal. While a few professionals devoted their lives to the care of the sick, and many non-professionals served the sick in a caring and compassionate way, the sick population was largely neglected and exploited. The poor consulted anyone with a reputation for treating certain illnesses.

Health care was a serious problem in all of the interior towns and villages. Since there were no health facilities outside of Itacoatiara, the people who lived in the interior relied even more on the local shaman and home remedies. The health clinic in Itacoatiara was the mecca for the sick of the entire area. Family and friends would transport their sick to Itacoatiara by canoe or larger boats. The trips were long and difficult. Once in Itacoatiara the long wait would begin. Because there were no public hostels available, people would have to find their own shelter, set up housekeeping, care for their sick, and go each morning to stand in line at the clinic to obtain a ticket. The clinic staff and doctor could only attend to a designated number each day, so tickets were allotted to regulate the flow of patients. No matter how many hours they worked the line of sick people never shortened. Emergencies took precedence, and they were common-place. The town always had a floating population of sick people from the interior with their families. A sick person requiring daily and prolonged treatment for a serious illness depended on family in every way. So families had to remain with their sick in the town in a precarious makeshift shelter, far from home and always without adequate finances.

The health clinic charged a minimal service charge. Providing services was hampered on a number of fronts. The long lineups of waiting sick were endemic. The clinic's drug and medicine supply (always inadequate) often failed to arrive. Because of these problems many families simply opted for the services of the many pharmacies in town. These services came with a hefty price tag since drugs at the pharmacy were costly, and the diagnosis and treatment often depended on whatever expertise the druggist had gained by experience.

Judging from North American standards, you could easily criticise the glaring failures of the state health system. But we marvelled at the outstanding service the staff at the Clinic in Itacoatiara performed for such a huge population and with such limited resources. In the early years of our presence in Itacoatiara, the doctor, nurses and staff serviced an area with over one hundred thousand people.

Malaria had all but been eradicated in the area. Leprosy and tuberculosis had effective outreach programs. Several preventative programs, such as better hygiene in living habits, were being taught throughout the area. Vaccination for small pox, measles and malaria was carried out on a regular basis. There were courses provided for midwives and pregnant women. But, for many reasons, health education among the illiterate was difficult. There were never enough staff, and how could the few staff reach such a population spread over hundreds of kilometres.

Resources for health care were much better in Manaus. As well as a large public hospital there were three or four private hospitals and a number of private clinics. The medical profession was well represented with specialists in all branches of medicine. So, those with the financial resources travelled to Manaus for consultations, treatment, and better hospital care.

The larger population of poor people had to rely on what was available locally. There were always long delays at the clinic. As strangers in the town, the poor from the interior flocked to the "padres" for assistance and intervention. They were often in need of financial aid to buy medicines and drugs. Frequently, when we returned to Itacoatiara from our pastoral visits in the interior, we brought with us the sick who needed medical help. Our residence was often turned into a makeshift hostel for those arriving from the interior.

Working with the sick and their families never ceased to be a heart-wrenching experience for me. I felt frustrated and helpless. They often arrived on our doorstep with few if any material resources. Having no relatives or contacts in Itacoatiara they were out of their element in a strange surrounding. Their desperation and vulnerability made them easy victims to unscrupulous charlatans. How many times were wrongful drugs administered? How many died because of maltreatment, or no treatment? It seemed in such circumstances that these poor people were second class citizens. Their lives were expendable. We could reach out and help only a few, but the majority would be left to their own resources, and the sad fact was that in the world around them they really did not matter!

My involvement with the sick who daily came to our door seeking help, and the many who asked for passage onboard the *Santa Teresinha* on our return trips from the interior, was a profound learning experience for me. I was exposed to the reality of the world of the poor first hand. When his wife or child is gravely ill, needs medical attention immediately and his financial situation is precarious, what does a poor man do? He is forced to beg from anyone. His self-esteem, his pride and dignity go out the window. A promise of help from anyone is like a lifejacket to a drowning person.

Our inability to respond in an adequate fashion to the desperate needs of these people was a constant source of frustration and anger. Frustration with a system that caused such poverty, anger with one's own helplessness to solve the dilemma, and anger at the total loss of self-esteem and dignity that the poverty-stricken poor had to endure. In such circumstances I often questioned the reasons for our presence in the midst of these poor and sick people! I questioned the unequal distribution of wealth and resources in the world! Being objects of our charity, of anyone's charity, should not have been the role of so many daughters and sons of God.

Something had to be done. Health care professionals at the local clinic, and a few municipal administrators were as concerned as we, their pastors, were. Again, a committee representing the concerns of the local citizens was set up, and negotiations were begun with the state health officials in Manaus.

In conjunction with our request from Brazil for medical help, the Scarboro Society in Canada consulted with a number of religious medical professionals explaining the health problem in Itacoatiara. The Sisters of St. Joseph from Peterborough responded to our call for help. They also wanted to be part of the North American church that accepted the invitation of Pope John XXIII's to assist the Latin American church. In 1964, while home on furlough, Paul McHugh and I visited with the sisters to explain first-hand the deplorable state of health facilities throughout the area. We also briefed them on what their future lives in the Amazon would be like. They agreed to finance and send a team of professional medical sisters to operate and staff a small hospital.

In Itacoatiara our meetings with the local administration proved fruitful. An unfinished building, originally planned as a maternity hospital, was made available to us. Financial contracts were worked out with the state and the municipality, and a construction crew began work to complete the hospital. Five sisters, four of them medical professionals, were appointed to this new mission. They began preparations in Canada to refocus on what was to be a completely new life for them.

The new maternity hospital, equipped with a medical laboratory, was fully operating by late 1965. A doctor had been contracted to work at the hospital with the sisters. The hospital and its operation were beset with a multitude of problems in the ensuing years. It certainly did not solve the medical and health care problems of the town and neighbouring municipalities, but it became an important cog in making the dream of accessible and adequate health care for all more of a reality.

The Sisters of St. Joseph who came to staff the hospital were not missionaries. They had not been educated or trained to work in what might be termed a missionary setting. They were professionals in health care in Canada, who volunteered to respond to an immediate need. Their dedicated service and presence in Itacoatiara alleviated the sufferings and the sickness of thousands of people over the years. First-hand experience made them missionaries. Their work and contribution in Itacoatiara and the surrounding area was invaluable in setting up a health care system that reached out to the poor and to villages and towns in the interior where health care was non-existent. The sisters, in many ways, revolutionized health care in Itacoatiara.

But in no way did it detract from the work of the many local health professionals who were committed to the care of the sick. Many of the doctors and nurses who came from larger cities and towns to work at the state health clinic in Itacoatiara were tireless workers who reached out to the poor and gave of their time. One of the doctors who arrived in Itacoatiara a few years after our arrival was a young woman from the south of Brazil. Doctor Annelore Foltz brought her professional expertise to the poor of the area, and was totally committed to the well-being of the sick. She set up programs for the victims of leprosy and worked with them for years. She continues her medical profession in Itacoatiara to this day. Many of the local nurses served and cared for the sick and the destitute with a Christian commitment that was truly remarkable. And the field workers were pioneers in their long and tedious trips to the interior, working to eradicate malaria.

By 1980 a new state hospital, staffed by three or four doctors, a good number of nurses and supporting staff, was opened in Itacoatiara. The hospital had thirty-five beds, was open day and night, and usually had an adequate supply of medicines. The clinic continued to attend to the sick from the interior, and the sisters used their small maternity hospital as a laboratory and X-ray clinic.

We tried our best to help the plight of the poor people we served. But I soon realized that charity was not enough. More had to be done, and that *more* made me re-think the very reasons for being a missionary.

CHAPTER 15

The Lessons of Inculturation

The 1960s were a decade of radical change. As the winds of change swept the globe, change was also unfolding in our new world of the Amazon. Those initial years, between 1962 and 1964, were a training camp for learning and gaining experience. We moved from classroom theory to daily immersion in the culture, tradition and history of the region and its people. For the most part, our pastoral work was carried out among a Christian and Catholic population whose religious expression of faith identified with their Portuguese colonizers. Our own religious expression had originated from the early French missionaries in Canada, and was flavoured by our Anglo-Saxon backgrounds.

We soon learned that the cultural life of the people we had come to serve had its origins in their Portuguese, Indigenous and African backgrounds. Their social and political life had been fashioned by their colonial past. Their rural agrarian way of life was a throw back to the time of the colonial land barons. A frontier of untamed jungle, with a hot, humid tropical climate required an ability to change and adapt if we were going to survive. In those first few years in Itacoatiara we were exposed to the harsh life they experienced, and to the ingenuity they used to overcome it. Understanding the mentality of the people would depend on how well we adapted to their historical and religious history, and how well we understood their way of life. Like them, we had to physically and mentally adapt in our new world if we were to be a positive and constructive presence among them.

Many aspects of the Amazonian people were easy to accept and could be readily embraced Their sincere hospitality and openness to the stranger, their deep family ties and reverential respect for their elders all demonstrated Christian values. Their eternal optimism, their love of life and their acceptance of life on life's terms were values that we too could make our own.

We found other traits more difficult to accept. The *festa* celebrations and how they honoured their patron saints required change and understanding on our part. Slowly, we came to understand that the patron saint of their village, town or chapel, was not just their protector, but also gave identity to their community. It was what bonded them as a people.

For the villagers the *festa* was a religious event, an important opportunity to celebrate the heavenly patron of their village. It was time to honour the heavenly intercessor that spoke to God on their behalf. It was time to party! The Eucharist and attendance at Mass, which were all-important in our lives, were secondary in theirs. After all, the Eucharist and Mass were religious extras for the majority who lived in the interior, and who had been accustomed to one or two pastoral visits a year.

The choosing of an influential person in the community as the *padrinho* (godfather) for a child, was a very important choice that was made with a great deal of deliberation. The influence and help of such a godfather gave the child a fighting chance in life. To our foreign minds, a godfather's influence and social standing were not as important as their strong moral values or being a practising Catholic.

I labour the point, but these daily encounters with another culture and religious expression could either be a positive step or a stumbling block in our effectiveness as missionaries. For us, these local customs were not easy to accept, but if we were to serve the people we would have to adapt.

Our first years in Itacoatiara were a time of settling in, of becoming part of the town and part of the people. We bought an old home in the town square, and moved in after making renovations. Each of us was assigned to pastoral areas in the town. Consulting the leaders of the various church groups, we worked on a plan to renovate two of the devotional chapels for regular Sunday services.

A small number of elite families controlled the economic and political life of the town. These included the merchants and bankers, the owners of the local industries, jute, and rubber factories, and a lumber mill. The bosses of the five or six political parties ran the municipal bureaucracy as well as the state-run agencies. There was a small middle class made up of clerks, municipal workers, teachers, and port workers. A labouring class worked in the industries mentioned above, and included farmers and fishermen who supplied the local market with the stable food supply that fed the city. The majority of the population was the poor who eked out a daily living in one way or another. A small number of this group farmed small plots of land on the banks of the river close to town. The port workers had a union, but all other workers depended on either their merchant/industry patrons or political patrons for employment.

We continued the pastoral plan inherited from Aclides and Pinto. This was considered the best avenue to follow, as it gave the people an opportunity to get to know us, and it gave us the time to become familiar with what was happening around us.

Our frequent visits to the sick in the town acquainted us with leprosy and tuberculosis. Both diseases were very prevalent. Many of the lepers lived segregated from their families in small huts at the rear of the home. Some had suffered for years and the ravages of the disease had disfigured them terribly. I got to know and became friends with many of these people. Most of them were isolated and cut off completely from the community, but their families treated them with love and compassion. Leprosy was feared and people kept their distance. Some were following treatment under the program initiated by Dr. Annelore; others were encouraged to get medical help. It was marvellous to witness the recovery of many and their subsequent integration back into the community.

From each of the patients I visited I learned so much. Jose, who was being treated for leprosy, became a friend and a mentor for me in the local history, relating much of the folklore of the area. Antonio, who suffered from tuberculosis, taught me a great deal about the river, the surrounding jungle and its animal and bird life. He had grown up in the interior where he became a hunter and fisherman. Taddeus, an old teacher, helped me to become more articulate in the language. Like so many that serve, I received more than I gave.

Like many of the locals we all had bicycles to travel around the town. The central market was the supermarket of the town. Here you could meet parishioners on any weekday morning, or find someone to deliver a message to an interior community. As well as buying local produce and tambaqui or pirarucu (two of the many species of fish), you could have a visit or set up a meeting over a morning cup of coffee. In the market you could also listen to the latest news and gossip.

As the "rich", newly-arrived friendly foreign padres became known, there was soon a daily lineup of the poor at our door asking for food and medicines. We were rapidly becoming involved in the lives of the people and coming face to face with the economic situation of the poor majority. It was evident that something had to be done.

The *Alliance for Progress*, a brainchild of the Kennedy administration, was a massive food distribution program for the poor of Latin America. Its stated objective was to better the relations between Washington and its Latin American neighbours at the grass roots (with just the right amount of good old American propaganda thrown in). The program was to serve as a sign of America's willingness to reach out to the poor of Central and South America.

Our Redemptorist mentors in Manaus were in charge of the plan for the Amazon area. It was a massive charity program involving the disbursement of tons of food and used clothing. All of the pastoral sectors or dioceses in this area of the Amazon were organized down to the parish level. Local groups saw to the distribution of food and clothing to the sick and elderly, the poor and expectant mothers.

In practical terms, for us, the program involved the setting up of volunteer committees that would maintain lists of worthy recipients, and distribute the food to the needy every six weeks, both in Itacoatiara and in the towns and villages of our area. Our boat, the *Santa Teresinha*, travelled to Manaus every six weeks when shipments came from the United States, loaded our allotted tonnage and returned to Itacoatiara. The parish centre served as the organizational office for our parish volunteers. Distribution centres were set up throughout the town and the interior. Hundreds of people swelled our lists, and due to the good work of our volunteer teams the food (milk, cereals, oil and clothing) reached the most needy. A minimal charge was levied to most recipients to cover operating costs.

Initially, most of us heartily endorsed the program in view of the staggering poverty around us, but as time went by we began to have problems with it. It was a give-away program with few strings attached. While in the short term it supplemented the food intake of the poorest sector, some of us questioned its worthiness. Without an educational program were the poor not being made even more dependent?

We operated the program for two years, all the while debating the nature and purpose of development aid. It was a frequently discussed issue at our pastoral meetings and with our volunteers. Heated discussions and arguments, both for and against the program, were debated on an ongoing basis. Finally the majority of us voted down the program much to the chagrin of its loyal supporters. I was vocal in my opposition to the program. We did continue an educational program for expectant mothers and distributed a monthly milk supplement and medicines to them.

Several of us had also become involved in setting up a study group to interest our parish leaders in credit unions and co-operatives. This study with local workers helped us to grasp a deeper understanding of the economic reality; it also educated a small group of men who were in favour of beginning a credit union. While our success was not great in the initial years, a housing co-operative was eventually founded, land was bought and about twenty homes built. A farming co-operative was eventually established as well for the buying and selling of farm produce. These were our initial forays into the socio-economic lives of the people.

All sectors of the population, from the very rich and privileged class to the poorest, participated in varying degrees in church life. As well as attending to the regular spiritual and devotional needs of the people, we started to set up study sessions for adults, eventually introducing the reforms and teachings of the Vatican II Council. There were also preparation courses for baptism and marriage.

Our work at the parish level, our presence at the school and our involvement with the co-operative movement introduced us to many of the townspeople. Lasting friendships were formed. We were getting to know the movers and shakers at the parish and community level, and were soon privy to the political scene. Since we had not stepped on any political toes as of yet, we were able to dialogue in the social forum. Through our efforts some reforms and concessions took place; I believe these were of benefit to the general population.

Brazilian males, it is said, have three passions: politics, football and women. Whether or not politics is their top priority is not for me to say, but it was pretty close, at least until the revolution in 1964. Federal, state and municipal elections were preceded by many weeks of intense campaigning. Party loyalists were expected to sell the "party line." It was old time electioneering with a great deal of wheeling and dealing. Candidate rallies and speeches were carried out in a carnival-like atmosphere with promises for everyone. And the party that carried election day always took care of its own. Political parties usually swept into office, not because of programs or policy, but on the popularity of its leaders. Candidates on the campaign trail openly sought endorsement from the church. They would also take advantage of every village and parish festa to make their presence felt. Patronage was always prevalent. While we avoided partisan politics, we often went to public officials, monitoring their promises and presenting petitions for better health facilities and more schools, both for the town and the interior.

All this was going on at the same time that the Second Vatican Council was taking place in Rome, from 1962 to 1965. Then in 1964, the government of Brazilian President Joao Goulart was overthrown. It was a bloodless coup that caught the country by surprise. The military dictatorship that took control of the government was to take over every aspect of Brazilian life and initiate a police state that would rule for more than twenty years.

Both our pastoral work and our immersion into various social and developmental programs were unfolding at the same time as these larger events. It would mean radical change in our missionary lives, and in the religious and political life of the Amazonian people.

CHAPTER 16

Expanded Horizons

The General Council of Scarboro Missions had taken on the mission in Itacoatiara and surrounding area with the understanding that it would eventually be made a diocese and a bishop would be named. We had frequent visits from our Superior General and Council members in our first years. Their visits were undoubtedly to encourage us in our work. But the Council was also interested in how the mission was progressing and how we, the first group of missionaries, were making out. With a good number of ordinations each year, our mission group was increasing with two new missionaries yearly.

Early in 1965, with more personnel on the scene, our work expanded. The Archbishop of Manaus, Dom Joao de Sousa Lima, had been insisting that we take over a parish area on the outskirts of the city. Two of the original group, Vince Daniel and Doug MacKinnon were appointed to Manaus. They began initial preparations to take over the parish once negotiations with the bishop were completed. In addition to responding to the needs of the people in the area, we would have a base of operations in the capital city.

It was also felt that we could better serve the needs of the people by setting up a permanent parish in Urucara, one of the towns that had previously been serviced as a mission parish out of Itacoatiara. George Marskell and I were assigned to this parish. Urucara had a population of over a thousand within the town, and another five thousand living in its interior regions. Another town, Sao Sebastian, with a population of about two or three hundred was about two hours away by boat.

We purchased a small one storey wooden home on the main street of Urucara that was adjacent to the river. The old church was in the main park a few blocks away. It had been constructed early in the 1700s and was in a sad state of disrepair. A foundation had been started for a new and larger church at the back section of the park.

Once again the people received us warmly, and they went out of their way to make us feel at home. Our pastoral work in Urucara included the town itself, as well as the towns of Sao Sebastian and Castanhal. We attended these on a weekly basis and set up a schedule for visits to the villages that were scattered about in the municipality. The Urucara River flowed southeasterly into the main Amazon, two hours down river from Urucara. Several villages were in this area. North of Sao Sebastian there were scattered settlements on the Jatapu and the Uatuma Rivers.

For the next three years I worked with Urucara as my home base. Construction began on a smaller version of the *Santa Teresinha*. This new boat would provide transportation for our pastoral visits and our regular trips to Itacoatiara and Manaus. We also bought a twenty-four foot canoe with a 25 hp. outboard motor attached to the back of it. This canoe was used for weekly visits to Castanhal and Sao Sebastian, as well as villages close by. Our colleagues in Itacoatiara sent us supplies once a week on the line boat. We were eight hours downstream by boat from Itacoatiara.

Living in Urucara was yet another great experience for me. Certainly we had to become accustomed to living without many of the conveniences one takes for granted. We were quite isolated both from our colleagues and from access to almost every type of supply. Hardware, building materials, food and medicine came from the outside. But we learned to live with the basics. In such a small town we came to know the people and develop, not just pastoral ties with them, but close and binding friendships. The people came to know us with all our shortcomings, and we came to know the community quite well.

Having priests live and work alongside them was a new experience for the townspeople. Their connection with the church and the clergy had been through pastoral visits a few times a year. Their pastor had been a local Amazonian priest. We were foreigners from Canada, but our permanent presence with them, sharing our lives and working with them in their daily struggles, gradually broke down barriers. We slowly became part of the life of the town.

With our regular pastoral work we built up a strong rapport with the youth of the town. They became our leaders with the school children in teaching catechism and forming a choir. They became an active group for church, social and recreational activities. My involvement with the youth would include several duck hunts during October each year. These excursions to the interior lakes with this group helped forge great friendships. The ducks from our hunt would be cleaned and roasted in a local oven by the women of the parish. On Sunday evenings, following church service, everyone would get a chance to bid on the roasted fowl, and the proceeds would go toward the new church.

In the dry season as the rivers dried up there would always be a run of tucunare, a large fish similar to lake trout. Outings, similar to the duck hunt, were times of camaraderie and recreation. Such encounters gave rise to invitations to accompany some of the fishermen on their nightly fishing forays.

George Marskell had a real gift for working with young people. His small groups met on a regular basis for study, to instruct catechists, plan liturgies, and develop special events around the major *festas*. The *casa paroquial* or parish house would always have some group or other working on some project. Both George and I frequented the local school on special occasions to do religious education.

As in most interior towns and villages the lack of medicines and health facilities was a major concern. Working with a group of concerned towns' people we petitioned state authorities for permission to use an abandoned health post. Three young women worked and studied with the sisters in the hospital in Itacoatiara. When they completed their studies, the health clinic was opened to serve some of the needs of the townspeople. Medicine was made available through co-operative buying. Some courses in prenatal care were introduced.

We were fortunate in having the presence of Clinton and Phyllis Thomas in the town. They were American Church of Christ missionaries and were professional medics. Clint ran a small clinic attached to his residence and was always ready to help out in any major crisis.

The Thomas family - Clint, Phyllis and their three young boys - arrived in Urucara about the same time as George and I. They had previously worked in Macapa, the capital city of the state of Amapa on the Atlantic seaboard, north of Belem. As Protestant missionaries they had suffered at the hands of the Catholic Church there, and so with good reason were leery of the new priests in town. Our first meetings were somewhat cool, but in a short while we became friends and then worked together in our mutual concern for the sick.

About eight months after beginning our work in Urucara, George Marskell was asked to return to Itacoatiara to work alongside Paul McHugh, who had been appointed the ecclesiastical prelate of Itacoatiara. I was appointed the local superior of the Scarboro group. As superior of the Scarboro priests it was my responsibility to encourage them in their work, discuss any problems they encountered in their life in the Amazon, and to work with the new prelate, Paul, in assigning our colleagues to pastoral work in areas that would best serve the people. Paul, as prelate and chief pastor, had the overall responsibility of administering the ecclesiastical area. Tim Ryan, Bill Smith and Ray O'Toole, who had arrived a few years earlier, formed the rest of the Itacoatiara pastoral team.

Justin MacInnis, also a new arrival, joined me in Urucara. In addition to his regular pastoral work in Urucara and visits to interior villages, Justin became deeply involved in the health problems in the area. He studied medical journals and case histories of sicknesses common to the area. He knew the Merck pharmaceutical manual as comprehensively as any doctor did. The sick came on a daily basis for medicine and diagnosis. Day or night Justin was available to attend to their needs.

In Urucara, as elsewhere in the interior, the prohibitive cost of medicines was a major problem. Supplying medicines and drugs was a lucrative business. Even though there was a proliferation of drugs in the country, the bottom line was always profit. Local merchants in the interior bought their supplies in Manaus, then added a markup usually between fifty and one hundred percent. Until we opened the church's first-aid clinic, and began buying our own medical drugs and supplies, we were always confronted with this problem. The poor simply could not afford to buy necessary drugs and medicine at such exorbitant prices.

Although there was a fair amount of division in the town because of political cliques, the people by nature were open and possessed good will. Rallying them to the challenge of building their church helped to dissipate much of this division. The majority of the families were dirt poor, but over the next three years everyone worked together with the objective of building their church. This was a common good around which all of the people could come together and build community.

As pioneers living and working in isolated areas, they had a strong custom of *puxirum*, of pulling together. Their accumulated building funds were invested in bricks and cement. When possible we transported the bricks from Itacoatiara to Urucara. The youth of the town would unload the boat or the barge, and men, women and children would carry the bricks up to the building site. When a barge was not in use, we would attach it to our new boat the *Sant'Ana*, and with a gang of youth take off for an afternoon of swimming up near the town of Sao Sebastian. Part of the excursion, of course, would involve loading the barge with sand using five-gallon tins. The work of unloading the sand back in Urucara was the same as for the bricks.

In the ensuing months there were countless *puxirums* on many a moonlit night. Countless hours of volunteer work by the townspeople moved tons of sand, hundreds of roof tiles, and thousands of bricks to the building site. Slowly but surely the walls of the church went up. Working together created deep bonds of community spirit and served to bring people together. One of the final *puxirums* in the church construction was the *lagem* of concrete and steel wiring that bound the walls together at roof height. When the forms had all been readied we called for a *puxirum* that was to begin on a Saturday morning at seven. Concrete had to be mixed by hand and then carried in buckets up to the roof section of the church. Well over a hundred men and youth worked in stages from Saturday morning around the clock until Sunday afternoon to complete the work. The women cooked pots of fish and beans to feed the workers.

Such goodwill and the giving of themselves were beautiful traits of the people of the interior. They had not lost that spirit of pulling together for the common good. The church was eventually completed; bricklayers and carpenters did their work. But the church was built really by the sweat and with the hands of the people; it was truly their church.

Urucara exemplified the *patrao* or patron system that controlled the economic life of the people. There were five or six principal merchants in the town. The majority of poor farmers in the area looked to them, their patrons, for grocery and hardware credit, for crop funding and loans in case of extreme need. In exchange for credit and loans the farmer would promise to sell to his patron his yearly harvest. Principally this was jute, but included other lesser crops as well.

The merchant was comparable to the company store in mining and lumber towns of Canada. Buying on extended credit meant higher prices, and selling one's crops for the price the merchant decided on. The unscrupulous often exploited the situation to the detriment of the poor farmer and his family. Bargaining on an equal playing field just did not exist. The merchant always had a stacked hand. Such economic dependence meant a *patrao* or patron exercised not only economic control, he also could exercise political control over his dependent farmers and their families.

It was not unusual for the farmer to call on his patron to be the godfather of his children. This created a religious and social bond between the patron and the farmer. It was the farmer's security to have his patron become a guardian for his child and be obligated to look out for the well-being of his godchild. In practise it usually meant a cheap source of labour for the patron. In 'caring for the godchild', the patron at times would take the child into his home as a domestic. Under the care of the patron, the godchild would have food and lodging and be sent to school, but would always remain subservient to the patron and his family.

During an extremely bad crop year a parish committee and I met with the merchants. We presented a plan for controlled prices on basic necessities. One or two backed us fully, the others reluctantly agreed. We posted the controlled prices throughout the town. The agreement held for about a month, but soon fell apart. There were innumerable ways in which the merchants could squirm out of their goodwill agreement. The farmers as well needed to be educated and organized before any real bargaining could take place. That would have to wait for a later time. That year I remember that at least four or five farmers that I spoke with had less than three hundred dollars in hand after selling their crops of jute, and squaring their debts with their patron. No security whatsoever was part of their lives. The majority possessed no authentic land titles. Good crops were contingent on good weather, and the price of their produce was decided upon by people in Manaus and Belem. Epidemics such as small pox, measles, fever were beyond their control. But despite all of this they were a people of hope, and they lived that hope; they dreamed that things would be better for their children.

The example of our cook, Dona Bebe, was always a powerful lesson for me. She was a single woman in her late thirties who lived with her two sisters and their families a short distance from our house. Her grandfather had been a slave in the northeast. When emancipation came and people were being encouraged to leave the arid states of Ceara and Pernambuco, the grandfather journeyed by land to Belem with his family. From there they came upriver by boat to Santarem. After a few years working in the area of Santarem they again moved upriver to the Urucara area in search of land.

A merchant-trader from Manaus hired Dona Bebe as a young girl to work as a domestic in his family home in Manaus. After years of service there she was taken by another family connected with the Brazilian government to Georgetown, Guyana where the family lived for five years. Upon their return to Manaus, Dona Bebe left their employ and returned home to Urucara. She had never been to school and knew little aside from the culinary skills she had learned in the homes of her employment.

She had been living with her family for several years when we arrived in Urucara. She was persuaded to come to work for the 'padres'. She was a shy, retiring person, but was proficient in her work. She was always on the job, and as she got to know us took on the task of caring for the 'padres'. But an employer/employee relationship was something entirely new to her. As a domestic her life had always been in the hands of others; they were the ones who commanded and laid down the daily list of tasks that fell to her responsibility.

She had never known employment where she had rights as well as responsibilities. As far as she was concerned it was up to us to tell her when she could take a day off, when she would be paid, when she could go home at the end of the day. It took many months of patient explaining on our part to bring it home to Dona Bebe that she could make independent decisions, that we were not in charge of her life. Slowly we developed a relationship and a friendship with her. As she grew to know us she allowed us to learn about her life as well.

Besides her dedication to us, Dona Bebe lived solely for her family. She had four nieces and one nephew who had large families. On our trips to Manaus and Itacoatiara, Dona Bebe would entrust her shopping list to us. It would include basic medicines, household items, and always the task of buying yards of cloth. The cloth would be made into clothes for her grandchildren. This was her pay day, and the only use she had for currency. It was to buy necessities for her extended family. On pay days Dona Bebe would never accept her salary. It was always left with us for that trip to Manaus, when she would present us with her shopping list.

Justin MacInnis and I left the parish of Urucara in 1968. Two new arrivals to the mission, Hubert den Tandt and Brian Manning, would replace us. The experience of living in a small isolated community was invaluable. One grew to understand and know a little better the *cabocolo* and his way of life. Their dauntless spirit of hope and faith in the face of whatever obstacles they confronted, was a humbling experience. They had their feuds and their grudges; they had their vices and at times shirked their responsibilities. But they were also the 'People of God' adrift in the desert, but marching slowly toward the Promised Land.

We, however, would see no Promised Land for some time. It was the desert experience that loomed in front of us, even though we were a thousand miles up the Amazon River.

CHAPTER 17

Challenging the Role
of Mission

From the time of our arrival in Itacoatiara we met as a missionary community twice a month to discuss our pastoral work in town and plan our trips to the interior villages. As we took on pastoral assignments in Manaus and Urucara our meetings were held every six weeks for two-day sessions. In these initial years all of us were united in following the pastoral program left to us by Alcides and Pinto. Certainly we had all agreed on the decision to have the Precious Blood Sisters take over the school in Itacoatiara and give more children a chance at education. We were in accord with the Sisters of St. Joseph from Peterborough, Ontario, coming to respond to the lack of health facilities and care. As a result of our meetings as a group were quite routine. The responsibility for major decisions and their implementation was in the hands of Paul our superior. At our meetings we gave our input and expressed our opinion, but our voice was always consultative.

In my formation years at the seminary, and as a youthful member of the Society, obedience was the virtue *par excellence*. Seminary life was based on the observance of the Rule. The Rule, a daily mandatory schedule of prayer, study and other activities, brought discipline into our lives, and order into the smooth operation of the seminary. It was there to help us grow spiritually in the virtues of humility and obedience. We were received into the Society by taking an oath of obedience to our lawful superiors.

Looking back on my formative years in the 1950s, there was little dialogue or input on the question of obedience. As subjects it was our duty and a virtue to obey a superior without question. It was always presumed that the superior would act in justice and honesty and for the common good. There was the implied presumption, as well, that a superior, by his office, would have the competence and good judgement to always make the right decisions. If we were told to do something, we obeyed. Obedience was the will of God. Our formation years provided very little information on authority itself, and how it should be exercised. The system was not unlike what the poor farmers had to endure with their patrons, and in a sort of offhanded way I could appreciate their struggle, although their struggle had much more severe consequences.

But times were changing. With the arrival of younger missionaries and the excitement of new ideas that resulted from the Vatican Council, we began to approach the problem of authority in radically different ways than we had in the past.

At our meetings some of us began to press for change. The traditional way of administering the large numbers of baptisms and confirmations, our whole sacramental approach; all of this was questioned. Should our pastoral visits to the interior towns and villages be scheduled at more appropriate times than at major *festas*? What type of catechetical approach would be more effective? And, as the documents from Vatican II began to reach us, questions of collegiality in decision-making and the role of the presbyterate (Council of priests) in planning the pastoral program, were all discussed at our meetings. Life was certainly not dull.

Our superior, Paul, on the other hand, was very reluctant to make any major changes. He felt strongly that such changes should wait until the appointment of the new bishop. While all agreed that there was validity to this position, as the months went by we came to feel that some changes could not wait. We were all walking on new ground. The pastoral challenges of Itacoatiara and the new and radical changes emerging from the Council were before us! It was a time of growth for all of us! It was also a time of tension! As in much of the Catholic world, it was, unfortunately, also a time of division. As colleagues and fellow missionaries we had learned to live with differences in personality and temperament. But what to do when our theological perspective and missiology clashed, and dialogue ended?

The Archdiocese of Toronto under Archbishop Philip Pocock had adopted our work in May of 1964, in response to Pope John XXIII's appeal to help the Latin American church. The announcement that the Archdiocese would financially help the mission took place while Paul McHugh and Doug MacKinnon were on vacation in Canada. In response to the Archdiocese, Paul and Doug prepared a list of programs and the rationale for the programs that they felt needed funding. They sent their list to us in Itacoatiara with their reasons, explaining the situation and asking our approval. This situation would become the occasion of our first major disagreement over mission planning and policy.

Mission activity in Itacoatiara depended on financial aid from abroad. Certainly the hospital and the health care work depended on outside help. The new school system was financed in large part by Scarboro's mission budget. And now this new source of financial aid was being offered to us. Should we build up structures that depended on aid from outside? Christian charity was taken for granted, but who would support the slow work of building sustainable development programs? There was a responsibility to utilize these financial resources well. There was also a corresponding responsibility to those who would be the recipients of this aid.

When Paul and Doug returned to Brazil our first meetings focused on the list of programs that had been presented. Many of their proposals were rejected by the rest of us, some on the grounds that we were creating structures that were unsustainable, and others because the projects were not culturally acceptable. This negative reaction to the proposed list was the beginning of serious divisions within the mission. It was not received as legitimate and positive input for future mission planning as it was intended to be, but unfortunately as the questioning of authority.

Meetings on this topic were to become stormy sessions in the life of the mission. Those of us who had rejected some of the projects had presented our rationale. We felt that all such projects would determine how the mission would operate in the future. We believed that our theological views, the insights gained from our education, and our everyday experiences in our work in a new culture, were all factors that had to be considered in making our decisions.

In describing these early years in Itacoatiara I am attempting to show the influences and circumstances that had shaped our pastoral work. There had been no serious long range planning. We tackled problems in each area as they were forced upon us. In a sense we had adopted a let's wait and see policy. Our team had not studied even the pastoral plan of the Brazilian bishops for the country. We were awaiting the appointment of a bishop, and then would come a pastoral plan.

With the advent of this new arrangement with the Archdiocese of Toronto, the necessity of formulating a plan and policy for our work was a major concern for most of us. By 1968 there were two priests in Manaus and another eight in the prelacy. The young blood in our ranks wanted a pastoral plan in place, in much the same way as we had when we first arrived. With the openness to dialogue and collegiality that was prevalent at Vatican II, authority, as it was being exercised in the mission, was being questioned. Most of the time I agreed with the younger missionaries, and this could be interpreted as my challenging Paul's leadership and authority. Yet legitimate questions needed to be asked. Was mission policy and practice to be determined by one person holding the position of authority, or was it to be an exercise of collegial responsibility? In the traditional formation that some of us had received authority was vested only in the superior. His was the final word, and as subjects our role was to obey! But was that really the best way? Was it the most effective way for the future?

More and more, our meetings as a Scarboro group became confrontational. The heated debates often ended in opposing camps with different points of view. We were attempting to settle the issues of authority and obedience as we attempted to prioritize a list of programs funded from abroad. But our theologies, our vision of church, of development and of inculturation were at variance with one another and caused a deep rift between us.

Another instance where these questions of obedience, mission theology and understanding of development clashed was with regard to the *Alliance for Progress* program. As I noted previously, the Alliance was a handout program with no educational component attached to it. It was introduced as America's way of helping her poor neighbours to the south, and definitely had a political agenda attached to it. Generally speaking all of the various missionary groups in the region accepted the program as a necessary infusion of food and clothing to help the poor get on their feet. It was charity pure and simple. How could we criticize charity? Yet, as some of us began to judge it, the program was also terribly paternalistic. It was long on American propaganda and short on alleviating the core problem of why there was such poverty in the first place.

As we began to question the validity of the program, we brought some serious reservations to the table. From the point of view of mission and inculturation, should we be part of Uncle Sam's propaganda? Should we continue to be agents for American policy? Was this program not helping to hide the economic and political interference of the United States in the life of Brazilians? Did this image we were perpetuating as rich foreigners help our work in mission, or help us inculturate with people whose income averaged about seven or eight hundred dollars a year? Our decision to discontinue the program for all of the above reasons was a collegial one and not simply the decision of one person. If we had followed the traditional role of authority and obedience, the program would not have been closed down.

An example of where the traditional approach to authority did win out involved the language and inculturation schooling of young missionaries. The Society had sent its young missionaries appointed to the Dominican Republic to the language and cultural school founded by Ivan Illich in Cuernavaca, Mexico. The first group to Brazil had gone to his school in Annapolis. But following our year at the school no young missionaries to Latin America were sent to these institutes by the Society. The decision to discontinue our connection with Ivan Illich's schools in Brazil and Mexico was made by the General Council of the Society. Obviously, they had received complaints from either the superior in the Dominican Republic or Brazil, or both places. The methods of Illich and his team challenged the status quo and initiated change! There was never any consultation with the missionaries who had taken their studies at these institutes. Instead, the Society set up a language training program in Canada. Some of us in Brazil felt strongly that the program in Canada could not duplicate the experience of Illich's institute.

Our common purpose as missionaries held us together, and prayer united us by a thin thread, but the seeds of division remained. Through persistence we did hammer out a long-range plan that incorporated the Brazilian bishop's plan and would bode well for the pastoral and social work of the church in Itacoatiara. Taking equal responsibility for pastoral planning helped us to grow as persons and as missionaries. Experiencing dialogue and co-responsibility would help some of us to adapt to the major changes in the church that lay on the horizon. The collegial approach to decision making was not perfect, mistakes were made, but in my view it was a more mature way of dealing with authority and obedience.

My formation had been in a traditional church that provided all the answers. My role as priest and missionary had been laid out for me. I said my prayers and looked to the church for all the answers. By nature I was a peacemaker; I avoided confrontation. But this world that had been so familiar to me was being challenged. It was fast changing. And it was the church itself that challenged me. Ivan Illich's approach to mission, namely to question and to challenge the traditional approach, was taking hold in my thinking. Several other colleagues thought the same. As the senior priest of the Scarboro personnel, and as local superior, it was my responsibility to work alongside the bishop for the good of the people and the mission. But here I was along with some confreres apparently in opposition to the ecclesial authority. Our questioning of policy was not intended to be an act of defiance to authority, but a serious attempt to be faithful to our mission mandate. I was facing a "trial by fire" both personally and as a missionary.

CHAPTER 18

Lay Leadership

O ne of the major projects undertaken by the mission was the building of a pastoral training centre for lay leadership. This was the first of the approved projects that would be funded by the Archdiocese of Toronto. *Centrepi* (Educational Centre of the Prelacy of Itacoatiara), was constructed during 1966 and 1967 on several hectares of riverfront property on the outskirts of the town. Its first training session for lay pastoral leaders was held in October of 1967. Eighteen leaders from interior communities began a two-week session. This pioneer group followed a basic course in catechetics, community leadership, health care, and community worship services. There were basic classes in reading and writing. Local teachers from Itacoatiara were involved in planning and running the course. The sisters and priests contributed in the areas of our expertise.

The centre became one of our top priorities in our vision of a new church. Laeticia Oliveira, a specialist in basic educational techniques became *Centrepi*'s first supervisor. Over the years she was to develop a number of courses that would educate hundreds of lay leaders representing thirty-two communities from both the interior and the town of Itacoatiara. Scarboro missionaries Bill Smith and Omar Dixon, both of whom had studied catechetics, were part of *Centrepi*'s team that worked with Laeticia.

As the concept of basic Christian communities developed throughout Brazil, retreats, seminars, training sessions and extended courses were conducted at *Centrepi* by lay leaders and theologians from other parts of the country. These courses became educational opportunities not only for the lay leaders but for the sisters and priests as well.

In the centre's first years of operation the pastoral teams selected the lay leaders from the interior communities who would be trained. As we grew in experience it was the local community and the teams that presented the list of candidates. The scheduling of courses coincided with planting and harvest times. Nine or ten short courses took place throughout the year, as well as a longer two-month session.

The response from the laity throughout the prelacy to the courses of study offered by the centre was overwhelming. The young and the old sacrificed their work time, and accepted being away from their homes and families in order to come to the centre for training. While their communities contributed financially to the centre, the leaders who came for training were committed volunteers, dedicating themselves to the work of their local communities.

The centre opened whole new dimensions in the life of the church for the prelacy. Deep bonds of commitment were forged among the participants. We, as foreign priests and sisters, developed a greater understanding and knowledge of the people and their communities. We were dealing with people from the grass roots. The reality of their daily lives and struggles became a reality in our lives. The church as a people of God was being formed in a real way.

Not all of those who came for courses persevered as leaders in their communities. But many made lasting faith commitments to the building up of strong and active communities rooted in faith. I will always remember Geraldino de Freitas who came from *Terra Preta de Limao* (Black Land of the Limes). This was one of the poorest communities in the prelacy. The village where Geraldino lived was accessible only by canoe through dense swampland in high water from a tributary of the Amazon. In the dry season it meant a three-hour trek by foot. Geraldino, who was in his sixties, was a respected leader in his community. Though illiterate as far as formal education was concerned, he was a gifted leader with the wisdom and experience of his age. He came to *Centrepi* for successive courses over a five year period to improve his writing and reading skills. He immersed himself in biblical and catechetical courses and continued his leadership work in his community for many years. Each year he would bring two or three young people for training. His determination and desire for learning became an inspiration not just for other lay leaders but for all that knew him.

Centrepi was also used as a centre for weekend retreats, preparatory courses for baptism and marriages, and to train ministers of the Eucharist. As the number of communities and participants continued to grow a monthly newsletter became the vehicle for keeping leaders informed of the happenings within the prelacy.

Another project initiated during this time was to set up and fund an interior formation centre for farming in Urucara. Padre Augusto Gianola, who came to work in the prelacy from Parintins, was its first director. He worked with young farmers in the eastern area of the prelacy. Courses provided practical experience in the care and cultivation of local fruit trees such as oranges, limes, avocado and bananas. The school also experimented in growing vegetables that the climate and soil would sustain. A literacy program, financial management, and basic health and cooking programs were added as volunteers from Italy came to form part of Augusto's team. This project continued in the prelacy for seventeen years until Augusto's health deteriorated and funding ended. It was a great help to the local farmers, aiding them to improve and care for their crops, educating them in soil preservation, and providing them with the basics to run a small farm.

There were other projects that were funded by the Archdiocese of Toronto. A small brick-building venture proved unsuccessful. A portable sawmill was also bought for the Urucara and Sao Sebastiao area. This project functioned as a co-operative for a few years and then was bought out by two of the members and became a private venture. Funds were also provided for the digging of wells in isolated villages, and model latrines were built and distributed to the interior.

These projects, as well as our initial forays into credit unions and co-operatives, would bring us even closer to the reality of the social and political problems of the area.

As the 1960s came to an end the ranks of the original five Scarboro missionaries had grown to sixteen missionaries. The parish in Manaus had grown into a large active church community with two satellite missions. Pastoral teams were living and working out of Uricurituba to the east of Itacoatiara, and another team at the west end of the prelacy, as well as in Urucara. The Precious Blood Sisters had more than 360 students in their primary and secondary schools, and 34 students in the teachers' college. The Canadian Sisters of St. Joseph had two more sisters join them, and they set up a lab adjoining the hospital. They had a local doctor on staff. Small health posts had been established in many interior towns with a supply of basic medicines.

Father Paul McHugh, who had been named a prelate in 1965, attended the last session of the Second Vatican Council in Rome. In July 1967 he was named bishop of the prelacy and was ordained as bishop in Itacoatiara in October 1967. Paul was to be bishop until 1972 when ill health forced him to resign.

In 1967 and 1968 the Scarboro Mission Society held chapter sessions at headquarters in Canada. These were summer meetings called to study all aspects of mission in light of Vatican II, and to prepare for the election of a new administrative council. Bill Smith, the elected delegate from Brazil, and myself, as the local superior, would attend these sessions. At the 1968 chapter session George Marskell was elected to the Council at Scarboro. That same year Vince Daniel returned to Canada because of sickness.

In 1970 I was due to take studies in the south of the country. However, when the military closed the designated seminary I returned home for what I thought would be a year of study. As the first decade of Scarboro's presence in Itacoatiara came to a close four of the five original missionaries had returned to Canada; two because of ill health, George Marskell to serve on the General Council of the Society, and myself for a year of study.

In 1972, with the departure of Paul McHugh, Doug MacKinnon was appointed to serve as administrator of the prelacy. Cardinal Paulo Evaristo Arns of Sao Paulo had expressed interest the previous year in a mutual exchange program of personnel. One of Doug's first decisions was to enter into negotiations with the Archdiocese of Sao Paulo. These negotiations resulted in the prelacy being adopted by the Archdiocese of Sao Paulo. The objective of the exchange program was to expose the respective churches to each other's life and reality. By late 1972 three priests, two sisters and three lay volunteers arrived in Itacoatiara. It was the beginning of a pastoral experience that would last for thirteen years and would be of immense benefit to the prelacy. Scarboro missionaries would now have the presence of Brazilian pastoral agents, priests and religious working alongside them.

The full expectation of the exchange program was never completely realized however. Several Scarboro priests did work in Sao Paulo as volunteers for several years, and two lay leaders worked briefly in a poor section of Sao Paulo. But the prelacy of Itacoatiara never managed to send special pastoral teams. The pastoral work of the prelacy benefited in a far greater way than the Sao Paulo church from the exchange. The teams of lay and religious personnel were committed to the vision of a new church. Their Archbishop was one of the outstanding bishops of Latin America. He was committed to the poor. The men and women who came to Itacoatiara, under the auspices of Arn's diocese, had all been active in parish ministry. They brought with them their ties to the Brazilian church in the rest of the country, their knowledge of the current political happenings, and their strong links with the aims and objectives of the pastoral plan of the larger Brazilian church. Their involvement with the church in Itacoatiara was a major contribution not only to the people, but also too our understanding of and integration into the reality of life in Latin America.

As this chapter of life was unfolding in our little world of Itacoatiara I now write about the broader social, political, and religious situation of Brazil, the context in which we lived and worked as missionaries.

CHAPTER 19

Brazil: A Country of Contradictions

As my journey reaches another bend in the river, I feel that it is necessary to give you a more in-depth knowledge and understanding of the country of Brazil. The mission in Itacoatiara in the state of Amazonas was thousands of kilometres from the heart and soul of the country. Our mission presence in this area often referred to as the 'green hell' might be compared to five or ten Brazilians working with the Inuit people, in a small northern area of Iqualit, far from the mainstream of Canadian life.

Most Brazilians refer to their country as the *terra de Deus*, the land of God. It is the largest country in South America and the fifth largest in the world, with more inhabitable land than China, the United States or Canada. It's population today (2003) is more than 175 million. The three metropolitan areas of Sao Paulo, Rio and Olinda-Recife have a greater combined population than the whole of Canada. It is the most technically advanced country in the southern hemisphere, and is a land of rich resources. Yet, it is a country overburdened with social problems, an inheritance from its colonial past. Geographically, this giant of a country can be divided into three broad areas: the hot humid Amazon valley marked by a vast water system, the half-desert/ forest expanse of the northeast, and the highlands and plateaus of the central and southern area. It borders on all the countries of South America save for Chile and Ecuador.

Paulo Freire, a Brazilian philosopher and educator of international repute, created a methodology of educating the illiterate through a process he called conscientization (*conscientizacao*), or consciousness raising. The objective of the process was to educate illiterate peasants through an awareness of the political, social, and cultural reality in which they found themselves. As missionaries in Brazil we went through that process in our early years in the Amazon. The following study of Brazil and its history will hopefully conscientize you to the reality of Brazil, its people, its culture, its political and social life, and the Catholic Church in that country.

Brazil was the only Portuguese colony in Latin America. The Treaty of Tordesillas of 1494 gave the Portuguese Crown the right to explore the Southern Hemisphere. Six years later, in April of 1500, Pedro Alvares Cabral landed in today's state of Bahia in northeast Brazil. With the establishment of a settlement of 400 men in 1520 by Martin Afonso de Sousa, Portugal began the exploitation of its newest colony.

In the following years the colonizers were to move south from Bahia down the eastern coast of Brazil establishing a settlement in Sao Vicente (1532), close to modern day Sao Paulo. The Portuguese colonizers like the Spaniards came to conquer and carry new riches to the motherland.

In the 16th and 17th centuries the new colony was to become a major producer of sugar, cotton and coffee. Gold and rubber would be discovered and become the commerce of the 18th century. An indigenous population of 7 million would be enslaved as the beasts of burden for this new found wealth. The sugar and cotton plantations would depend on the importation of millions of slaves from Africa. A flourishing trade in this inhumane traffic was to see Brazil build up the largest slave population in South America.

The initial years of colonization would see a gradual move from the coastline into the interior of the new land. Expeditionary forces from Sao Vicente, called the *bandeirantes*, pushed inland both to extend the boundaries and enslave the indigenous populations. Fiefdoms and captaincies were established which granted huge tracts of land to Crown administrators and officials. The Dutch established a foothold in Brazil for 24 years from 1630-1654, but were forced out by the Portuguese.

As in the rest of Latin America the legacy of colonization has been the exploitation of the lower classes, namely the indigenous, the black population and those of mixed blood. Land, wealth and power were concentrated in those favoured by the Crown, while the majority of the population lived in abject poverty. Patronage and corruption became a legacy of colonization even as the country moved toward democracy in this present century.

Napoleon and the French invaded Portugal in 1807. As a result, King John VI fled Portugal, came to Brazil and established a monarchy. Returning to his homeland in 1820, the King left his son Dom Pedro I, as Regent. Within a year, in a bloodless coup, Dom Pedro cut ties with Portugal and established a Republic. Eight years later Dom Pedro was forced into exile and was succeeded by his son Dom Pedro II. The second Dom Pedro was by all accounts a benevolent ruler. Slavery was officially abolished in Brazil in 1888, but the sugar and cotton plantations kept thousands in bondage for years afterwards.

Joaquim da Silva (Tiradentes), a Brazilian dentist formed the first group that advocated freedom from the rule of Dom Pedro II and independence. He was arrested by the Crown and hung as a traitor in Rio in 1792. Although independence came to Brazil in 1889, long after Tiradentes death, he is recognized today as the father of independence.

In the 20th century, Getulio Vargas was Brazil's most famous authoritarian President. First elected in 1930, he rewrote the Constitution and managed to centralize the government. Prior to Vargas, Governors in the twenty states gave scant notice to the central government. Most were populists and elected to office with the backing of the land barons who were the powerbrokers. Vargas was overthrown with the establishment of the Second Republic in 1945.

But he returned to power in 1950 and ruled as a dictator until his suicide in 1954.

The 1900s witnessed the arrival of thousands of immigrants from the Ukraine, Poland, Germany, Italy and Japan. Its population is one of the most cosmopolitan in the world and while often proclaimed as a model for other societies, the truth is that Brazil is divided by class, with racism and elitism ever present.

Juscelino Kubitcheck (1956-1961), a popular President, was the visionary who built the new capital of Brazilia. Janio Quadros, the brilliant but erratic mayor of Sao Paulo was elected to the Presidency in 1962 but resigned eight months later. He was succeeded by Joao Goulart, his Vice-President. Goulart, of the Brazilian Workers Party, assumed the Presidency during a turbulent time of social unrest and labour strife. The country was ripe for revolution. He attempted to form unsuccessful alliances with Carlos Lacerda and Leonel Brizola, two of the country's most powerful politicians. Goulart was a leftist who recognized the necessity of agrarian reform and the promotion of the rights of the working class. His program of reform and his leftist views alarmed the power brokers and big business. In March of 1964 a protest march of more than 400,000 in Sao Paulo, organized by the right wing of the Catholic Church, signalled his downfall and brought the military from the barracks. Goulart went into exile in Uruguay as the military took control of the country.

Brazil is the largest Catholic country in the world, although in recent times fundamental sects have threatened the monopoly of the Catholic Church. There has always been a scattering of Lutherans, Presbyterians and Anglicans throughout the country. Afro-Brazilian religious syncretism has been prevalent in the rites of Candoble and Macumbo, and Spiritism came from Germany in the 18th century.

During colonial times the church's main focus was to convert the indigenous population. It could be described as a paternalistic, yet benevolent institution that espoused gospel values while walking in step with the colonial powers. Along with the colonial masters, the church accepted a culture of poverty as the norm. Little effort was expended to correct the terrible imbalances that existed in the social structures of the country. As always there were heroic attempts by individual churchmen, such as the Jesuit Jose Anchieta, who worked tirelessly on behalf of the indigenous peoples.

While it was a colonial church, like-minded religious like Anchieta worked for the betterment of the marginalized populations of slaves and indigenous. The Social Encyclicals of Pope Leo XIII, written in the latter part of the nineteenth century, had a resurgence in the late 1940s with the beginning of the Social Action movements within the church. The Young Christian Students and the Workers Movement developed a new breed of church leaders and activists who advocated for the poor and the oppressed. Visionary leaders were being formed who began to break ties with the ruling elite, committing the church to radical social involvement. This change would not come easily. Colonial ties were strong and entrenched.

Archbishop Geraldo Proenca Sigaud of Diamantina, in the state of Minas Gerais, provides one such example. A wealthy landowner and an opponent of agrarian reform, he was one of the founders of an organization called "Tradition, Family and Country" (TPF). An ultra-conservative group, it favoured the *status quo*, objected to the reforms of Vatican II, and opposed the church's presence in the social arena. The TPF promoted their cause by an all out war against communism, and by launching a crusade to return to the church of the Middle Ages. Sigaud and the TPF became allies of the military dictatorships in Brazil, Chile and Argentina and stopped at nothing to protect the private property of the elite. They received undisclosed financial aid, and were willing allies of the military in their fight against the progressive church. Much to the embarrassment of other conservative prelates, Sigaud accused Bishops Pedro Casadaliga and Tomas Balduino of being communists, and denounced many others as being subversive.

But another story was unfolding at the same time. The conference of Brazil's Bishops initiated a national pastoral plan in the early 1950s through the efforts of a youthful Dom Helder Camara, who was then auxiliary bishop of Rio de Janeiro. Camara, who became deeply involved in attempts to eradicate the *favellas* or slums that surrounded the city of Rio, became the conscience of the Brazilian Bishops' Conference.

In 1962, facing a grave social situation, the Bishops' Conference called the nation's leaders and the faithful to action. "We possess no magic formula that can transform the world in a day, but... pastoral action, following the church's social doctrine in the world of labour, business and the professions with the highest moral principles... can carry the country to its destiny of progress... looking to the human needs of people, health, food, education and housing... agrarian reform, working in a Christian climate of love and unity. We exhort men of government not to forget the important principles of church teaching when they are concerned with public affairs." (National Conference of Brazilian Bishops 1962, *Scarboro Magazine* 1964.)

Archbishop Carlos Gouvea Coelho of Olinda-Recife, in the drought-ridden northeast where endemic poverty ruled, followed with this statement: "The church cannot remain insensible to the tragedy of inhuman living conditions. Millions of our brothers and sisters vegetate in such conditions, ... We have to have the formation of a common conscience, a new economic and political system, paternalism will not suffice, there must be a just and human social order to living the gospel." (Conference of Brazilian Bishops: Northeastern Sector 1962, *Scarboro Magazine*, 1964.) During the same year, the National Bishops' Conference spoke against communism and against the criminal control of the economy through corruption in politics, the uncontrollable appetite for gain and the deteriorating political, social and economic situation of the country. "Government leaders must work not just for the interests of privileged groups, but for the good of all. Atheistic communism actively exploits the situation while liberal capitalism, no less atheistic, profits from communist agitation. Certain groups, on the pretext of combating communism, nourish the propaganda of subversive ideas and exhaust the patience of the poor". (Conference of Brazilian Bishops 1962, *Scarboro Magazine* 1964)

Bishop Helder Camara with his group of young Catholic leaders targeted the underdeveloped northeast. Church and government collaborated to found the Northeast Development Agency. More than a million inhabitants of the over populated area were encouraged to resettle in the states of Maranhao and Bahia. Radio schools were set up and Paulo Freire's educational techniques taught thousands of illiterate adults to read and write. The Natal Movement developed a vigorous program of evangelization and social action for those who were poverty stricken.

Awakened by the Second Vatican Council, the church in Brazil and her prophetic leaders would join like-minded visionary bishops and theologians throughout Latin America and come together at the Council of Medellin in Colombia. At this famous conference attended by Pope Paul VI, the bishops would formulate their gospel response to the dangers of communism, the social ills, the grinding poverty, and elite capitalism that marginalized millions of Latin Americans. But this new direction would bring terrible consequences that would see a mobilized campaign of slander and persecution against the Latin American church.

At the same time that my Scarboro colleagues and I were dealing with the initial problems of establishing a mission presence in the Amazon region of Brazil, our insignificant trials and difficulties would pale in comparison to the trials that would engulf the citizens of Brazil. On April 1, 1964 the government of President Joao Goulart was overthrown by a military dictatorship. The Generals of Brazil's Armed Forces, wary of Goulart's commitment to socially progressive reforms, overthrew Brazil's democratically elected government in a decisive coup. In support of the armed forces of Brazil, an American naval task force was sent to the southern Atlantic. This American force included an Aircraft carrier, destroyers and tons of arms and ammunition.

General Humberto Castello e Branco was installed as President of Brazil. Thus began a reign of terror that would go on for twenty years.

Initially the military acted with some restraint, purging - as they called it - the political and social system by arresting and imprisoning people they perceived to be opponents of their regime. They dismissed thousands of civil servants, military personnel and politicians.

From 1967 to 1971 a violent reaction to the military took place. There were student demonstrations and uprisings calling for a return to civilian rule. Small urban guerrilla groups initiated acts of retaliation. They kidnapped the American Ambassador Charles Burke Elbrick and some prominent Brazilians, holding them for ransom. President Castello e Branco died in a mysterious plane crash.

The hard-liners within Brazil's Armed Forces were waiting in the wings to take over. They set themselves up as the great defenders of freedom against communism. Led by General Coutu e Silva they imposed the 'Doctrine of National Security' on the citizens of Brazil. Following the Second World War, Coutu e Silva and other Generals who had served with the Americans in Italy, had established Brazil's Advanced War College. Here, military strategy and special courses were developed for both young officers and business people. With close ties to the Pentagon, Brazils' Generals emulated American military policy on security and nation building.

The new god, according to them, was the state. It was the omnipotent power, the supreme deity and within that state citizens were to relinquish their intellect and will to that power. Any thought or expression that differed from the aims and objectives of National Security was considered treason and an act of subversion. The sacredness and infallibility of the state's program was protected by the fact that, according to the Generals, there was a "state of constant war both within and outside the country." Thus, the rights of citizens had no place because the state took precedence in all matters. If citizens could not or would not accept this doctrine then they became "enemies of the state." It was the state's responsibility and duty to imprison, to torture, to murder or to exile any dissidents or enemies of this new god. The military was the avenging angel of this god; war was war, and the secret police and a national network of intelligence had to control the civilian population. Barbaric acts of torture and imprisonment were justified by the sacredness of the state. Political parties, labour unions, student federations, all were outlawed, and the state controlled the press.

The Generals worked from the premise that civilians were not capable of running a government. It was ironic that many of these generals had fought against a similar type of fascism in World War II against Hitler and Mussolini.

Fr. Jose Comblin, a prominent theologian and missionary in Brazil has written extensively on the Doctrine of the National Security State (a Creole version of fascism, says Comblin) in Latin America. Military dictatorships were common enough, but the strategy employed by the military in Brazil was to wield total power over the daily lives of citizens. Comblin notes that a special ploy was to keep people convinced that communism was the only enemy. Using this ploy the military were able to manipulate many church leaders and were able to divide the church. Although General Coutu e Silva and many in the military dismissed the Catholic Church and religion as irrelevant, they recognized that rallying the religious forces was an indispensable factor in their strategy to win over the masses. In their anti-Marxist ideological campaign the military allied themselves with certain sectors within the church such as TPF, offering an alliance that would further the aims of the church to build a moral society. This alliance would hold out the carrot stick of lavish privileges within the state. (Jose Comblin, National Security State, *Scarboro Magazine*, 1979.)

At the same time this National Security State would persecute any church leaders who might oppose or question their aims and objectives.

In the overall scenario of what took place in Latin America it is important to recognize that the ideology of the National Security State is anti-gospel. Outside the state citizens had no value, their only identity was with the state. The state wielded power only by exerting repressive force. It encouraged a continuous confrontation of nation against nation and citizen against citizen. It left a legacy of torture, death and the disappearance of thousands on the South American continent. Cardinal Paulo Evaristo Arns, working with Jaime Wright, a Presbyterian minister, and the Human Rights office of the Archdiocese of Sao Paulo, published the book *Brazil, Never Again* in 1984. It was an expose of institutional torture by the military taken from their own jail records. The book became a best-seller in Brazil and created such revulsion in public opinion that it helped bring about the downfall of the military.

The doctrine of National Security had an ideology that complemented the strategy of the American government. Sadly, its imposition was carried out with the help of the CIA. The conversion of many high-ranking church officials to its way of thinking would be a revolt against what the Latin American hierarchy formulated at the Council of Medellin in 1968. It would be contrary to the conclusions of the Synod of Bishops held in Rome in 1971 which stated: "Action on behalf of justice and participation in the transformation of the world appear to us as a constitutive dimension of the preaching of the Gospel, or in other words, of the church's mission for the redemption of the human race and its liberation from every oppressive situation." (Penny Lernoux, *People of God*, Penguin Books, 1989, p. 35.) The church leaders in Latin America who supported the National Security State tacitly accepted the bloody repercussions, and the thousands of deaths and disappearances of innocent women and men. It would be the acceptance of the principle that evil is permitted if it brings about good for certain groups.

There were other bishops in the Brazilian church who spoke out and acted against the repression and ruthlessness of the National Security. Cardinal Paulo Evaristo Arns of Sao Paulo and other church leaders in the industrialized south demanded the right of daily visitation of the military prisons. The *Washington Times* commented that Arns' speaking out against the violation of human rights was the strongest and most courageous affirmation ever made by a Brazilian prelate. As a result, the church itself became a target of persecution and an enemy of the generals. As one institution beyond their control, the church became a prime target of the military. Dom Helder Camara, by now the Archbishop of Olinda-Recife, a leader in the organization of grass-roots communities, was declared a non-person and denied access to the media. He was subjected to daily harassment and persecution. His secretary, Padre Henrique Pereira Neto, was kidnapped on May 26, 1969, tortured and killed. His body was roped to a jeep that drove the streets of Recife. The intent was clear; the military had declared war on the church and her progressive leaders.

In Itacoatiara and other remote areas it was difficult to get news of what was happening in the rest of the country. Being neophytes in the political arena of Brazil the early months of the revolution did little to change our immediate lives except for two incidents that I will relate. Gradually, church links kept us informed, and we were immersed in the political realities of Brazil and soon the rest of Latin America.

The first incident that brought us into direct contact with the reality of the military coup of April 1964 was a letter from Archbishop Dom Joao de Sousa Lima. In his letter he requested that all bishops and superiors of the Archdiocese assemble in Manaus for a briefing on the objectives of the new government. This briefing was to be presented by the new military commander of the Army's Northern Command in Manaus.

We assembled in Manaus in the spring of 1965. While the Archbishop was the convenor of the meeting, the new military commander planned the agenda. As I recall it, the general began by thanking the Archbishop and all those assembled for being present. His speech was no more than a propaganda ploy justifying the military takeover of the government. He spoke of the corruption within the civilian political system, the economic and social crisis that confronted the nation, and the threat of communism, the enemy of both the church and the state. He called on the church for support in helping the military bring stability and morality back into government. He assured us that his government was fighting the same enemies as the church, the dangers of communism and immorality. Church and state had to work together to attain such ends for the good of Brazil, a Catholic nation.

The majority of those present at the meeting were foreign missionaries and we were all working in remote areas of the state. Few of us had direct contact with what was happening in the rest of Brazil, although rumours and some reliable information were reaching us. At the time our knowledge of what the National Security State was all about was limited. So, the meeting did not appear to be confrontational, although some seriously questioned the loss of democracy. Were we not being invited to work along with the government for the welfare of the people? As Brazilians are accustomed to do, the meeting was cordial. The Archbishop thanked the General for his report and for the opportunity of the church's collaboration.

In his closing remarks the General invited all of us to a luncheon and a get-to-know-you gathering at army headquarters. We were also informed that all missionaries as visitors to the country would be required to register at police headquarters in Manaus for new identity cards.

During coffee break and at the closure of the meeting many of us exchanged our reaction to the Generals' remarks, and any information we had on the overall situation of the country. We lamented the loss of democracy, but the General's alert to the danger of communism overshadowed any negative feelings we had at the time. Still, a number of us felt uncomfortable about going to the command headquarters to lunch and decided not to attend.[1]

---

1. The above incident is my recollection from memory. I had not saved any notes on this meeting.

CHAPTER 20

The Waiwai-mari Atroari People

Sociologists tell us, and history confirms it, that in the 1500s, when Pedro Cabral came ashore in Brazil, the country was populated by between six and nine million indigenous people. By the 1900s the indigenous people in the same area numbered only one million, with half of the 230 tribes in Brazil now extinct. And today the indigenous population of Brazil numbers less than 200,000.

Like their sisters and brothers in the rest of the Americas, the native Peoples of Brazil have been the victims of the white man's greed and exploitation, and the diseases that followed in his wake. Today, on the brink of extinction, they continue to face insurmountable odds in their quest to be recognized as Peoples with the same rights as you and I.

When Scarboro was assigned to the Brazil mission in 1961, we were told that a future assignment and pastoral responsibility would be with the Waiwai-mari-Atroari People. This tribe of indigenous people lived on the northern edges of our mission territory. They had had little or no contact with the outside world.

Before we were able to initiate any plan to make contact with these people the Military Government had taken over the country. The government's Federal Indian Affairs Department, known by its acronym FUNAI, had received orders that prohibited any outside contact with the Atroaris or other tribes, and furthermore, that travel in Indian Territory was restricted.

I remember very clearly in our first year in Itacoatiara being called to the door to see the "Indians." Our home at the time was almost adjacent to the river. Looking out the front door I saw two braves accompanied by a New Tribes missionary (A fundamentalist Missionary group from the U.S.A.). They were coming from the riverbank and heading toward the municipal buildings. Clothed only in their loincloths, they passed by with great dignity despite the stares of onlookers. They were sturdy, healthy individuals, ill at ease in their surroundings as they walked up the street followed by a crowd of young people. That was my only direct contact with the indigenous people who lived only several hundred kilometres distant from us. Through others, I did come to know of them as a People, and of their sad history.

During the years 1966 and 1967 the military announced plans for the construction of a highway between Manaus and Boa Vista, the capital of the neighbouring state of Roraima to the north of Amazonas. The highway was to eventually reach to the borders of neighbouring Guyana. The initial construction of a rough BR-174 highway commenced, and several months into construction newspaper reports indicated that highway crews were being hampered in their work by bands of indigenous people. Later newspaper stories reported the death of several construction workers after clashes with these indigenous people, a tribe called the Atroaris.

Sometime in the summer of 1968 work was suspended on the highway, and it was announced by officials that a peace expedition was being assembled that would attempt to make contact with the Atroaris. The expedition was to be headed by a young missionary by the name of John Calleri. The objective of this peace expedition was to peacefully seek out the Atroari people, befriend them, and over a period of time move their villages further into the jungle.

Fr. John Calleri was an Italian missionary, belonging to a group of missionaries calling themselves the Comboni Fathers. These missionaries worked out of Boa Vista, in what was at the time the Territory of Roraima. Much like the Scarboro Fathers they pastorally cared for the populations of the town of Boa Vista, and the small towns that dotted the territory. They also ministered to several tribes of indigenous Peoples.

Since his arrival in Brazil nine years earlier, John Calleri had spent his pastoral ministry with one of these tribes.

The Superior of the Comboni Fathers was approached by the Government. They were searching for a seasoned missionary, one who had experience with the indigenous Peoples, to head the peace expedition to the Atroaris. The peace plan elaborated by the Government officials looked good; it seemed to be concerned with the welfare of the Atroaris, and their resettlement further inland. So Calleri was chosen, and he set about preparing for the expedition. From the outset Calleri was not all that enthused about the government's plan and was often at odds with them. He had made a list of proposals as part of his collaboration with the project. There was to be no further highway construction and a long period of preparation and planning for the project. While construction on the highway stopped, the military would not accept a longer period of preparation. Calleri reluctantly went along with the tight schedule forced upon him to assemble and prepare the expeditionary group.

The Atroaris apparently massacred Fr. John Calleri and his nine companions less than 160 kilometres from our mission in Itacoatiara. The tragic climax of the Calleri expedition into Atroari territory occurred on October 31st, 1968. Calleri had thought long and seriously about undertaking his peace mission. Everything, however, seemed to indicate that he was the man for such a dangerous task. He was committed to the well-being of the indigenous Peoples and was deeply versed in their habits and customs. His soul-searching had led him to finally accept the government proposal.

Fr. Bill Smith, a Scarboro missionary in Manaus recalls Calleri saying, "when God gives you a special gift, you've got to use it." His gift, he believed, was an ability to show the native Peoples that he was their brother. So, Calleri used his limited time schedule to plan the expedition. He assembled a team of men and women who would accompany him. Officials from the Indian Affairs Department had chosen most of these volunteers. Calleri's plan was to enter Atroari territory with his group, make contact with the tribal leaders and spend a few weeks close to their *maloca* or village. Through this contact and dialogue he wanted to show the Atroaris that the group meant no harm and that the "invasion" of a road in their territory would not infringe on their ancestral lands.

His plan called for a strengthening of the bonds of friendship over a two-year period. It was hoped that after that period the Atroaris could be persuaded to move their village from the vicinity of the planned highway. The estimated 600 Atroaris would be free to live according to their tribal customs. The dilemma, as Calleri saw it, was the competing interests between so-called progress and the "child of nature." His first priority in the planning was always the safety and protection of the Atroaris. Two women volunteers had been included in the group as a gesture of good faith, and to show the Atroaris that the expedition was not an attempt to steal their women.

The peace expedition left Manaus on October 12th. Their destination was Sao Gabriel, about 40 kilometers from the Atroaris settlement. At this time several planes also began daily flights to drop basic food staples and other gifts close to the village. The expedition then proceeded by canoe up the Sao Antonio River to a locale close to the Indians. Calleri reported to Manaus via radio on October 22nd that they had made contact with the Atroaris. Over the next few days daily reports from Calleri indicated that all was well, that the group was camped close to the Atroaris.

On October 25th a message indicated that once again contact had been made with the Atroaris. On the 26th the news was still positive, the expedition was camped alongside the first village, and although the Atroaris appeared reserved and shy, they had offered their guests bananas and native bread. They also helped their guests to build a hut, and at dusk the same day gifts were presented to the Atroaris by Calleri and the group. Although the Atroaris carried their bows and arrows, the *cacique* or chief embraced Calleri. This first encounter seemed to bode well for the expedition. For the next two days everything continued on a cordial basis. Calleri made plans to push on to the next village. On the third day of contact, however, the Atroaris began to show signs of discontent and Calleri made the decision to return to the original campsite.

The sole survivor of the massacre, Paul da Silva, testified that the Atroaris accompanied the group back to the original camp but en route began to become aggressive. At the camp, da Silva reported, they refused to eat with Calleri or the group. That was when da Silva made his decision to abandon the expedition; he left at nightfall and returned down river. Da Silva reached Manaus on the 14th of November to recount his experience firsthand.

The Brazilian Airforce initiated a search operation on the 4th of November. The remains of the doomed expeditionary members were discovered on the banks of the Sao Antonio River and were returned to Manaus for identification and burial. Following the tragedy there were many theories advanced as to what caused the massacre. A lot of questions went unanswered. There was the possibility that treachery was involved, and it was well known that many wanted the expedition to fail. On December 1st, those who undertook the expedition, including Joao Calleri, were laid to rest in a common grave. The massacre itself and the reason behind it remained shrouded in mystery.

As Superior of the Scarboro contingent of missionaries I travelled to Manaus for the funeral of John Calleri. His superiors had spoken with us regarding John's work with the peace expedition, since his work would be within the pastoral area of the prelacy of Itacoatiara. I joined John's colleagues and fellow missionaries in mourning his tragic death, and the death of those who had fallen with him.

According to Da Silva's report of the final meeting between John Calleri and the chief or *cacique*, Calleri waved a shotgun in the chief's face, and finally fired the shotgun in the air. Calleri's colleagues dispute this allegation as completely foreign to the person of Calleri.

What we do know as fact, is that the government wanted the highway BR-174, to be constructed. Construction resumed during the following year and the highway was completed between Boa Vista and Manaus.

A decade later, testimony regarding the fate of the Atroaris comes from a different source. Egydio Scwhade and his wife Doroti came to Itacoatiara in 1978 to work in the Indian Pastoral. Egydio is a former Jesuit and was a co-founder of the Indigenous Missionary Council (CIMI). This Council was created by the Brazilian Bishops and operated within the Bishops' Conference. The Indian Council had been created in the aftermath of the military coup. Accusations of Indian genocide had been levelled against the military by many, including Archbishop Antonio Ramos, the deceased Archbishop of Belem in the state of Para. The mandate of the Council was to promote and protect the rights of the indigenous Peoples of Brazil.

Egyidio's credentials are indisputable. He has always been an authentic defender of the rights of the indigenous tribes, at both the national level and at the prelacy level. His whole life, along with that of his family is dedicated to the well-being of their rights. As a sociologist he has both studied existing historical material on the Waiwai-Atroari nation at the University of Manaus, and has presented the results of his personal studies.

In the period 1979-1980, Egyidio and Doroti Schwade were successful in moving into Atroari territory and living with a small group of Atroaris, whom Egyidio refers to as the "survivors." They lived with this group of thirty odd Atroaris for several months, until they were expelled by the Indian Affairs Department. According to the Scwhades, he learned from the chief who was less than thirty years of age, that all of their elders had been destroyed by huge birds in the sky that rained down clouds of dust upon them. Other birds spat down small lethal projectiles. Egyidio has the crude drawings that were drawn by these people, portraying the death and destruction rained upon their families. (Sylvia de Oliveira Aranha, *E Deus visitou os seu Povo*, Edua, Manaus 2003, pp.165-169; personal interview with Egyidio 1984.)

According to the Scwhades there were over 2,000 Atroaris killed between 1971 and 1975. The government proceeded with the huge Balbina Hydroelectric Project, and mining explorations by the Paranapanema Taboca Mining Company continue to invade the reserves of the Atroaris to this very day. All this, Eygidio claims, shows that the true motives of the Brazilian state behind the massacre have been revealed. The small band of Atroari 'survivors' struggle for the rights to their ancestral lands to this day.

Throughout Brazil, the church's Indigenous Pastoral Council (CIMI) continues the struggle for justice, and for the demarcation of their lands. In the frontier town of Presidente Figureirdo, a town under the control of Mining interests and the Eletronorte Company which constructed the Balbina dam project, the dedicated commitment of Egyidio Scwhade continues to bother the collective conscience of the townspeople. He, his wife Doroti and their family, are living testaments that the Atroaris' dream for a new life and land of their own, will prevail someday.

Egyidio and Doroti live and work in this frontier town situated on the BR-174 highway, not far from the site where the Calleri expedition met its tragic end. They were strong activists, as was the prelacy of Itacoatiara, against the Balbina Hydroelectric Project. This was a major project initiated by the Brazilian Government in 1979, which flooded 3,000 square kilometres of the Atroaris ancestral lands. This huge artificial lake was the product of the hydroelectric dam and generators built at the headwaters of the Uatuma River. When the Balbina Dam complex was officially inaugurated in May of 1989, it could only produce 75 percent of the projected kilowatt hours of power. It had become such a national embarrassment, that then President Jose Sarney refused to attend the opening ceremonies.

CHAPTER 21

The Medellin Conference

The Conference of Latin American Bishops in Medellin, Colombia in 1968 was the pastoral response of the Catholic Church to the dominant political systems and governments of Latin America. In most cases, either dictators or corrupt patriarchal systems totally marginalized the majority of the population from any real participation in civil society and kept them in abject poverty. The conference itself was the brainchild of Bishops Helder Camara of Brazil and Manuel Larrain of Talca, Chile. The documents that emerged from this conference were to become the Magna Carta, as author Penny Lernoux calls it, of a socially committed church.

This meeting of all of Latin America's bishops was only the second time in Latin American history that its leaders would come together. The Medellin meeting initiated radical changes in the pastoral life of the Latin American church. The centuries-old colonial alliance of the church with the military and the wealthy elite finally came to an end. It marked the official entry of the church into the political arena, not as a political party, but as the moral conscience for its entire people. The church was to move beyond its social base with the middle and upper classes to the world of the poor and marginalized.

During the 1950s dramatic change in church thinking was evolving in Peru, Chile and Brazil. Individual church leaders were speaking out against the prevailing economic systems. These voices questioned the marked inequalities and criticized what they saw as an unjust society. They called for land reform, better wages, and a more just distribution of wealth. The Brazilian Conference of Bishops was especially judgmental in its pronouncements against the ruling powers.

The Medellin Conference was the result of methodical planning and study by the local church's intellectual progressives. They included such theologians, sociologists, social analysts and economists as Gustavo Gutierrez of Peru, Jon Sobrino of Uruguay, Jose Comblin of Brazil, Juan Luis Segundo of El Salvador and Enrique Dussel of Argentina. These clerical scholars came to the Medellin Conference in 1968 armed with staggering statistics that illustrated the following:

- the obsessive desire for profit and riches on the part of the ruling classes.
- the abject poverty of the marginalized masses.
- wide-spread illiteracy, sickness and disease, and the official disregard for any adequate educational and health programs.
- the obscene living standards of the rich and powerful, and complete disregard for the poor.
- the futility of elections and other trappings of a superficial democracy and no civil participation by the majority.
- the failure of developmental programs (*Alliance for Progress*) and political parties endorsed by the church (Christian Democrats) to improve the situation.

Many prelates shared the observation of Archbishop Marcos McGrath of Panama, namely, that capitalism was not the vehicle for achieving economic and social reform in Latin America. In many ways it was as much an enemy as atheistic communism. While the bishops were not political analysts they encountered evidence on a daily basis that the political and economic system was corrupt and ineffectual for the majority of their populations. In the face of such overwhelming evidence the bishops would vote for radical change. They were readily supported by the Latin American Religious Conference (CLAR), an association that represented thousands of religious and clergy.

The Latin American church at Medellin would make an historic choice for the poor and their integral liberation. A new church of the people was to take flesh in the lives of those long subjugated to the powerful vestiges of colonialism.

A new theology was to emerge from this historic gathering, the theology of liberation. Religion in the past had served as a repressive political tool for the masses, now it was to become an instrument of their political liberation. Liberation and participation were the goals of Medellin:

- Liberation was to be understood in the biblical sense of both physical and spiritual salvation.

- A liberating education based on the educational techniques of Paulo Freire the Brazilian educator. The poor must be educated to understand freedom.

- Participation would be achieved through small gatherings of people who share similar jobs, problems and aspirations. They would come together to pray, study the bible, and be part of a consciousness-raising process that would lead to their taking responsibility for their lives. This was the beginning of Basic Christian Communities (CEBs) that would multiply by the thousands in the Latin American church. They would become a vehicle whereby the masses could participate in the political and economic life of the community.

Pope Paul VI had travelled to Colombia to give his blessing and support to the Medellin Conference. He set the tone for the Conference upon his arrival in Bogota, the nation's capital. Paul stated that he wished to personify the Christ of a poor and hungry people. He called for the elite and those in power to be sensitive to the needs and cries of the marginalized masses that, he said, look for justice and active participation in society. Pope Paul expressed worry that the present economic injustices prevalent in Latin society would initiate a revolution of despair. His encyclical, *On the Progress of Peoples*, and his words were a powerful endorsement for the assembled prelates.

The Medellin Conference was to articulate the church's "preferential option for the poor." This option was not an exclusion of the rich and middle classes but a focus on the desperate needs of the poor and the marginalized. Institutionalized violence was the social sin that had to be eradicated. This revolutionary call of the church to work for social justice would bring it into open conflict with the ruling classes. *The Rockefeller Report* of 1979 (following Nelson Rockefeller's Latin American tour) would conclude that the Catholic Church in Latin America should be closely watched by the American government. (Penny Lernoux, *Cry of the People*, Penguin Books, 1982, pp.37-47.)

While this new pastoral approach had the strong support of the progressive bishops and of the Latin American Religious Conference, many conservative prelates would question whether they had not gone too far in severing their long-standing presence in the corridors of power. This would cause major divisions within the church in Latin America as social unrest boiled over into armed revolution.

This new church fashioned by the Medellin documents did become the moral conscience of her people in relation to the ruling governments. The bishops recognized the potential for class conflict that they blamed on the polarization between rich and poor. While the planners of Medellin utilized Marxist analysis, they had no time for left-wing guerrillas.

Prior to Medellin the conservative current within the church meant that religion and politics did not mix, even though the church was always aligned with those in power. The church at Medellin moved from this position. This new current of thought claimed the church's mission was more than religious – "salvation concerns not just in the spirit but the physical and the world. The spirit and the physical are called to the reign of God. Religion is authentic only when it expresses the reality of justice, the reality of a love characterized by solidarity and the reality of mercy, all lived and experienced and not merely proclaimed or ritualized" (Leonardo Boff, *Faith on the Edge*, Orbis Books, 1991, pp. 4-5.)

The post-Medellin church took on a new image, one of solidarity with the cause of the poor and of courage to face up to an authoritarian state. As well as a defender of the rights of the downtrodden, the church became a presence amongst the poor. Thousands of Basic Christian Communities (CEBs) were created and led by their pastors, where people gathered to pray, reflect as a faith community, and organize for their betterment.

The Medellin Conference reflected both a church acting on the conclusions of Vatican II and, local autonomous churches acting in a collegial manner. This plan of action was a radical blueprint for an institutional church long connected to the 'status quo.' As well as the conservative reaction, many young priests would interpret Medellin as a call to revolution and to take up arms. These radical groups of clergy confronted their pastoral leaders and demanded radical change immediately. It is true that many bishops present at Medellin, as well as clergy and laity did not fully understand the documents, or failed to implement them.

Many intellectuals in Latin American society hailed the documents as a blueprint for peaceful, social change. Obviously there was upheaval at all levels of society. Some in the hierarchy of the church later plotted against such a blueprint and threw in their lot with the state. The middle and upper classes felt the church was abandoning them. The elite and powerful looked upon Medallion as a declaration of war. The militant left condemned it as inadequate and promoted violent revolution.

The spirit of Medellin, however, took hold and was implemented at the national levels of the Latin American church. The Medellin documents became the pastoral tool for missionaries and local clergy alike; a plan to implement social change in a peaceful way. The methols of liberttion theology and the initiation of Basic Christian Communities became the instruments to conscientize the poor. However, conservative forces within the church would continue to work against the reforms of Vatican II and Medellin.

Two committed Christians in particular, both Catholic priests and scholars, influenced the bishops present at the Medellin Conference. Camilo Torres and Gustavo Guttierez were among the forerunners of those thinkers who critically questioned the role of their church in the lives of Latin Americans in the 1960s. They also influenced my own thinking and that of most missionaries in Latin America.

Both these young men entered the seminary, studied and were ordained as priests in a post-colonial church; Torres in Colombia and Gutierrez in Peru. They radically changed the face of Catholicism in Latin America, and initiated sweeping changes in theological thinking that would bring their church's pastoral approach into direct conflict with the rulers of power and wealth for decades to come.

Although both were committed to the same Gospel values, and shared the same dreams for reform, their backgrounds, and their future journeys in faith were radically different. Camilo Torres of Colombia, the son of a wealthy Bogota family was to die as a revolutionary guerrilla. Gustavo Guttierez, an indigenous Peruvian peasant, was to become the father of liberation theology.

Both young men had been sent to Rome and Louvain for post-graduate studies. From their sociological studies both realized that the church had to be involved in the grave social problems that affected the masses of people in Latin America. Torres was the social activist, reformer, and finally the revolutionary guerrilla. Guttierez was the thinker and theologian. Torres' revolution for social change ended abruptly, almost before it began. Guttierez's theological revolution and reform continues to the present day.

Camilo Torres

Torres' homeland of Colombia was a country marked by a long history of violence. As in the rest of Latin America there was an educated, elite class that comprised 15 percent of the 34 million Colombians (1960). The other 85 percent were the rural, uneducated illiterates. Two main political parties (both of the elite), the Liberals and the Conservatives, ruled the country for years. But there was bitter antagonism between the two parties.

In 1948 the Liberal leader, Jorge Elizer Gaitan was assassinated after an attempted reform. Following his death there was a nation-wide uprising against the Constitution and the government. The Army was called in to quell the unrest and restore national stability. During these years of political turmoil over 300,000 people died in a civil war known as "La Violencia." Several military coups occurred in the 1950s when the country's politicians warred against each other. In these years guerrilla activity began for the first time. Several other political parties emerged as well, but the Liberals and Conservatives formed a coalition and made peace. Between 1954 and 1974, through constitutional changes, they were the only two parties allowed to represent the Colombian people.

In this climate, Camilo Torres, like an Old Testament Prophet, stormed onto the scene in Bogota in the mid 1950s. He set out to convert the middle and upper classes of society. In the practice of their faith Colombians were those most religious but also the most conservative in all of South America. Colombians were fervent church attendees, so Torres felt that his Colombian brothers and sisters, as well as the church hierarchy, would be fired by the same deep commitment to reform as himself.

In reading his presentations and treatises, it is easy to conclude that Torres was a devoted follower of his church, on fire with the love of Christ, but committed to reforming that same church. He was scandalized by the church's political liaisons with the governing elite and the military. Torres seemed convinced, in a naive way, that by properly implementing the social sciences the church would immerse itself in the reality of the marginalized masses, and successfully fulfil its divine mission in building the Kingdom for all the people of God.

Torres made efforts to initiate and structure an authentic Latin American sociology. He introduced his university students to the stark reality of the marginalized masses around them. He spoke of the necessity of land reform and the problems of rural emigration. He railed against the colonial subculture of the elite and their exploitation of the land. His programs looked at the city of Bogota, with its small core of elite being inundated with the mass migrations of the rural poor, and the resulting squalor and lack of social services.

As his first years unfolded, Torres gathered a few disciples who shared his utopian dreams, but he was soon confronted with major obstacles. Very few of his Catholic Colombians shared the same Christian commitment for social change. His Colombian society was a society that ruled by violence. The elite and the powerful would never be the agents of social change.

His conservative church entrenched in its ways soon reached out to rein in their impatient prophet. Torres was asked by his Archbishop to withdraw from his university chaplaincy. Torres and Cardinal Luis Concha, the Archbishop of Bogota, had the highest respect for one another, but as Torres became more and more immersed in the social and political life of Colombia, they each had to follow their own conscience.

By 1964-65 Torres had organized a political platform and launched his "United Front of the Colombian People." He was now on a continuous circuit of rallies, attempting to put forth his ideas and plans for a revolution and a new Colombia. Through his preaching, teaching and political rallies he attempted to gain mass support. He was also eyeing upcoming elections. But his United Front appeal demanded a social commitment to radical reform that the majority of his Colombian sisters and brothers were just not prepared to follow.

With very little support from the majority, who had never been conscientized or politically educated, Camilo Torres suddenly announced that he was continuing his commitment to reform and revolution by joining a guerrilla band in the mountains. Torres was never a communist, and he pointed out publicly that his Christian commitment could never allow him to accept atheistic communism.

The struggle that went on within Torres is evident in his writings: "I was elected by Christ to be a priest forever, motivated by the desire to devote myself completely to loving my fellow man. As a sociologist I wished this love to become effective through science and technique.

Upon analyzing Colombian society, I realized the need for a revolution that would give food to the hungry, drink to the thirsty, clothing to the naked, and bring about the well-being of the majorities in our country." (Camilo Torres, *Revolutionary Writings*, Herder & Herder, 1969, p. 163.)

In one of his final messages to the Colombian people, his fellow Christians, Torres wrote, in a sense, what came to be his final testament. "I have given up the duties and privileges of the clergy but I have not ceased to be a priest. I believe that I joined the Revolution out of love of my neighbour." (*Idem*, p. 173.) Shortly after writing this last message Camilo Torres left Bogota for the mountains and joined up with a group of guerrillas. Less than a month later, on February 16, 1966, he was shot to death in the early morning mist on a mountain trail by an Army patrol. He was thirty-seven years of age. His revolution had ended, but his death was to mobilize the social conscience of his church.

Gustavo Gutierrez

Peru, the homeland of Gustavo Gutierrez, was a country plagued with the same social and economic problems as the rest of Latin America. Cardinal Juan Landazuri, a man of foresight, a theologian, and a man of the people headed the Archdiocese of Lima. Landazuri had welcomed the reforms of Vatican II, and was a strong but silent force in pushing for reform in the church. He was a strong voice in the planning of the Conference of Latin American Bishops at Medellin.

The social ills of the country were more than evident in the sprawling *favellas* or shanty towns of the poor that engulfed the nation's capital. Lima, an old colonial town built for a population of two million, had swollen to seven million. The poor and the disenfranchised had come to Lima seeking a new life. In the late 1950s the church reached out to be a presence amongst the poor. The pastoral approach of the Archdiocese made use of the tools of the time, food banks, co-operatives, credit unions, adult education, and farming projects.

But Landazuri realized that although such a pastoral approach was an aid for the poor, it was not a solution. The problem lay in the prevailing economic and political systems that dominated the continent. So, off to Europe and America went the intellectuals from amongst Landazuri's clergy to learn and perfect scientific techniques that would help the church analyze the social situation and develop strategies to change the political systems that enslaved the majority of the population.

Gustavo Gutierrez was one of the young intellectual scholars handpicked by Cardinal Landazuri. Upon his return from abroad he was appointed to the Catholic University of Lima, where Gutierrez, the intellectual revolutionary, began his career. Gutierrez was a man of faith committed to social change like his colleague Torres. Gutierrez, however, chose the Bible as his vehicle to implement radical change both within his church and society.

In his quiet way Gutierrez brought the words of the prophets, the plight of Israel, and the redeeming message of Christ to the classroom and to his writings. University students flocked to his lectures. In addition to his training and expertise as a biblical scholar and theologian, he brought the tools of modern sociology into play. He used the analytical tools of Marxism in the formulation of his Third World theology.

In the planning of the Medellin Conference of Bishops, Cardinal Landazuri was to have Gutierrez play an important role. At the Conference itself Gutierrez was to present his theological studies – his reflections would influence the conclusions of that historic Conference.

Gutierrez gained international status with the publication of his now famous work, *The Theology of Liberation*, first published in Lima in 1971. It was to become the handbook for pastoral planning in the progressive church of Latin America. He has published innumerable articles and continues to lecture throughout the world.

"Poverty is an act of love and liberation. It has a redemptive value. If the ultimate cause of human exploitation and alienation is selfishness, the deepest reason for voluntary poverty is love of neighbour. Christian poverty has meaning only as a commitment of solidarity with the poor, with those who suffer misery and injustice. The commitment is to witness to the evil which has resulted from sin and is a breach of communion." (Gustavo Gutierrez, *Theology of Liberation*, Orbis Books, 1971, p. 172.)

In his book *The God of Life*, Gutierrez identifies God as the "God of life, as the One who confronts the idols of death, greed and corruption, oppression and violence, and liberates us to enter the fullness of life. The God of the Bible is the defender of the poor who enters into a relationship of loving commitment with all people. Where do we find this God? In our practice, in the project of Jesus, in the life of faithful, solidarity and witness to life." (Gustavo Gutierrez, *The God Of Life*, Orbis Books, 1991, p. 7.)

When the Colombian bishops hosted the Conference of Latin American bishops in 1968, in the city of Medellin, the quiet, unassuming Gutierrez was very much a presence. In their pastoral and social analysis of the grave problems that faced the peoples of their continent, the bishops made the "preferential option for the poor" the chosen direction for their pastoral efforts for the next twenty years.

CHAPTER 22

Bringing the Message Home

A year prior to the Medellin Conference, Scarboro Missions began to revise its own role in mission activity. In light of Vatican II all religious groups within the church had initiated programs of study and renewal for their members. Our Society was officially a secular institute with members taking an oath of obedience to the Superior General, and agreeing to live in accordance with the Constitutions. We were not a Religious Order or Congregation *per se*.

Our Superior General during those years was Father Frank Diemert. He and his Council had been in office since 1958. Frank, or Deem, as we affectionately called him, had been a missionary both in China and the Dominican Republic. He also had been the Rector of the seminary during my formation years. Deem was open to change, and had hoped that the new mission in Brazil would serve as a model for progress, especially in view of the happenings of the Second Vatican Council. From my perspective the Council members of the Scarboro Mission were much more conservative and suspicious of change. Even with the changes of Vatican II, Deem had to work with Council members who were following the letter of the law, and were apparently not all that receptive to the open spirit of Vatican II.

In accordance with the spirit of renewal, and prompted by the Vatican Council, Scarboro Missions prepared for a general meeting of the Society called a Chapter. A Chapter committee was formed, and this committee worked with the General Council and the general membership. Documents that pertained to mission and to our work as missionaries were sent out to our mission regions for study and reflection. What was to be our role in this renewed church in light of the Vatican Council documents? Study seminars were set up for those at home and on the missions. All of us were encouraged to forward reports and suggestions on our governing structures, authority and collegiality.

This process went on during 1966 both at the regional level and at home. Theological experts were brought in to explain the church's new thinking. Questionnaires attempted to gather the input from the general membership. The various mission regions and groups in Canada elected extra delegates along with those who came according to our governing statutes to ensure a greater participation at the Chapter.

Elected delegates and the local Superiors were called home for six weeks of meetings in the fall of 1967. This was a meeting to prepare us for the Chapter sessions the following year. Bishop Cornelius Blomjous, a missionary whose career had been spent in Africa was chosen as our facilitator. Blomjous, a member of the Mill Hill Fathers (a group similar to Scarboro) had attended all the sessions of the Vatican Council in Rome. Each day we began our session with an address by the bishop on the renewed vision of Vatican II. There were study sessions and open discussion of papers prepared on various documents pertaining to mission and to our priestly lives. Our structures as a Society, authority, obedience, collegiality – all were examined. Committees worked on the preparation of Chapter documents for every matter that was to be discussed. The regions were informed about our discussions and the process for discernment that we were following. These were exhilarating times for the membership as a whole, but even more so for those of us involved as delegates.

Our Society was fifty years of age in 1967. Our personnel numbered close to 170, and the seminary was filled to capacity. There were missions in Japan, the Philippines, the Dominican Republic, Peru, Brazil, Guyana, Panama, the Bahamas, St. Vincent and St. Lucia. A new headquarters had recently been built at Scarboro for administration and promotion of the Society's work. An addition had also been made to the seminary of St. Francis Xavier. Scarboro as a mission society was a household name in most Canadian Catholic homes. The monthly magazine reached close to 90,000 homes.

With renewal and change in the air it was a challenging and privileged time to be part of Scarboro Missions. Father Frank Diemert, his Council, and the various committees, accomplished an almost impossible task in the preparatory work. Scarboro members for the most part responded enthusiastically. The mission regions prepared well for this preparatory meeting, and Chapter delegates were eager to represent the personnel of their regions.

This largest-ever gathering of Scarboro Mission worked diligently at their task of preparation. I was present as the Superior of the Brazil mission. With me was another delegate from Brazil, Bill Smith. Like those from other regions, Bill and I worked as a team to present the input and views of our fellow missionaries in Brazil. At the end of the six-week session, we returned to our respective missions intent on continuing the process.

The Chapter was scheduled for the summer of 1968. So, once again I flew home from Brazil to participate in this meeting of renewal where we sought to revise our role as missionaries. The intervening months had been busy ones. As well as our busy pastoral schedules, the regions had planned study days that reassessed the different aspects of our mission work. The Documents of Vatican II called on us to shape a new vision and understanding of mission. Reflecting on collegiality, a new constitution for governing the Society, the priestly life, and the church as a people of God, was an integral part of this preparation.

The solemn sessions of the Chapter meeting went on for over two months in the summer of 1968. An experimental Constitution for government was approved after much study. A visionary post-Vatican II statement of our purpose as a Society was drafted. A more democratic approach to communal life, authority and obedience was accepted through the implementation of collegiality and dialogue. A renewed spirituality challenged membership to live out their calling in close alliance with the daily lives of those with whom they worked. Attempts were made to break down clericalism.

As this historical Chapter began to wind down, the final task of the Chapter delegates was the election of a new Council and Superior General. Fathers Paul Ouellette, George Marskell and Ken MacAulay were given the responsibility by their Chapter colleagues to implement a radical and new vision for the Society. Paul, who was named the new Superior General, was a veteran of the Dominican Republic; George as Vicar General and second in command was my youthful colleague from Brazil. Ken MacAulay, my classmate, had served as Treasurer of the Society for several years and worked in the mission of Guyana. Their mandate was for a term of six years.

It should be more than obvious that a tremendous amount of energy, dedication, time, and finances were involved in such an undertaking. While members throughout the world were kept informed of the whole process, it was the responsibility of the new Council and the regional delegates to bring about the renewal of the Society. Personal renewal is difficult at the best of times. To renew the Scarboro Mission Society, as was the case in the universal church, would be a slow, painstaking process. Some people are convinced of the need for change while others are cautious or downright obstructive. Two steps forward, one step back, is the way with most change.

CHAPTER 23

Heading Home

O nce again, in July of 1970 I left my Amazon mission en route to Canada for a year of studies. My first stop was in Maryknoll, New York, for a six-week course in theology. The Maryknoll Missionaries were our American counterparts and had over a thousand priests and sisters stationed throughout the world. Our course of studies at Maryknoll examined mission practice in light of the documents of Vatican II. The two most important topics presented were those concerning our relationship with non-Christians, and the role of local churches in relation to Rome.

The church in the past had always approached non-Christian religions in a negative way. Our professors were from mission countries with large non-Christian populations, and they focused on what it might be like to be the subject of evangelization by Western missionaries. The course was meant to sensitize us as missionaries to other cultural traditions, and to understand other belief systems. It was an acknowledgement of their values and authenticated their honest pursuit in seeking God. In view of what was taking place in Latin America at the time, the role of local churches and their autonomy became an important topic from my perspective as a missionary.

Although my year at home was to be a time of study and reflection, I would become more involved than ever with the Latin American church because of these studies and the things that were happening around me. Renewal was evident in Scarboro's outreach at home. It was gratifying to see the conclusions of our Chapter meetings being implemented. The content of our mission magazine, *Scarboro Missions*, was reflecting the new concepts on mission work. Scarboro was forming ties with ecumenical groups throughout the city of Toronto, and offering support to groups involved in what was happening in Latin America. An Education Department was keeping those in the missions updated by preparing study kits. They also suggested renewal courses for those interested.

With seminary admissions dropping, Scarboro offered its facilities to like-minded groups for seminars, study days and retreats. The Society was becoming more and more involved with justice and peace issues. It was opening its doors, not just for seminars, but also as a place of refuge. One of the first groups of people to come to Scarboro were the Mexican migrant farm workers led by Cesar Chavez. They were initiating their now legendary boycott of California grapes in the Toronto area. After Chavez's grape pickers, families and individuals exiled from Chile, Brazil and Argentina came to take up residence at Scarboro in the 1970s. These individuals, along with Chavez, put flesh and human faces on the theological study and reflection that was dominating my life.

While home for Christmas vacation, Bishop Alex Carter of North Bay called me to a meeting at his residence. In the restructuring that followed Vatican II, Rome had recently appointed Bishop Carter and Bishop Emmett Doyle, of Nelson, B.C., to be the National Directors of the traditional Mission Societies that gathered funds for its universal mission work. These Societies were called pontifical, in that they were umbrella fundraising organizations for the Vatican; they were world-wide with branches in Canada. Their objective was to educate the Catholic laity on the importance of mission, and to raise funds for the work of evangelization throughout the world. The funds were administered through a central office in Rome.

These Societies were active in all of the dioceses of Canada. The Society of Sts. Peter and Paul, and the Society for the Evangelization of Peoples, had their national office in Toronto. A third national organization, the Society of the Holy Childhood, had appointed Bishop

Thomas Fulton, an Auxiliary bishop of Toronto, as its Director. Its office was in St. Catherines, Ontario.

Every year on Mission Sunday in October, the Society for the Evangelization of Peoples focused on the church's primary work of mission and made an appeal for funds. It also published a monthly mission magazine. The Society of Sts. Peter and Paul focused on the education of seminarians in mission countries. It encouraged Catholics to support the education of seminarians through sponsorship. The Holy Childhood was a program aimed at school children. It educated children on the importance of the mission work of the church. The funds raised through the Holy Childhood sponsored youth activities in mission countries such as schools, catechetical programs and health clinics.

In the aftermath of Vatican II, these Societies needed evaluation and restructuring. What now was the role of the church's proselytzing? This question needed to be asked specifically in light of the documents that recognized the values and truths inherent in all the religions of the world. The new approaches and new thinking on these important issues of evangelization questioned the traditional way we looked at it. This was a major concern for Mission Societies, for the church itself, and certainly for the laity.

During my meeting with Bishop Alex Carter we discussed all these issues and how best to proceed. Carter wanted an Executive Secretary to implement this new vision of mission, and to restructure the Societies. So it came about, that, after finishing my year of studies, I was appointed Executive Secretary of these Papal Mission Societies. A new phase of mission involvement began for me in May of 1971.

For several weeks I worked with Monsignor William Davis at his residence in Toronto. Davis had been National Director for many years. I then set up new offices at St. Augustine's Seminary in Scarboro, Ontario. Our first priority was the reorganization of the Societies of the Evangelization of Peoples, and Sts. Peter and Paul. As Director, Bishop Carter corresponded with all of the diocesan directors in Canada, informing them of his appointment, and the renewal and organization that would begin. In the interim, the staff of the Holy Childhood Society was to continue its work from their offices in St. Catharines.

As Executive Secretary, I set out to initiate change by concentrating on the magazine that went out to 140,000 homes in Canada. An assistant editor was hired, and with the help and advice from Scarboro colleagues who had experience in magazine work, we launched a totally new magazine. It was to be our educational vehicle for Canadian Catholics. We had access to excellent resource material and mission photo services. We sought out articles for publication from missionaries.

Mission Sunday was universally celebrated in the church each year. Through our educational material, we attempted to inform Canadian Catholics on the new vision of mission that came from the documents of Vatican II. With the collaboration of the Directors in the dioceses across Canada, this material was sent out to every parish and local Mission Council.

Several worthy programs were launched in 1972. The first was the formation of a Mission Team comprised of a missionary Sister, and four missionary priests. The team, in collaboration with the Mission Director in Bishop Carter's home diocese of Sault St. Marie, prepared a mission history of the diocese from its earliest years. The audio-visual Team at Scarboro Missions collaborated to produce a multimedia presentation. One program was for use at the parish level, and another for youth work in schools.

Bishop Carter launched the project in the fall of 1972, and for the next four months the Team visited and presented the program in every parish and most of the schools of the diocese. It resulted in the formation of a diocesan Mission Council, and mission groups were formed in most parishes. It was a pilot project that was to be followed in other dioceses across Canada. At a concluding ceremony, Bishop Carter stated that it was one of the most significant events ever held in the diocese while he was bishop.

Bishop Doyle invited the Mission Team to Nelson where again it brought the new vision of mission to all of the parishes and schools of the diocese. The program was successful because of the preparatory work that was done in the diocese by Bishop Doyle, his mission group, pastors and teachers.

The second program developed a cross-country tour of those involved in mission at a national level. It toured fourteen dioceses in Western Canada. Two representatives from the Religious Conference in Ottawa, the Director of the Mission office of the Bishops, the Director of the Home Missions office (the Church Extension Society), myself, and Mr. Raphael Legarria, a lay missionary from Mexico, drove from Toronto to Vancouver. We had scheduled meetings with the local bishops, the local directors of mission societies or groups, and representatives from the schools. These meetings were an attempt to put forth the vision of mission that emanated from Vatican II, and to initiate discussion and dialogue with the hope of forming active Mission Councils in these dioceses. It was a considerable undertaking.

We also attempted to work with a fledgling lay missionary group, the Canadian Lay Missionaries. This group had been formed in the early sixties, and found a home base in Wawa, Ontario. They had received some support from the diocese of Sault St. Marie, and had managed a training program for lay missionaries at their headquarters in Wawa. More than a dozen lay missionaries had been trained by this group and worked overseas, principally in Africa.

There was plenty of goodwill, and a strong desire to establish their group on a sound financial basis. This group looked to the hierarchy for endorsement as a Canadian lay missionary institute. They needed the financial support of the official church to establish a good training program for the laity. They also relied on established groups for solid spiritual preparation.

Unfortunately, there was only token support from most bishops, and our mandate at that time was incapable of responding to the enthusiasm and commitment of these lay missionaries. It was a lost opportunity, and I honestly believe we failed them. The Canadian Lay Missionaries disbanded as a group shortly afterwards. But their pioneering efforts and their dream of a Canadian Lay Missionary group eventually did come about when both the Spiritan Fathers and Scarboro Missions inaugurated Lay Mission programs in their organizations. Vatican II had emphasized, as never before, the role and vocation of the laity in the life of the church and in the missionary enterprise of the church. Yet, when it came to bringing to birth this legitimate and honourable calling of the laity to mission, it was a difficult and prolonged process to gain the whole-hearted support and endorsement of the clergy to the cause of the laity in mission.

The Holy Childhood Society needed an Executive Director who could implement a creative and new approach to mission; an approach that could be integrated into the new catechetical programs within the primary school system. Sr. Barbara Ann Schnarr, a School Sister of Notre Dame, took on the task and began her work with Holy Childhood in St. Catharines in 1972. With her knowledge of catechetics, teaching experience, and enthusiasm, Sr. Barbara brought new life to the work of the Society on behalf of mission. Her creative programs brought to Catholic children an understanding of mission and mission work.

My work with these Societies was first and foremost to educate, to bring home to Canadian Catholics what the mission of the church was about, and their role in that work. Since the educational aspect was the implementation of the new understanding of mission that the Vatican Council had envisioned, it was pioneering and exciting work. I do believe that the work of the Mission Team, our mission magazine, and the new approach to Holy Childhood programs in the schools, made a significant and valuable contribution. At the parish level, it made the reforms and teachings of Vatican II relevant in the lives of Canadian Catholics.

My strong conviction was that the work of the Mission Team could have been carried out throughout Canada and would have contributed to the formation of strong, knowledgeable, and committed Mission

Councils in every diocese in the country. Our experiment in mission education served as a model for others. There was much more work to do here, but my life was about to take another unexpected turn.

CHAPTER 24

Not Just Another General Chapter

In July of 1974, Scarboro Missions Superiors and delegates came together once again for another Chapter meeting. Throughout their tenure of office the administration of Fr. Paul Ouellette and his Council had diligently implemented the decisions and direction that the Society Chapter of 1968 had initiated. The mandate of the new Chapter was to evaluate the decisions and changes made in 1968 including the experimental Constitutions. The Chapter was to look at missionary formation for clerical candidates and the feasibility of creating a lay group of missionaries as part of the Society.

My participation at the 1974 Chapter, I thought, would be limited to that of an observer at some of the sessions. After the formal opening, a major decision was made to immediately begin the election process for the Superior General and Council. Elections had always been held at the end of Chapter. As we began this new process a group of colleagues approached me and asked if I would allow my name to be on the slate for Superior General. I took what little time I had to reflect, consult, and pray on where this would lead me. Encouraged by the confidence and solidarity of my colleagues, I became a candidate for the office. It was another opportunity to serve the Society and mission. If I was chosen, collegiality would be the mandate under which the Council would operate.

On the first day of the balloting a list of the proposed candidates for the office of Superior General was posted, and ballots were passed out to the delegates. To my surprise, I was elected as the new Superior General with a sizeable majority on the first ballot.

In the follow-up elections for Council, I proposed a new format for the election process of the two Council members. My proposal was radical in that the election process would be influenced by my input. From the list of potential candidates for Council I would submit a list of those with whom I felt I could form a working team. The Chapter graciously acceded to my request and two colleagues, Clair Yaeck from Japan, and Robert Smith from Santo Domingo, were elected as Council members.

The new mandate of a smaller Council was for four years. The 1968 Chapter had reduced the size of the governing Council from five to three members. This revision had also seen the creation of a Cabinet, formed by those responsible for Formation, Finances, and the Mission Department. Regional Superiors could also be called at times to form part of the Cabinet. This new forum was to promote teamwork, assist planing within the Council, keep departments informed, serve as a think tank, and be an advisory board to the Superior General and Council. I felt confident that, as the new Superior General, the Council and I would govern in the collegial manner and spirit that was demonstrated by Vatican II. Once the elections had taken place, the Chapter proceeded with its deliberations and the newly elected Council took part in all of the sessions.

A major decision of the Chapter deliberations was for the Council to set up a formation and training program for laity. This decision was to be a contentious issue in Society life for years to come.

With the closing ceremonies of the 5th General Chapter of the Society, another phase in my life began. Arrangements were made for an interim director to take over the work of Papal Missions, and I immediately moved to Scarboro headquarters. The new Council began its work with intensive briefing sessions from the previous Council. These briefings brought us up to date on personnel, finances, and the problems and successes of the various mission regions.

One of our immediate concerns was the formation and training of laity. Vocations for the missionary priesthood had fallen dramatically, and our seminary adjacent to our headquarters had only two or three candidates. The major decrease in seminarians studying for priesthood was a new phenomenon that many had difficulty in accepting. For over thirty years there had been an abundance of priestly candidates. Now seminaries were emptying. At the same time the church was experiencing a world-wide exodus from the priesthood. What was the underlying cause? Uncomfortable with this new crisis, many within the Society felt that too much emphasis was being placed on lay involvement in mission.

Since Vatican II ecumenism was a new priority in the Catholic Church. Efforts were made to be much more open to other churches and to work toward the common goal of unity. In the late sixties, one of the major breakthroughs in ecumenism in the Toronto area gave birth to the Toronto School of Theology. This resulted in the close collaboration of theology professors from five major denominations: the Anglican, United, Presbyterian, Baptist and the Roman Catholic Churches. Theological students and seminarians could follow approved theological courses taught by professors from any of these major denominations. The Roman Catholic School was set up around the campus of St. Michael's College.

Catholic theological students took their courses at St. Michael's and at the other Christian institutions in downtown Toronto on the campus of the University of Toronto. Gradually, houses of formation were set up by the various Catholic religious orders, congregations and groups from the Toronto area.

Scarboro had established two houses in downtown Toronto for the lay mission program in the early seventies. From these residences lay missionaries followed a program of studies at the Toronto School of Theology, and followed a formation program of one year at these two residences. In 1974, because there were only a few seminarians and a few candidates for the lay program, a common residence for both seminarians and lay candidates was opened in the Kensington market area.

This was indeed a major change for Scarboro Missions. At the same time that it was embarking on an experimental program for the formation of lay candidates, it was moving seminarians from the hallowed halls of the seminary into a residence with both male and female candidates.

At the time, Scarboro had one or two major seminarians, and two or three candidates for the lay program. They would be in downtown Toronto, exposed to an immigrant population, close to their studies, and living a common life of study, prayer, work and domestic life in a small, manageable residence. Their future lives as missionary priests and lay missionaries, would be in small communities overseas under similar circumstances. For those in formation, it seemed logical to move in this way.

Candidates were to visit headquarters once a week, and were encouraged to build friendships with Scarboro priests. They were to learn of the workings of the Society and study its history. Important topics such as celibacy and spiritual and communal life were to be part of their group discipline. Missiology courses and a history of our involvement in mission countries were topics given by the Formation Director. Society personnel were encouraged to join the candidates for meals and recreational evenings. Missionaries on furlough were invited to speak to the group and present their missiological convictions and experiences. But it was not the old seminary, and it was not the disciplined, traditional spiritual formation. It was something new; it was an experiment that included both clerical and lay candidates. This was major change. Seminarians were being moved from an isolated, institutional, and regimented program for clerical celibates to life in downtown Toronto, rubbing shoulders with lay candidates. Change such as this was unheard of, and for many in the Society it was just too much.

The innovative approach to formation for both clerical and lay candidates became the cause for a minority opposition groundswell within the Society. Both the 1968 and 1974 Chapter visions for change and renewal were now being questioned. This move away from the seminary provided more reason for this opposition to question the manner in which the Superior General and Council went about implementing their mandate.

The experiment in this type of formation and training carried on for ten years. While the lay program attracted candidates, few seminarians for mission priesthood finished their studies.

By the early 1970s the honeymoon was over. What was happening at the level of Scarboro as a mission Society was also taking place throughout the Catholic world.

Even though Claire Yaeck had been Rector of the seminary, and involved in seminary formation of students for a good number of years, we realized that this first major decision as a Council was being questioned. It brought home to us that not everyone in the Society shared the same vision for its future that we had. The changes that our recent Chapter had legislated were not being received by all with the same enthusiasm. It was a rude awakening, but one I should have expected.

One of the chief responsibilities as Superior General was to visit members of the Society in the various mission areas, and to hold general meetings and round table discussions regarding the Chapter and its legislation. I decided to have the Chapter delegates from the particular missions to assist me in this task. The various regions and personnel received written progress reports from the Chapter sessions. Follow-up visits by the Council and myself were an attempt to bring the Chapter and its process to our members in the field.

It was also an opportunity to visit brother missionaries in the field. It was an important time for personal visits with individual missionaries. As the new Superior, I visited with each missionary on his home turf. In making myself available to my brother missionary, I was made aware in a more intimate way of his daily life, his work conditions, and the challenges he faced as a missionary.

While the travel and contact with so many different people could be exhaustive, it was also life giving and personally enriching. You were at the heart of what the Society was all about, and gained intimate insights into the personal commitment and faith life of your brother missionaries. Not everyone was a success story; there were failures to deal with, some who were bearers of "bad news" instead of the "Good News". Nevertheless, it was a humbling experience to witness the faith and commitment of brothers at work in the field. Even those with whom I might differ on theological grounds, gave witness to their total commitment and faith in the person of Christ, and their love for the people with whom they worked and lived.

What an opportunity to be educated! I was able to visit so many countries and peoples: Japan, the Philippines, Hong Kong, Indonesia, Singapore, Thailand, India, the West Indies, Guyana, the Dominican Republic, Haiti, most of Central America, Ecuador, Peru, Colombia, Mexico and Brazil. Not just as a tourist passing through these countries, but as part of a movement involved in both faith communities and the daily lives of people. Such an opportunity brought me into contact with people and places, and gave me a feeling for the culture, the history and the particular struggle of the country and its people – all through the eyes and ears, the heart and spirit of my brother missionaries of Scarboro!

I was aware that such a privilege does not come to many in their lifetime. Travelling to our mission areas became a very important part of my life. In a sense this became my daily fare. It more than compensated for the countless meetings, exhaustive travels and grinding schedules. During my tenure as Superior General I was able to visit these countries and my fellow missionaries on more than one occasion.

During the years immediately following the Vatican Council, great efforts were made by the Scarboro General Council to encourage missionaries to take renewal studies in theology. There were a good number of quality renewal programs available. These programs, offering theological renewal, had been initiated in many of the larger dioceses both in Canada and the United States, as well as by the various religious congregations of the church. It was part of the overall effort made by the church to help its priests and religious to become acquainted with the documents and the theology of Vatican II, and to integrate it into their lives and ministry.

Members responded to this invitation in two ways. Some availed themselves of the opportunities with enthusiasm, with an authentic desire for greater personal understanding and growth. They also saw that their knowledge of Vatican II would help their people understand the changes going on in the church. These colleagues recognized the golden opportunity for greater training, and the challenge being presented in the vision of Vatican II. What other group of professionals were ever offered time off to study new techniques, to follow courses under the guidance of experts in their field, and to become updated professionally?

There were other members of the Society who enrolled in these renewal studies reluctantly and with scepticism. Their attitude was negative, and anything that smacked of change was rejected. Many not only feared change, but also feared any commitment to study. What happened within the Society happened as well, within the ranks of the clergy on a world-wide basis.

The failure to accept the challenge for change presented by the Vatican Council, the reluctance, the negativity, and the fear, all compounded into rejection. Radical change is not easy to achieve even under the best of circumstances. It is a leap into the unknown. Most of us live in the comfort zone of the *status quo*. Thus, rejection could be easily legitimatized. Those who rejected change pointed to the abuses and extremes as their justification. Both abuse and extremes always follow radical change. The language of the documents of Vatican II was new and ambiguous, they said. The "loyal opposition" could easily mount a campaign to safeguard the faith in the name of tradition and orthodoxy It was easy, and at times convenient, to accept the documents of Vatican II, but reject the spirit envisaged by the Council. The changes taking place in the church beyond their zone of acceptance could easily be dismissed as reckless experimentation.

At a local level, the changes legislated by the Society's Chapter, and the forward thrust of Vatican II theology and thinking, divided the

Society and the church into two camps. The many renewal courses and statements of Conferences of Bishops and renowned theologians, could not unify the clergy and religious of the world. In many ways they only moved the two sides further and further apart. Many of us, as part of the institutional church, have witnessed and suffered from the division that followed. Such divisions have affected every religious order, congregation, society and group in the church. As a result, we have created small enclaves, each surrounded by its own "Berlin Wall" – protecting us from the thoughts of the other side.

Our Council attempted to keep those in residence at headquarters abreast of the decisions made by Council. Instead of healthy dialogue and exchange there was often bitter confrontation. Attempts were made to come together in prayer and reflection, but even here the divisions remained and became all too evident.

On the one hand it was a difficult time for the Society; yet on the other hand, it was a prophetic time that carried its own "cost of discipleship."

Village chapel in the interior of Brazil

Jute farmer on his way home with his harvest

Michael O'Kane and Dom Jorge Marskell, sfm

Communal fish fry

Feast of
Our Lady of Nazare,
Silves, Amazon 1982

Main street, Urucara, Amazon

Visit with Eygidio and Doroti Schwads, Amazon 1995

Meeting of old friends. Michael O'Kane and Leonardo Boff, 1995

CHAPTER 25

Where the Rooster Roosts

The Society sought to incorporate the changes of Vatican II and the Chapter legislation at headquarters in Canada and abroad. It accomplished this through the Mission Information Department and the Society magazine.

The Mission Information Department followed the Renewal Chapter of 1968. It had been set up as a clearing house for mission information especially for missionaries overseas. A library of mission periodicals, magazines, resource material and the latest in new publications covering all aspects of mission themes was maintained, and placed at the disposal of missionaries both at home and abroad.

Information that emanated from mission sources in Rome, and the many Conferences of Bishops in mission countries, was made available. Personnel in the department forwarded this information on a regular basis. Through this service our missionaries overseas could keep abreast of mission activity in the church. Biblical and theological scholars offered renewal seminars for personnel at home. Study days were added to our annual retreats. Local mission superiors were encouraged to build up and maintain their libraries with mission periodicals.

The Mission Information Department became an integral part of our Promotion Department. Promotion of the Society and its work had always had a dual purpose in the Canadian church. The first purpose was to keep an up-to-date list of donors and of all those who subscribed to our magazine, *Scarboro Missions*. The magazine was mailed monthly to 90,000 homes. Through our magazine Scarboro reached out to Canadian Catholics for the financial support necessary to maintain and expand the mission work in which the Society was involved world wide. The second and equally important role was to bring new blood into the ranks of the Society, by encouraging young men to become part of our venture as missionary priests in the Society.

Direct mailing campaigns and our monthly magazine were our major contacts with our Catholic constituency across Canada. A team of priests had also become an integral part of our overall promotion. They criss-crossed Canada preaching in churches, and visiting schools; their objective was to make the work of mission an important part of Catholic life and thought.

From its founding, the mission magazine of the Society had always been our mainstay. The Society had kept the mission message and the work of the Society before the eyes of Canadian Catholics from coast to coast. In the years following Vatican II, the magazine evolved from a "folksy" style to a vehicle for mission education. It attempted to educate the Canadian church on the new global reality and the new vision of mission. In doing so, it moved into the area of global politics and presented issues around world religions, justice, human rights, the plight of minorities, and the cry of the poor throughout the world. From a magazine with a style that was originally benign, it's new editorial content presented readers with contentious moral, ethical, and justice questions. Issues like the role of multi-nationals in the world economy, apartheid in South Africa, and the struggles of nations and peoples to be free were frequently covered.

All of this did not sit well with some members within the Society. As was to be expected, many within the Canadian church hierarchy, priests, and laity were also strong critics of our new approach. The critics stated that we were becoming too political, too left-wing. "Where was the message of Jesus in all of this?" they wondered. As in the Third World itself, questioning political and economic systems, and delving into the problems of justice, poverty and human rights, were not considered questions or issues that Jesus would, or should, address.

The work of the Mission Information Department, and the content of the magazine, had been sanctioned by both the 1968 and 1974 Chapters of the Society. The change came about precisely because the churches of the Third World, especially in Latin America, were asking for solidarity and support from the First World. As the Society became more and more supportive of these issues it saw that part of its mission was to educate Canadian Catholics about them.

With the Medellin Conference of 1968, and its "preferential option for the poor", the church in Latin America had taken on new life and meaning. The Society, with its missions, and the majority of its personnel working in Latin America, became deeply involved in the vision of church that emerged from the Medellin Conference. In its outreach to the Canadian church, Scarboro attempted to bring the reality of Latin America, its suffering and poverty, and its economic and political oppression, into the lives of Canadian Catholics and the Canadian church.

In the early 1970s, for the majority of Canadians, Latin America and its problems were but a distant echo. That echo, however, was to become part of the Canadian conscience by way of a humble Mexican-American. Cesar Chavez, head of the United Farm Workers of America, brought the plight of thousands of Mexican migrant workers to Canada. For a period of time he lived at Scarboro headquarters when he came to promote the grape boycott in Toronto.

He made Canadians realize that issues of justice did not only occur in far away places. Cesar Chavez pitted his migrant, poverty-stricken workers against the corporate and political giants in the California wine and grape industry. Yet, the quiet voice, and the inner spiritual strength and convictions of Chavez sparked a movement for justice in both the United States and Canada. Thousands of ordinary people, moved by the person of Chavez and his "voiceless" followers, took up a cause that had previously been remote from their lives. They joined in the boycott of California grapes and became part of a movement seeking justice for an immigrant minority.

Chavez, by his holiness and simplicity, became for many the prophetic symbol of the persecuted, voiceless, and impoverished masses of Latin America. The preferential option for the poor took on flesh in the person of Chavez and his movement.

Cesar Chavez's life and work illustrated the work the Society was attempting to do through the magazine and the Mission Information Department. He was living and preaching the gospel of non-violence, and the gospel call to justice and respect for the dignity and worth of every daughter and son of God. By his example, Chavez underlined that all Christians were called to the mission of building up the Kingdom of God.

Three other men, among others, who lived at Scarboro during the 1970s, in a far less public way than Chavez, complemented the work of the Mission Information Department. These three would leave their indelible mark on my thinking. Two of these young men were refugees and stayed briefly at Scarboro Missions. Alfredo was from Cordoba in Argentina, and Roberto was from Santiago, Chile. Both were in their early twenties and had been exiled from their countries after months of questioning, and physical and mental torture. During the military dictatorships in their respective countries, Alfredo had been involved in union work, and Roberto in student activities. Their stories and the suffering they endured at the hands of the secret police in Argentina and Pinochet's Chile made the horrors of the National Security State come alive for me.

No judge had ever convicted them of any crime. Yet, they had been imprisoned and declared enemies of the state on suspicion of being involved in illegal activities. When the state finished its torture and interrogation, these two young men were exiled from their families, their friends, and their homeland, and declared non-persons. They were viewed as being unfit for compassion, healing or reconciliation with their governments. National church leaders, and the Vatican by default, supported these governments.

Herbert de Sousa, affectionately known as Betinho, was another exile who, along with his wife and young child, lived at Scarboro Missions in the early 1970s. Herbert was an intellectual from Rio de Janeiro who opposed the military dictatorship in Brazil. Labelled a subversive for his criticism of the Security State he was arrested and imprisoned. Pressure from intellectual allies and the church forced the government to send de Sousa, a haemophiliac, into exile. Attracted to the Young Christian Student Movement as a university student, Betinho had worked for reform of the political system within the Brazil prior to the military coup. He became a voice for the impoverished masses in the *favellas* of Rio de Janeiro. With the imposition of the National Security State, de Sousa became a target of the military. In exile, de Sousa continued his work and planning for the poor of his country.

When he was allowed back into Brazil in the early 1980s Betinho founded IBASE, a non-governmental development agency. Through his contacts abroad he established a development agency that was able to help thousands of Brazilians build a better life for themselves. The programs of IBASE reached all sectors of the marginalized: the people who lived in the *favellas* of Rio, the landless farmers, the thousands of street children, and the countless numbers afflicted with AIDS. Betinho died in 1999, but his work continues.

During the years following Vatican II, the Society did become an influential force on the Canadian church scene. It attempted to bring home to Canadians the major social justice issues facing the Latin American church. Our magazine focused on the concept of "reverse mission", the notion that mission was not just one way, north to south, but that we had so much to learn from the south. The problems of justice and human development in the face of world poverty, and the reality of economic and political oppression, became common topics in the magazine.

The Society was influential in setting up the Ecumenical Institute in Toronto, the Canada-China Programme with other churches, the Latin American Working Group, and the beginnings of a number of Coalitions (with other church groups). All of this work was justice oriented and considered part of the Society's mission.

In mission countries, Scarboro was attempting to respond to the "church of the Poor" and the call of the churches of the Third World. This new thrust was taking place under the inspiration and vision of the reformed church of Vatican II. It was in no way a negation of the tremendous mission effort and committed lives by missionaries of a different era; it was simply a response to new realities.

You will recall that the 1974 General Chapter of the Society had voted to reduce the size of the General Council, and to establish a Cabinet or think tank that would serve in an advisory capacity. This cabinet was comprised of the Superior General and Council, the treasurer of the Society, the head of the Mission Information Department, and the head of the Formation Programme. As far as the Council and I were concerned, this model of leadership was a good one. We met once a month and the Council set the agenda. Cabinet members were encouraged to submit topics for the agenda that they deemed important. But before long there were rumblings that the Cabinet was unduly influencing Council decisions, and that it was the Council and the Council alone that had been duly elected to govern the Society.

Obviously, for those who resisted change any new model of governance would not adequately fulfil their needs. As I saw it, the rumblings against the Cabinet really stemmed from two major Chapter decisions: the resolve to establish a Lay Missionary program and to leave its implementation to the Council; and the decision to move our students to a downtown residence away from the Seminary, the traditional place for study, prayer and formation.

The Chapter had also made another substantial commitment that did not sit well with some members of the Society. In solidarity with the church of the poor, and with greater reliance on Divine Providence, the Society resolved to disburse to missionary efforts, any financial surplus over and above a three month operational budget. For many, this was like selling the Society out from under them. It was too radical a decision for them.

Yet, to be strapped financially, living in a sense from hand-to-mouth, was not something foreign to the Society. For most of its early years, and well into the late 1940s and early 1950s, the Society could hardly have been described as affluent. Sound financial footing had only come later, along with the financial prosperity that spread to the middle classes of Canada.

I must note that each of these major decisions were Chapter decisions, voted on, and passed by the majority of Chapter delegates. The Council, of which I was the head, aided by the counsel and expertise of the members of the Cabinet, had been mandated to act on these decisions.

The major and radical Chapter decision, to disburse Society finances, over and above the three-month budget plan, was implemented by the Council. The members of both Cabinet and the Council sent out questionnaires and consulted with various Mission organizations. Superiors in mission were asked to consult with their personnel and the local churches. The Council drew up a detailed plan of objectives for the disbursement of these funds. The funds were eventually disbursed to some seventy misson groups. The recipients varied from groups involved in proselytizing and catechetics to ecumenical and development groups. The disbursement was international in scope and the allotted funds varied in monetary size.

In my capacity as Superior General of the Society, it was my responsibility, along with the Council, to fulfil the decisions of the previous Chapters. I was also convinced that the exercise of leadership on my part should be collegial, with any major decision being made only after discussion and debate with my two Councillors. I believed my role was to encourage and support my brothers in the Society. I also looked upon my position as Superior General, along with my fellow Councillors, to be the "voice" of the Chapters. That mandate called us to take risks in the spirit of a renewed church. In that role we were to lead into unchartered waters in spite of criticism.

My conviction to this day is that as a Council we made ourselves available to our confreres in the Society, both at home and overseas. At headquarters, our doors were open to dialogue and discussion with individuals and groups. Frequent house meetings were scheduled at headquarters, open and frank discussion was encouraged. Superiors overseas were asked to hold similar meetings, and we asked for input from those meetings.

Both the 1968 and the 1974 Chapters of the Society had engaged the Society personnel in serious preparation for the Chapter meetings. Care was taken to hear the voice and concerns of all our membership by having a greater number of voting delegates present at these Chapters. Position papers on important issues were drawn up by committees made up of the delegates. Groups at home and on mission were encouraged to submit position papers on issues that they deemed important. The democratic process was followed meticulously in the debates on major papers, and the voting process that followed. There was little more we could have done.

Despite all this, the dark clouds of discontent and disunity loomed in Society life. It became more and more obvious that we were a divided community. Those residing at Society headquarters jokingly referred to the two groups as East and West Berlin.

In 1978, as preparations for yet another Chapter meeting were taking place, two representatives from what I call the "loyal opposition" asked for a meeting with the Council. We met with these representatives on three occasions. They spoke for a group of seven who had serious reservations about the direction they saw the Society taking. Their concerns became charges that questioned the Council's leadership in four principle areas: how our authority was being exercised within the Society, our membership, the use of funds, and our purpose as a Society.

The Council and I considered the group's charges as being very serious. They were questioning the exercised authority of the elected Council in carrying out the mandate of the 1968 and 1974 Chapters. This group consisted of veteran missionaries, some of whom had served in previous administrations. A number of them had been active voting delegates at the two previous Chapters. Though we did not agree with the concerns of this group, we respected these men and the

---

concerns they voiced. Some of them had been our mentors in earlier years.

It was my desire to alleviate their concerns and answer their charges. We discussed the Chapter decisions that were linked to the four major areas of their charges. We took their concerns and charges to the Cabinet. We consulted with an eminent Canon lawyer from outside the Society. We consulted with several bishops who were on our Board of Governors. The Council presented their conclusions and the opinions they had received from their consultation to the group. But the group was still not satisfied.

During their final meeting with us they presented a document, outlining their four areas of major concern. It was signed by seven members of the Society. Their first concern was authority and its exercise within the Society. Their document objected to the Council's collegial style of leadership. It objected to what they felt was the undue influence of the Cabinet. It claimed that the Superior General was not using the personal authority of his office. Their second concern was the lack of priestly vocations. They objected to the move away from the seminary; they said having lay and clerical candidates living together was destroying the clerical enclave necessary for good priestly formation. Implied in this concern was a questioning of the person in charge of formation. They were objecting as well to lay candidates being part of a clerical Society. Their third concern was related to our disbursement of funds that the Chapter had decreed. They questioned some of the groups to whom we had allotted funds. The fourth concern was about our purpose as a Society. The group was not happy with the contents of the magazine; they said it was too political, too justice oriented. They questioned our association with non-Catholic coalitions, and our opening of the seminary to such non-clerical groups as Chavez's farm workers and the exiles and refugees from Brazil, Argentina, Chile and Central America.

Since our talks with this group of seven had not resolved their concerns satisfactorily, and the Council was not taking immediate action, they had made the decision to go outside the Society. Their signed document was sent to the Ontario Bishops and to the Papal Nuncio in Ottawa. Needless to say, this course of action was a bombshell. Our authority and integrity as a Council was not only being questioned, it was also being judged as having failed in the exercise of its mandate by this small minority group with a few sympathizers.

The document presented to us made the claim that "the Council was leading the Society out of the church." They were asking Rome "to take whatever action was deemed necessary to bring about renewal within the Society, in the true sense of the word." (quote from their document). Of the seven signatures, four of those signing had been present at the 68 Chapter; two had been present at the 1974 Chapter, and two others were entitled to be at the 1974 Chapter as observers, but declined to attend.

To my mind this was a serious assault on both our mandate as a Council and our authority to govern the Society. It was questioning the decisions of both previous Chapters. These men were presenting arguments and views that they had expressed at Chapters but which had not been supported. Their actions were a sad and tragic commentary on the impasse that resulted within the Society from our attempts to incorporate the reforms and renewal of Vatican II.

Over the years I have tried to understand the mentality and the reasons why my confreres acted as they did. Their Society and mine had diligently prepared for Chapters, and made every effort to educate and inform the members on the changes of Vatican II, and the results of the Chapter proceedings of 1968 and 1974. As I look back now on those difficult times, my sympathy goes out to those brothers who just would not, or could not, face and accept the changes taking place in the church. They did not want *their* Society changed, or the church. They were in the camp of the traditionalists and the reformists, while I had been converted to the progressive camp. It was true that we had very different views, but surely we could have kept the lines of communication open. I found it ironic at the time that these men, when they were our mentors, had taught us that a missionary was a journeyman. He moved from place to place, through his preaching and teaching helped to establish a local church, and then moved on. Our presence in any one place was never to be permanent; so the very essence of the missionary spirit rested on the premise that change and insecurity is a part of the vocation.

As Chapter time rolled around in 1978, it encountered a shaken Council. Personally, I was demoralized and depressed! As Superior General with two wonderful, faith-filled Councillors, my administration had failed to rally the troops. The Chapters of 1968 and 1974 had responded in a Spirit filled way to the vision of Vatican II. But to implement that vision the Society had to be a unified, cohesive, hope filled group.

The Bishops of Ontario had responded to the document written by the group of seven members by stating that it was an internal problem that should be resolved by the Chapter. The Nuncio in Ottawa gave a similar reply. At the 1978 Chapter the document was given a day of hearings on the agenda of the proceedings. Most of the delegates dismissed the "loyal opposition" and their charges as completely unfounded. The Chapter then moved on to other business. While Chapter delegates downplayed the protest as normal in a time of renewal, neither Clair, Buddy nor I allowed our names to be on the slate for re-election.

I saw in this whole sad affair not just a judgement against the current Council of Scarboro Missions, but really a tactic to avoid the much greater call of Vatican II for renewal and change. The whole experience, far from being faith filled and life giving, was tearing the Society apart. This was a premonition of things to come and my feeling was that it was a lost cause. Although I hoped for the best I wondered whether the Society would survive.

As expected, the Chapter of 1978 confirmed the direction the Society had taken in the two previous Chapters. It opened dialogue with Rome on canonical matters that pertained to the governance of Societies such as ours. The experiment with the Lay Mission program was to continue. A new Council was elected with Ken MacAulay as General and Gerald Curry and Fred Wakeham as his assistants. Gerry Curry had worked in Japan and Fred Wakeham in the Philippines. The new Council did everything it could to bring about reconciliation with the general membership of the Society. Obviously there had been sides taken by members of the Society over this incident. Personally, I remained mystified by the rift, and as a result went into a long period of disillusionment and searching.

CHAPTER 26

Change for Renewal's Sake

W hy do committed and loyal men find it difficult to grasp the spirit of renewal? Was it not expressed with eloquence and inspiration by the documents of Vatican II? Why do we fear change when it calls us to do something out of the ordinary? Is it wrong to desire change? Is there anything wrong with not wanting change and trying to keep things as they have always been? Are things ever really as permanent as we imagine them to be? These larger questions began to consume me and would give me no rest.

The division that occurred within the Society during my leadership drove me to look in a new way at the age old questions of conversion and grace, of good and evil. If the gospel was such good news then why did not everyone accept it? Why did I not give my whole life to it? Where do my own pockets of resistance reside? Why were those in power in the Americas unwilling to bring about change for the poor? Why could we not find ways to change the system so that the majority, and not just the few, could benefit from the wealth of the land? Why was their so much resistance to change if it was for the best? Where was God in all this? Where was the church in all this?

I knew that my searching would not resolve these questions once and for all, but I felt a need to look at how institutions start out with a spirit of change and innovation, and slowly become inflexible to the very spirit that inspired them in the first place. What better way to examine this perplexing issue than to look at the history of the Society to which I belonged?

I present this analysis as my understanding of Scarboro Missions history and of the individuals involved.

Scarboro Missions is a group of priests founded in 1917 to work in China. From the beginning we were intended to be a "missionary" Society for the purpose of evangelizing and preaching the Gospel to non-Christians. We were a unique group within the Canadian Catholic Church at the time, different from the religious orders and religious institutes such as the Jesuits, Dominicans or Franciscans.

A small band of followers gathered around our founder, John Mary Fraser, and went with him to the mission fields of Lishui, in the province of Chekiang, China. Our numbers in the 1930s were small, and the mission work in Lishui was hampered by the Chinese-Japanese conflict of 1932-1939, and later by World War II. This was followed by a period of internal conflict that saw the forces of the Communist leader Mao Zedung overthrow Chang Kai-shek.

Up to and including the time of the Communist victory some forty-five Scarboro missionaries had served in China. Some of these men spent their entire missionary careers in China under very difficult times. Three had died there. Others fled the ravages of war and made the long trek to India. Most of the Scarboro missionaries suffered confinement at the hands of the communists or were expelled from the country. All were marked by their Chinese experience.

By the early 1950s our largest mission was in the Dominican Republic in the West Indies. Prevented by war from sending missionaries to China, the Society had sent missionaries to help out in a Christian country that had few local priests. Many of the priests that had served in China finished their missionary careers either in the Dominican Republic or in other missions taken on by the Society. The Japan Mission was opened by the Society in 1947. Other than China, it was the only non-Christian country where the Society was engaged.

Although it was our original purpose, our mission history in non-Christian countries was limited to our experiences in China and Japan.

The focus of Society work for over half the members of the Society was now in Christian countries with a Spanish flavour, and in proximity to Latin America.

In the Dominican Republic the first priority for the missionaries was the important task of bringing the sacraments to the majority of the population who were baptized. These people had little knowledge of their Catholic faith. Scarboro priests in the Dominican Republic during the 1940s and 1950s gave of themselves in establishing parishes and building churches. They visited their parishioners in interior towns and villages, traveling by horseback or jeep to minister to their needs. In the Dominican Republic they worked alongside the local church and clergy. But, while they were working in a Latin country with a culture, history and language, different from Canada, they functioned much like their counterparts in Canada. They had the basic theological formation of their era. Their busy lives allowed no time for study.

They worked in a milieu that was Christian historically and traditionally. Their ministry was primarily a sacramental one, and within this ministry the focus was that of evangelization. They baptized thousands of children and adults, spent countless hours in the confessional and celebrated Catholic marriages. They set up church structures, built churches, established catechetical centres, and trained catechists. In the early years, with few roads at their disposal, they spent days and weeks traveling to isolated hamlets and villages to bring the sacraments, and to celebrate Mass. As a young seminarian and priest I spent many hours listening to the "tales" told by these experienced men.

It is relevant here to consider the circumstances under which they worked. The Dominican Republic was under the dictatorship of Raphael Trujillo Molinas. Trujillo ruled the Dominican people with an iron fist. His power was absolute and he tolerated no opposition. His army of thugs and assassins ensured that no political freedoms existed. Yet, because he was a foe of communism, he was looked upon as a friend and was supported by the American government.

The Archbishop of Santo Domingo, Ricardo Pettini recognized the dilemma of trying to work with a despot dictator. At that time in history, Pettini believed that rather than challenge the government on the lack of freedoms, working to build up the church and protecting its freedom to do charitable work among the population would attain greater results. The constant risk of being banned from the country was real, and hung over the church's foreign Archbishop. He made it clear to the other foreign priests coming into the country that they were to avoid any political activity.

So, the ministry of the Scarboro priests was predominantly pastoral and sacramental. Justice and human rights were not on the agenda. They did become heavily involved in helping the poverty stricken masses through charitable organizations. As the years went by some of the priests became involved in establishing credit unions and market co-operatives, but their *modus operandi* was to do charitable work while avoiding any vocal opposition to Trujillo.

By the early 1960s the mission of Scarboro in the Dominican Republic had over forty priests. The mission work for the veterans and the priests that followed them continued to be the strengthening of the local church, using all the traditional movements. Through great personal sacrifice and tireless pastoral work these men built up the church, and their charitable works alleviated the misery in the lives of many people. Their apostolate did bring hope to the masses.

For these men this was the focus and the thrust of their mission activity. The majority of the priests followed this agenda, although a few had very serious problems of conscience as they tried to cope with the flagrant violations of human rights that they witnessed under a terrible dictatorial regime. Some found expression for their frustrations by working with the poor through education and the co-operative movement.

A form of McCarthyism was prevalent in church circles at this time in the name of the John Birch Society. Communism was seen as the great evil, the anti-Christian devil incarnate. Even a despot like

Trujillo, because of his anti-communist stance, was looked upon as an ally in the war against communism. And as opposition groups began to mobilize against the despotic rule of Trujillo, these movements were all judged to be communist inspired and financed. In fact some were, but there were many others that sought legitimate change to better the terrible conditions of the Dominican people. Unfortunately, even these groups were labelled as communist and their genuine concerns conveniently dismissed.

But winds of change were blowing, not just in the Dominican Republic but throughout the world. In the 1970s, the young priests arriving to work in the Dominican Republic had a different formation and a different focus. They were a different breed of missionary. The change in thinking that preceded the Second Vatican Council emphasized that social justice be an integral part of evangelization. This was a departure from the theological formation of former times, and was at odds with the pastoral approach upon which the veterans had built and spent their lives. Social justice was an integral part of evangelization for this new breed. Both groups found it difficult to reconcile the others' approach to ministry.

Even before Vatican II officially initiated change, a difference in theological studies and mission practise was unfolding. In their enthusiasm, young missionaries in the early 1960s were often critical of the old way of doing things, without being sensitive to the sacrifices and labours of their elders. Many times they acted imprudently in their zeal for reform, and in their rejection of what they considered to be antiquated pastoral practises. Naturally, the veteran missionaries took a defensive attitude and looked upon the young as troublemakers. It seemed there was little or no dialogue. Some of the young men left their mission and the priesthood. Their elders carried the scars of these confrontations. Errors in judgement and approach were made on both sides.

The scene, in many ways, was a reenactment of the "Parable of the Workers" (Matthew 20: 1-16). The Master of the Vineyard went out in the early hours of the morning, and hired workers for the day;

again he went out at mid-day; and then he went out at the ninth hour. The early workers grumbled on receiving a pay equal in amount to those who had come late! They had endured the heat and the long hours. How come these newcomers were considered as equals? On the part of the new missionaries, their presence, and their youthful exuberance and fresh ideas were not always appreciated. The old guard, for their part, felt this new theological thought passed negative judgement on their years of toil. New theological thought clashed with old tradition and practice, and left the deep wounds of division!

One of Scarboro's young priests, Father Arthur MacKinnon, an activist for social justice, was shot to death in his parish of El Seibo in 1965. His death had followed the political unrest that occurred after the assassination of Raphael Trujillo. The Dominican people were revolting against years of tyranny and oppression. Justice and the liberation of the poor became a Gospel mandate and a rallying call for this new breed of church activist and missionary, not just in the Dominican Republic but throughout Latin America.

I have tried to provide some historical background for the tension and the deep division that grew within the Society following Vatican II. It is an attempt to explain some of the reasons behind the turf wars that were fought within the Society in the Chapters that followed Vatican II (1965) and the Latin American Bishops' Conference in Medellin, Colombia (1968). Put simply, the young guard with their new theology that emphasized a new vision of church became pitted against the old guard who looked upon much of this new vision as the destroyer of their church, their traditions, and their Society.

The protest of the group of seven, was not just against my tenure as Superior General, nor even against Chapter renewal and revision, but was for the historical reasons outlined above, a fear of all things new. Ultimately it was a rejection of the spirit of the Second Vatican Council. This was a devastating realization for me.

CHAPTER 27

Stormy Weather on the River

In my own journey as priest and missionary, the irony remains that my background and training had been similar to that of my "protesting" colleagues within my mission Society. I had been nurtured within a traditional Catholic family and church, and was ordained in the 1950s. Like them I accepted the church as "my Mother and my Guide" in living out my faith and my missionary calling.

To this day, I strongly believe that the vision and challenge for the future so well expressed in the Documents of Vatican II, had called me and my colleagues to a radical conversion, and to a new approach in the building of the Kingdom. That conversion embodied a difficult process for all of us; one that was filled with risk-taking. It was a new and untravelled road. The progressive church of Latin America that had courageously embarked on these unchartered waters had challenged those of us involved in mission to help in the building of the Kingdom of God for all peoples. This kingdom was never intended to be just a heavenly Kingdom, but an earthly one as well. It was to create a just, economic and social society where all women and men could live out their dignity as daughters and sons of God.

Some might feel that such a vision is utopian, but I fervently believed in it. Was this not the central message of the Gospel? In this matter I had been converted to pursuing such a world, not just by the documents that came out of the Vatican Council, but more so through daily contact with the poor in Brazil. My personal experiences with people like Roberto, Alfredo, Herbert de Sousa, and Cesar Chavez at Scarboro headquarters, together with my study of the lives and theology of Camilo Torres and Gustavo Gutierrez, had left a lasting impression on me.

It was also becoming more evident to me that the church of Rome was retreating within the fortress walls of the Vatican. The small group of protesting brothers within Scarboro had powerful allies all over the world. With the call to renewal and the real action that followed, a powerful conservative and reactionary movement was gaining momentum throughout the church, one that was backed by the Roman Curia.

My frustration and disappointment was fuelled by anger at how the institutional church was becoming an obstacle to the very reforms it had officially promulgated. I felt a profound sense of betrayal. I had reached a crisis in my priestly life that would make or break me as a person. What was I going to do with the rest of my life? Answering that question would take me on a painful journey of soul-searching for the next eight years. That journey would lead me away from my past. I would choose new life outside of the traditional understanding of priesthood and mission.

Following the 1978 Chapter, I stayed on in Canada at the request of the General Council. I was appointed Director of the Mission Information Department and editor of our magazine, *Scarboro Missions*. But my life as a Scarboro missionary had reached a crossroads. My hopes for a unified, vibrant, and renewed Society and church animated by the spirit of Vatican II had suffered a crushing blow. I stayed on for two years in my new position. I devoted as much enthusiasm and energy to my work as I could muster. But my heart was not in it. My heart and my head were straying from the Scarboro Foreign Mission Society.

During my seminary days I had renewed a friendship with a high school friend from North Bay. Lorne Devine and his wife, Norine, lived close to the seminary. At that time I visited their home whenever possible and the bonds of close friendship grew deeper over the years.

The family supported me with their love and their support for mission. Their nine children became very much a part of my life. Norine and Lorne were active members of a lay group that supported the mission work of Scarboro Missions. They were always a strong moral support in my personal life over the years.

Scarboro headquarters became less attractive for me, and the wounds of division and suspicion did not make for a happy family community. So I began to lean heavily on the Devine family. In retrospect I must have imposed on them by my presence, yet they were always there for me. To this day they continue to be a supportive and intimate part of my life.

My Irish-Canadian roots did not make me adverse to a good time being enhanced by a few drinks. Over the years I drank with gusto and enjoyed every minute of it. But, during my last years at headquarters, and again later during my last sojourn in Brazil, I became aware that my drinking was becoming a problem. My anger and my drinking fed on one another as my frustration with the church grew. I had two 'tigers' sitting on my back at this stage in my life.

In 1978 I celebrated 25 years as a priest and missionary with Scarboro Missions. Over those years I had had my difficulties with the celibate life. Meaningful relationships with women had developed throughout those years, relationships that for me had been both lifegiving and supportive. I had been in love and been loved. Those relationships had been healthy, loving and life giving, as well as difficult because of my vow of celibacy. I had never really questioned the celibate lifestyle that went along with my priestly vocation, and had always attempted to balance those relationships with my celibate life. As a priest/celibate my life and passion had been wholly consumed by the mission enterprise in which I was involved.

But now I was coming into conflict with my church, the religious mentor to whom I had given my life. I felt the church had betrayed me both theologically and pastorally. From my point of view, the service I was called to give involved the wellbeing of millions of fellow humans! We could not feed their souls and be bystanders to the causes of their poverty.

Now the question of celibacy was becoming an issue! To what extent does the church have control over my life and my growth as a human being? In 1979 I renewed a relationship with Carol Spencer who was a Religious Sister. We had known each other from the early 1970s and had become friends when she worked on a Mission Team under my supervision. From that time we had corresponded occasionally with each other. A chance meeting brought us into a closer relationship in 1979. Carol was a Sister of St. Joseph from North Bay, my hometown. Her religious vocation had started as a teacher in the separate school system in northern Ontario. She had also worked in Guatemala as a missionary, and was now stationed in the Bahamas. During a visit to the Bahamas we met again and our relationship deepened. It took hold and the magnetic quality of love and attraction began to have a profound effect on my life.

In the following six years that attraction and love would grow through correspondence and occasional visits in Canada. Carol also visited our mission in Brazil in 1982. While our attraction to each other was growing we remained committed to our respective callings in spite of the fact that we both questioned the direction our church was taking. The bonds of love and friendship were growing. Yet, having lived within the discipline and tradition of the church for so many years our options were limited. And so we mutually decided that it would be best to continue in our calling and commitment to mission and the church for the time being. These intimate feelings are difficult to share and to articulate. However, my journey would be incomplete without such a sharing. As the philosopher Blaise Pascal once wrote, "The heart has its own reasons which reason knows little of." (*Pensées*) In one sense these years were my "dark night of the soul", but in another sense, something new was beginning to germinate.

My enthusiasm and interest in the Latin American church, and especially the church in Brazil, remained a central focus of my life and ministry. The concerns of Brazil never strayed far from my heart.

During my ten year hiatus in Canada, I continued to follow the struggles of the Latin American church. I retained a glimmer of hope that somehow if things were to be turned around in the larger church, it would happen through the church in Latin America.

A new pope had been elected to the throne of Peter, John Paul II. The followup meeting to Medellin of the Latin American bishops had been delayed for a year. However, it did took place in Puebla, Mexico in October of 1979. John Paul II inaugurated the Puebla conference. Although Cardinals Lopez Trujillo and Sebastiao Baggio had attempted to control the agenda for that meeting, the progressive bishops and the theology of liberation seemed to have won the day. The conclusions of the Medellin Conference were reaffirmed. Rome, in spite of a conservative Curia, officially appeared to agree with the Conference in it's preferential option for the poor.

With guarded optimism I made the decision with my superiors to return to the Brazil mission in late 1979. My superiors were well aware of both my personal crisis and my conflicts with the church. They recognized that my heart was no longer in my assignment at home. The Itacoatiara mission in Brazil could use my experience. Bishop Jorge Marskell, my friend and colleague, aware of my crisis urged me to return. I am sure these friends felt that if I immersed myself in the work of the Brazilian mission, a ministry close to my heart, I might perhaps overlook what was happening at the universal level of the church. In fact, the exact opposite happened.

CHAPTER 28

Brazil Revisited

During the 1970s the military in Brazil, in staging its covert war against the church, restricted the entry of Catholic missionaries into the country. By the early 1980s those restrictions were beginning to be eased. So it was with some apprehension that I applied for re-entry into the country and for a work permit. I began the process in mid-June 1980, and by late September I was fortunate to be granted the necessary documentation.

In early October 1980 I flew to Sao Paulo where I had arranged to work in a large urban parish for several months. The pastor of the parish, Celso Pedro da Silva, had worked with Scarboro in Itacoatiara. My stay in Sao Paulo would give me the opportunity to reacquaint myself with the political happenings within Brazil and to be exposed to the social and economic problems that pastoral workers encounter daily in the largest city in South America.

Sao Paulo had been the scene of violent confrontations in 1978 and 1979 between the military and thousands of steel workers. There had been a paralyzing strike by the steel workers, that closed down the steel industry. The strike had been organized as a protest against the economic policies of the government. Mass demonstrations and frequent clashes with the military became the order of the day. The church, under the leadership of Cardinal Paul Evaristo Arns, sided with the workers and the churches in the city became sanctuaries for the protesting workers. It was a long and bitter struggle, but in the end the workers forced the government to the bargaining table. From this struggle the Workers' Party was born. During the ensuing years it was to become a strong opposition voice for reform, and a voice for the poor, both at the national and local levels. Ignacio da Silva, known as "Lulu", a Union president elected to head the Workers Party, became a strong contender for the Presidency of the country, following the fall of the dictatorship.[1]

My stay in Sao Paulo was to acquaint me with the many changes that were taking place in the country during the military dictatorship. My missionary experience in the Amazon in the 1960s was now enhanced by this brief immersion in the pastoral work of the Sao Paulo church, the largest Archdiocese in the world. I saw firsthand how this church endeavoured to implement both the reforms of Vatican II and the preferential option for the poor.

The phenomenon of internal migration in Brazil was more than evident within the parish boundaries. Like most large, industrial cities Sao Paulo had always been a beacon of hope for the poor and landless. They flocked from the arid northeast by the thousands to Sao Paulo in search of work. The landless masses from the south, that had been removed from their traditional way of life, also looked to life in the city for a better future. By the early 1980s the population of greater Sao Paulo had grown to seventeen million.

My visits to the basic christian communities that were linked to the parish showed the strong presence of the church in the life and the struggle of these poor migrant workers who faced the grim realities of life in such a large metropolis. Pastoral workers worked alongside the natural leaders of each small community to form strong faith communities of mutual support. In addition to meeting on Sunday to worship, these communities met several times during the week for Bible study, prayer, and problem solving. During my short stay in the parish I visited these communities regularly, staying with host families. These folk were like strangers in their own land, coming from the arid northeast and the south of the country. Their stories of their

---

1. In 2002 Ignacio da Silva was elected President of the country.

migratory journeys by foot, by truck, and by bus, with their few earthly belongings, and with meagre finances, was not unlike the trek of the chosen people to the Promised Land.

Within the boundaries of the parish there were many old stately homes. Many of these had been bought up by speculators and turned into rooming houses. With lax health regulations and a severe housing shortage, they became a means of exploiting the poor and destitute migrants. It was not uncommon to visit fifteen or twenty families with four or five children living in cramped quarters in these old homes. Sanitation systems were overworked; water and electricity were in short supply. Such places created a whole new type of *favella* or shanty town.

I found it ironic, too, that as I made preparations for returning to Brazil, one of the major stories in the Toronto area was the closing of the Goodyear Tire plant in the Oshawa area, and the loss of jobs for several hundred workers. The reason given for its closure was the lack of tire sales. In fact, it was being relocated to Brazil. During the first week in my new home in Sao Paulo, one of the pastoral workers showed me the new plant not far from the church. Globalization had already begun. Here in Brazil, Goodyear would not have to worry about unions and environmental laws, and they would be assured of a steady stream of cheap labour.

Several times a week, Francisco, one of the seminarians living at the parish, would spend the morning helping me brush up on my Portuguese. There were scheduled weekly visits to other parishes and communities to observe different pastoral approaches. It was another opportunity to witness the dynamics in community discussions. A Scarboro colleague, Father Doug MacKinnon, was living and working in a nearby parish. He was a volunteer in the exchange program between the sister churches of Sao Paulo and Itacoatiara. We got together every two weeks and he used the visits to take me to the communities where he was working.

Following these eight weeks in Sao Paulo I made my way to Itacoatiara. By this stage in my journey I had in many ways left the bark of Peter, and was journeying alongside a similar but different vessel, the church of the poor.

I was returning to a different church than the Itacoatiara church I had left in the 1960s. Internal migration had reached the state of Amazonas and the population of Itacoatiara had grown from 15,000 in the 1960s to close to 100,000. There was a large military base in the city, and the military kept a close eye on the activities of the church. There had been community skirmishes with large fishing vessels that invaded the lakes and rivers. Community vigilante groups had been formed to protect the fish population. Individuals and companies were moving in from the south buying huge tracts of land for cattle farms. These land take-overs resulted in the expulsion of farmers who had lived and worked their small tracts of land for several generations. The prelacy was involved in protecting the rights of such farmers and their families. A large mill operation producing laminated chipboard was in full operation and employing four hundred workers. The church had become involved in the operation by monitoring worker safety and wages.

Coming back to Itacoatiara meant returning, as well, to work with a close friend who was now the chief Pastor, Bishop George Marskell. Jorge (his Brazilian name) and I had come to Brazil together in 1961. We had formed a close friendship, working together both in Itacoatiara and Urucara. We shared the same dream and hope of what the mission of the church should be.

Jorge had returned to Brazil in 1974 after serving six years on the General Council. Four years later, in 1978, he had been ordained bishop of the prelacy in Itacoatiara. I had represented the Society at that ceremony. Jorge's dedication and commitment to his people, to their social needs, and the way he gave voice to them as a People of God came from his strong belief in a liberating Christ. These were the pastoral gifts we had seen in Jorge and the ones we shared with Rome in 1977, when we recommended his nomination as bishop.

At the time of my return to the prelacy the personnel consisted of 9 priests, 11 religious sisters and five lay volunteers. A pastoral plan for the prelacy based on the Brazilian Bishops Conference was in place. The 92,000 sqare kilometers area had been divided into seven pastoral areas. Pastoral teams lived and worked out of the towns of Silves, Urucara, Uricurituba and Presidente Figureirdo, as well as Itacoatiara. The personnel in Itacoatiara worked the town itself and two other areas by boat. There were now over 140 basic communities, and each community had its own lay ministers. Our training centre, *Centrepi*, continued to run educational and training courses throughout the year for the leaders and ministers of the various communities.

It is only fitting that these local community leaders be acknowledged for what they were to the overall running of the pastoral program of the prelacy. These were the men and women who helped their villages grow in faith and build a solid community spirit. These volunteer leaders, like others in the village, struggled for a daily living, yet gave of their time and talents to build real faith communities. Without their sacrifices and commitment no lasting work could have been accomplished. The work of community building was a constant uphill struggle, marked by success, failure, and starting over again.

To keep the whole operation functional and operational, doses of goodwill, flexibility and faith commitment were the necessary ingredients for all involved. Jorge Marskell, as shepherd and leader, cemented the above ingredients together with his gifts for promoting dialogue, listening attentively, and providing the power of his example.

It was not long before I was immersed in this vibrant pastoral life. I was appointed Vicar General and took over the prelacy finances. My responsibilities in Itacoatiara included being pastor at the Cathedral and several smaller faith communities. I became part of the team for marriage preparation, and for pastoral work among the workers.

All of the priests working in Itacoatiara also had their charges in the Amazonian interior. I joined the pastoral teams that were responsible for the town of Silves (four hours by boat from Itacoatiara), and the faith communities linked to Silves and the Urubu River. I also was responsible for the visitation of five communities on the highway that linked Itacoatiara to Manaus. Co-ordinating pastoral work in Itacoatiara with scheduled visitations to the interior obviously meant planning well with the members of the teams with whom I worked.

Our scheduled trips to the interior communities were usually one or two day visits, depending on their location and size. Visits would be set up so that we could cover all the communities in the area on successive days. Communities were visited about four times a year by the pastoral team.

Each year there was a seminar/retreat for all the pastoral and community leaders of the prelacy at *Centrepi*, our training centre. This was a time when we came together for five days of reflection, prayer and planning. There would be a special facilitator, usually a theologian from southern Brazil, who would focus our biblical reflections on some aspect of evangelization.

The pastoral visits to the interior and our pastoral work in the main towns concentrated on some aspect of the overall pastoral plan for the prelacy. This was very much connected with the social and economic life of the people. It was always attempting to make the gospel message relevant, and a source of strength and hope in the everyday life of the people. There were also the sacramental and liturgical celebrations that were central to pastoral activity.

Every year each one of the parishes and communities celebrated a *festa* in honour of the parish patron saint. It was a time for devotion and prayer, but most of all it was a time to set aside the problems and worries of everyday living; to celebrate life and bring together all of the community.

Although demanding, the work was both satisfying and diverse – and always a challenge. I experienced first hand the daily lives of the people, how they struggled to live off the land and provide for their families. This was a ministry where I rubbed shoulders with the poor in their milieu. By the end of an interior trip, I always returned home humbled by the quiet dignity of the villagers, and the simple aspirations of the men and women in each community. Though isolated from Itacoatiara, the villagers and their communities became a part of my life. Their lives were a source of energy and renewed resolve in my life. The communities, I suspect, drew their strength and direction from the pastoral team, just as we did from them.

I acquired a 14-foot aluminium boat with a 35hp outboard that was used for my monthly trips to Silves, and on most of our travels into the interior. But some of the communities would send a boat to meet the team at a designated site. We would travel there by car or jeep, and then be transported to the first community by motorized canoe or by strong paddlers. After our designated stay at the first community, the second community boat would arrive to transport us on to the next community, and so on. In this way we made our way from community to community. Our visits would always be marked by a community meal. Naturally, there were no hotel accommodations and so we would sleep in hammocks either in the chapel, community centre, or with a family.

The pastoral life of the prelacy was vibrant and healthy. It was fuelled by the leadership of Dom Jorge, the commitment of the members of the pastoral teams, and the lay ministers in the communities. The shortage of personnel was always a major problem. The vision of Dom Jorge was that the prelacy reach out to all without exception, and try to respond to their needs. This was a tall order, in view of a scarcity of personnel. The situation pushed the teams to their limit. During my years back in the prelacy (1980-1986), we would see priests and lay volunteers finish their commitments and move on to other work, with few to take their places.

One of Dom Jorge's dreams was to have a small rural seminary, a facility where ten or twelve young men could pursue their high school studies in a communal and prayerful atmosphere. For several years he and other priests had been counselling and encouraging a number of young men who felt a call to missionary service in the prelacy. These young men from Itacoatiara and the interior needed both moral support and financial help.

With the approval of the Pastoral Council, a plan for the operation of the facility was put into operation. Valeriano dos Santos, a priest from the Sao Paulo exchange program and pastor of Urucara, volunteered to be responsible for the students and to live with them as their counsellor and Rector. Terry O'Sullivan of Scarboro Missions, who was a pastor in Manaus, was appointed to head the pastoral team in Urucara. I was asked to supervise the planning and construction of a modest residence and chapel. So, the rural seminary was built on property the prelacy had acquired, about eight kilometres from the town on the Itacoatiara-Manaus highway.

Four months later the Oscar Romero Rural Seminary became a reality, and seven students along with Valeriano took up residence. The students followed a daily program of work, study, and prayer. They also attended one of the local high schools in town. Valeriano and volunteers from the pastoral teams, handled supplementary studies for individuals, classes in church history and spirituality, and counselling.

The Oscar Romero Seminary and *Centrepi*, the pastoral training centre, were very important entities in the life of the prelacy. They were both educating, training and forming future leaders who would continue the pastoral work of the prelacy, and preparing pastoral workers for the various communities. As well as those responsible for the daily operation and programs of the seminary and the centre, other necessary maintenance work was carried out by volunteers.

With the priest shortage being an ongoing problem in Itacoatiara we reached out to the Yarumal Missionaries of Colombia and the Guadalupe Fathers in Mexico. They were two young missionary groups that I had come to know while in administration back at Scarboro. Both groups had young missionaries available. I made several trips to Medellin and Yarumal, Colombia, in 1984-85 to investigate the possibility of the two Societies working in Itacoatiara. By 1986 both Societies had committed themselves to working in the prelacy.

Another dream of Dom Jorge's was to conduct a synod, or what came to be called an Assembly of the People. This was a meeting of delegates from all of the communities together with their bishop and pastoral teams. It was a meeting to assess and evaluate the pastoral work going on in the prelacy, and to be the "voice of the people" in helping the bishop and his council formulate a pastoral plan.

The first Peoples Assembly took place in Itacoatiara in 1982. The plan was to hold similar meetings every two years in a different locale within the prelacy. It was to evaluate the work of the previous two years, and plan for the following two years. But it was also an opportunity for all of the communities to come together, to mingle as brothers and sisters, and to get to know one another. It represented the family of faith of the prelacy coming together to pray, reflect, and plan the work of the Gospel for their brothers and sisters throughout the breadth and width of the area. It was also a time for Dom Jorge, as bishop and shepherd, and his pastoral teams to rub shoulders, pray, and celebrate the faith life of the whole prelacy.

These assemblies served as a decision making body as well. Delegates were elected by their respective communities, and so each community had a voice in planning the pastoral programs for the prelacy. This was certainly collegiality in action. These first Assemblies were truly history making events. There was much preparatory work and planning by many people. There was also much goodwill, generosity and volunteer work on the part of the host community that would house, feed, and support close to two hundred people over a five day period. It was truly a faith event and a living example of the church of the people.

Dom Jorge was also vice-president of the Land Pastoral of the National Bishops Conference. He attended meetings of this council in the south of the country. He used these trips outside the prelacy to search out religious and priest volunteers to work in the prelacy. It was evident that there would be few if any missionary priests coming from Scarboro Missions, as the seminary back home was empty. There were thirteen young men studying at the rural seminary in Itacoatiara. Another seminarian was completing his last year of theology and two were studying philosophy at the regional seminary in Manaus.

So it was that I found myself back in Brazil, working as part of a church that was attempting to live and breathe the spirit of Vatican II. It was a church that had made "a preferential option for the poor." It was part of a national Brazilian church that was viewed as one of the most progressive in the world.

At this time in my life I felt it was a privilege and a challenge to be part of that whole process. My prayer life continued amidst a busy and active life. Did I neglect my inner soul searching in the midst of all the activity? I did wonder at times. However, I can say that the strength and faith of the people in the many communities strengthened my faith. I was nourished, too, by the faith commitment and leadership of Dom Jorge and my fellow pastoral workers.

Even in this far-flung place, the direction of the church was always a subject that was very much a part of our lives. Although Dom Jorge was saddened, and at times dismayed, by what was happening within the church universal, his mission to the people in the prelacy was steadfast. He resolutely followed his pastoral vision, to be a bishop and shepherd, not *of* his people, but *with* his people in all their struggles and hopes. Their struggle was his struggle – that included working for the freedoms of economic security and full recognition of their place in Brazilian society.

On my part, I saw him living out the spirit of Vatican II that is so poetically expressed in the opening passage of the *Pastoral Constitution on the Church in the Modern World*:

> "The joys and hopes, the grief and anguish of the men
> (and women) of our time, especially those who are
> poor or afflicted in any way, are the joys and hopes,
> the grief and anguish of the followers of Christ as well.
> Nothing that is genuinely human fails to find an echo
> in their hearts. For theirs is a community composed
> of men (and women), who, united in Christ and guided
> by the holy Spirit, press onwards toward the kingdom
> of the Father and are bearers of a message of salvation

for all. That is why Christians cherish a feeling of deep solidarity with the human race and its history." ("The Church in the Modern World", *The Documents of Vatican II*, Walter M. Abbott, sj, editor, America Press, 1966, pp.199-200.)

But I could not escape what was happening within the universal church and it haunted me on a daily basis. The Second Conference of the Latin American Bishops in Puebla, Mexico in late 1979 appeared to have defeated the conservative elements within the Curia and reaffirmed the conclusions of the Medellin Conference. Evidence was mounting throughout the Catholic world to the contrary. The episcopal appointments of Vatican hardliners were replacing Vatican II vision- aries and shepherds who were in tune with the needs of their flock. The pope, and not just the Vatican Curia, was putting his men in place throughout the Catholic world. The official statements of the church were for justice; the practice seemed to prefer the existing state of affairs.

In 1984, Archbishop Jose Cardoso Sobrinho became the Archbishop of Olinda-Recife, replacing the beloved Helder Camara, long the voice of the poor in Brazil. Helder Camara was given no voice in the choice of his successor. Sobrinho wasted no time in dismantling the work of Camara. He closed the diocesan seminary, and dismissed theologians for being tainted with liberation theology. He was signalling Rome's intent on cleaning house in Brazil. It became more and more evident that the progressive bishops of the Latin American church, and their pastoral plan to create a moral and just society for the majority, were being scuttled by the policies of the Roman Curia. It was demoralizing for me and I began to lose all hope in the institutional church.

In 1985, when Father Leonardo Boff, the Brazilian liberation theologian, was silenced by Cardinal Joseph Ratzinger, we invited him to spend time with us in the prelacy. I had known Leonardo since 1975 when we had met at Scarboro Missions in Toronto. At that time, we had become friends. In 1984, Boff had been called to Rome to defend his writings on liberation theology. Cardinals Paulo Evaristo Arns and Aloision Lorscheider, leaders of the Brazilian hierarchy, accompanied Boff to Rome and were his defenders. At the time Boff felt that the attack on his writings was really an attempt to embarrass the Brazilian Conference of Bishops. Nevertheless, he had come home from Rome, confident that the progressive church had made its case in Rome.

During Leonardo's stay with us in the prelacy he often chided me for my cynicism toward Roman policy. " Miguel", he would say, "don't lose hope. You have to have hope in the institution." Imagine him saying this to me! At this time in his life, facing the major problems he had to contend with, he was still able to encourage me to have hope. I suspect, though, he saw the writing on the wall. A few years after my departure from active ministry, Leonardo too, was to leave, and he was quoted in the press at that time as saying, "there is no hope in the institution."

CHAPTER 29

Difficult but Life-giving Choices

T he Fall of 1986 seemed to be the opportune time for me to take my leave from Brazil, and decide on my future path. My heart was with Dom Jorge and the church of Itacoatiara, yet my head (and part of my heart too) was telling me that this shining example of the church of the poor would somehow be dismantled by Rome. The Yarumal and Guadalupe Fathers were sending three missionaries to the prelacy, and so I felt less guilty in leaving the people and my colleagues who were so much a part of my life.

With the approval of my Superiors I had enrolled in a Spiritual Renewal Programme that was to begin in February of 1987. This was to be followed by a Society Chapter in July, that I was to attend as a delegate. Unexpectedly, I left Brazil much more quickly than I had planned. On a trip to the interior in late June, I was a victim to food poisoning. Doctors in Manaus advised that I leave for Canada and have an operation as soon as I was well enough to travel. I was leaving Brazil but not the people or the vision I had witnessed there.

Once back in Canada I went through a series of medical exams and tests, was treated and began to regain my strength. Surgery was scheduled for later. The convalescent period allowed me a few weeks to visit with family in North Bay and Sudbury. By this time Carol was back in Canada studying at St. Michael's Theological School. She was also working with the lay volunteers at a Scarboro Missions residence for the Lay Programme in downtown Toronto. Together we had time to discern our future.

Since the death of my parents, I had always made my home with my sister and her family. So I spent time with Geraldine and Ken Barry and their children in North Bay. Ken had been diagnosed with cancer. He, Geraldine and their children were coping with this upheaval in their lives. As the priest in the family, my presence with them was a support and help. It also gave me some justification to put my own difficulties on hold while they confronted sickness and loss.

Being from a close-knit family, my time was divided between visiting my brother John's family in Sudbury, and Russ and his family and the Barrys' in North Bay. While family members may have suspected that I was going through a personal crisis, our primary concern remained focused on Ken, our brother-in-law and his family.

Before I left Brazil I had made a retreat given by Cardinal Alosisio Lorscheider in Manaus. At that time I sought out his counsel regarding the "tigers" on my back. His counsel was compassionate and direct. I was to deal with one problem at a time, but the "tiger" of anger with the institution was first and foremost. My relationship with Carol, my problems with the church, and my future would be dealt with after I had first dealt with my inner anger.

Again, in the Fall of 1986, with Ken's cancer in remission, I spent time alone on the shores of Manitoulin Island in a retreat setting, and attempted to come to terms with my anger at the institution and try to deal with it objectively. Not an easy task! That year I spent Christmas with family in North Bay and Sudbury. During January 1987 I was with my sister Geraldine and the Barry family in North Bay. It was a difficult time for all of us. I was fully aware that Ken had but a few months to live. So our time together was precious and mutually supportive.

While the Barry family were unaware of my struggles, I suspect that Ken sensed there was some kind of crisis in my life. Some of his comments during our time together seemed to indicate this awareness. He was aware of my opinion on the negative policies of Rome. On our last morning together as we said our goodbyes, knowing we would not see each other again, we spoke of our many good times together, and all that we had shared. Aware that I was heading for New Mexico and a long spiritual retreat, he asked for prayers for himself and the family, and added that I should pray for myself. "Reflect on the gift of life," he said "and how precious it is. It is a gift to be lived to the fullest and with inner peace." Needless to say, his words to me made for a reflective drive to Toronto.

A close friend and Scarboro colleague, Gerry Curry, was also enrolled in the program in New Mexico. Our 100-day sojourn "into the desert" was to begin in mid-February at the Sangre Retreat Centre close to Santa Fe, New Mexico. Gerry and I had planned to drive to Santa Fe and to visit Las Vegas and the Grand Canyon en route. The trip placed us in good space as we made our way south. We had time to relax, leave behind our everyday concerns, and prepare ourselves for this time of renewal. The long road trip gave us ample opportunity to share and confide with one another. I think we both realized that not too many people in the secular world had the opportunity that was being presented to us.

The Spiritual Renewal Programme was directed by the Christian Brothers on the outskirts of Santa Fe. The disciplined program was marked by a daily routine of prayer and reflection, and was set up for religious women and men facing a mid-life crisis. We were a group of thirty-four coming from many different pastoral activities and experiences. But we were all there for one purpose – to renew ourselves both as spiritual and human beings.

The program began with a five-day silent retreat; this time of silent prayer and reflection was to be repeated again mid-way through the program and at its conclusion. We had quality time to commune with God through prayer, scriptural reflection, and the beauty and silence of creation around us.

Daily sessions in scripture, and moral and dogmatic theology were presented by well known theologians. This daily input was augmented by input from professionals in the field of human living. The program offered us a spiritually wholesome environment and a safe place to drink at the well of spiritual and human renewal. I was provided individual counselling and group support sessions once a week.

What did the program do for me and my 'tigers'? I think it offered me a once in a lifetime experience to come closer to my God and the Jesus of the Gospels, and to wrestle honestly and without fear with the issues I was facing. I looked as objectively as I could at the possibility of continuing service in the church. In my conscience I finally concluded that it was no longer possible. From the perspective of my conscience, I felt that the Vatican was undermining the church of the poor, and I could no longer serve such an institution.

Even though I had become more aware that I was in love with Carol, it was still inconceivable for me to think in terms of leaving the priesthood at this point. But during the latter half of the program one of the theologians, a disciple of Teilhard de Chardin, brought home to me that I was not leaving my priesthood; I was only changing direction, and could live priesthood in another way.

To come to this understanding lifted a major weight from my shoulders. I still wrestled with the guilt of being unfaithful to my calling, but my spiritual director gently led me to the possibility of looking forward to a loving marriage with Carol, and a future that would bring healing, enhance our lives, and still be grace filled. Over the following weeks my inner turmoil gradually disappeared and an inner peace returned. I was a child of a loving Creator who beckoned me to new life. The theological and scriptural presentations at Sangre also confirmed for me that the thrust and intent of the Latin American church, in its crusade for a just society, was consistent with the path of Jesus, the Liberator. At this crossroads in my life I was embraced by loving sisters and brothers, who were spiritually searching out their futures like I was. I had made a major decision as to the direction of my future life.

As the program at Sangre came to a close in early May, I received word that my brother-in-law Ken was dying and that my sister Geraldine had suffered a mental breakdown. The family wanted me home so I made a hasty departure for North Bay.

While sickness, suffering and dying are part and parcel of our daily lives, this was a major crisis in the lives of the Barry children who had to cope with their dying father and their mother's hospitalization at the same time. Thirteen years earlier they had been subjected to another crisis. Their mother had suffered a brain aneurysm, and in the midst of her slow recovery they had lived through the trauma of a gas explosion that destroyed their father's place of business. The tragedy killed their father's partner, his secretary, and six other people, and injured twenty-nine others. It was a trauma that deeply affected their lives as well as those of their parents.

Ken died two days after I got home, and as a family we coped with their father's death, and their mother's breakdown. We mutually supported each other and grieved the loss of their dad. Again, I kept my plans and future prospects to myself during this time of family crisis.

In mid-June I returned to headquarters at Scarboro Missions for the Chapter sessions that went on for a month. Parts of the concluding sessions of the Chapter were directed toward healing and reconciliation, which had been a major focus of the Chapter. This focus allowed me to be reconciled with many of my Scarboro colleagues, and with my personal decision to start anew down a different road in life.

Following the close of Chapter I sat down to discuss my future plans with Ken MacAulay, the outgoing Superior, who was a classmate and close friend. During one of our sessions, Ken brought up the matter of my drinking. He gently suggested that since I had previously spoken with him about having a problem with alcohol, that this was the time to address the problem. As I shared my decision for a new life in marriage, he reaffirmed the spiritual way in which I had come to terms with the problems of priesthood, and my anger with the church during my stay at the Sangre Retreat Centre. Should I not now deal with the problem of drinking in the same way? Ken was a trusted colleague who had my wellbeing at heart. He suggested that I bring the matter up with my close friends, the Devines, and with Carol.

Both Carol and the Devines echoed the sound advice of Ken MacAulay. The spiritual time at Sangre, the love and concern of good friends allowed me to embrace their counsel and suggestions. I readily accepted both the suggestion of Ken MacAulay, and the offer of the Society, to follow a program that would look at my drinking problem. This was certainly another spiritual awakening for me, and an opportunity to cleanse my own house and start anew.

I will be forever grateful to Ken MacAulay, Carol, the Devines and others who gently led me to look at what had become, or was becoming, a major problem in my life. Alcoholism is a disease that destroys the lives of many. Its insideous claws had reached deep into mine.

CHAPTER 30

Saying Goodbye

The conscious decision to leave my Society and the active priesthood had been made. My "dark night of the soul" with all its turmoil and unrest was over. In many ways, the liberation of the peoples of Brazil and Latin America from the "tigers" of marginalization, poverty and social injustice that had become my mission had now been granted to me personally. As Teilhard de Chardin had written in his book, *The Divine Milieu*, "God did not come to diminish our splendid responsibility, that of becoming our own self." I possessed the freedom of a child of God. So I was to continue my journey up the Amazon of life, no longer in the "boat" of the Latin American church, but rather in a canoe with Carol as my companion, paddling alongside that church.

Carol had already left her religious community after going through a similar discernment process. Together we looked to a new life together and planned our marriage. Now we started on a different journey up the Amazon River of life. Saying goodbye to our lifelong friends in our religious communities and publicly announcing our decision to family and friends was to be another epic event as we made this major transition.

We both owe a debt of gratitude to the support, the love and the understanding of friends in our respective communities. Obviously, there were others in our communities or the Catholic community at large who did not have the same understanding. For many, our decision was tantamount to a betrayal of faith and a negation of God. You have to come from a traditional Catholic background to fully understand why some people might think this way. We certainly understood their feelings, and accepted the fact that some people would never understand.

Making our decision known to our families and close friends was our next step in this process. Both of us were what might be described as high profile persons within our own communities, in our mission work, and certainly within our Catholic communities of North Bay and Sudbury, our hometowns.

Our decision, while personal, also affected the lives of the people close to us. So we went about announcing our decision both separately and as a couple. In the majority of encounters we received the love and support of family members and friends. Some perhaps did not agree with our decision, but nevertheless accepted us as responsible and faith filled individuals, and were happy for us.

My parents and Carol's father were deceased. It was time to speak to Margaret Spencer, Carol's mother. Carol had frequently visited her mother and family members in Sudbury after her move to Toronto. She had received her mother's support when she had left her community. In November of 1987 Carol had informed her mother of her intention to marry me. A few weeks later we both journeyed to Sudbury to speak with her. Margaret Spencer was a devout and loyal Catholic with a traditional background. I am sure that facing this major announcement at this time in her life was difficult for her. But she received me in a most gracious way, and listened to both of our soul searching stories. Although she came to a greater understanding of those stories in later years, on this occasion she reluctantly gave us her consent and her love. Her one request was that I apply for the required permission from Rome as soon as possible, so that our planned marriage could be blessed by the church. This permission would involve a process called laicization.

Our married life began on March 5, 1988 with the celebration of the Eucharist at our new apartment in the Portuguese area of west-end

Toronto. The marriage ceremony, conducted by a friend, Rev. John McGibbon, a United Church minister, took place at the Hart House Chapel of the University of Toronto. It was a small but special group that gathered to celebrate with us. Several close friends from both our religious communities, Lorne and Norine Devine, and representatives of our families, were with us for this very meaningful occasion. It was special both for Carol and myself to have my sister Geraldine with us. She was making a recovery from her long illness.

Carol and I celebrated our happiness with our friends as another new and exciting stage in our lives began. We flew to Florida to honeymoon with close friends, Joanne and Bob Ling. They too, had stepped away from religious life into marriage a few years prior to us. Carol had worked with Joanne and Bob in the Bahamas.

As a couple we had given close to 70 years of dedicated service to our church and our communities. Now began a new life. Our story, put succinctly, was that we had fallen out of love with the church (but not our faith), and in love with one another.

Many of our friends and family were rightly concerned about our prospects of finding employment in middle age. Thankfully, this was not a major preoccupation for either of us. We had faith that providence would lead us to where we would both find work, sure we would be able to utilize our past experiences and our professional skills.

Carol enrolled in a program for Hospital Chaplains (CAPE), and successfully completed it. As she began a course to further her qualifications, an opportunity opened for her as a chaplain at Sick Childrens' Hospital in Toronto. Good friends, Pat and Bob Michener, helped me prepare a professional resume that I submitted to twenty or so agencies where I felt I could use the expertise in social work that I had gained over the years.

In May of 1988 I was the successful candidate for the position of community development worker for St. Christopher House. St. Christopher House, a social service agency in the downtown core of

Toronto, had been involved in working with new immigrants to Canada for many years.

It was a time of new learning and growth for both of us. Our new positions committed both of us to work with people in areas that were not unfamiliar with past experience. The transition was difficult, but adaptation had always been a part of our lives, and we could count on the support of new professional friends and fellow workers. We grew into the work in the next few years, and gave ourselves to the aims and objectives of our respective employers. Carol, with her pastoral and spiritual experience, quickly proved her worth as a chaplain at Sick Childrens' Hospital.

St. Christopher House, as a community based agency, and with a professional staff dedicated to helping recent immigrants, was an ideal workplace for me. My new colleagues, as professionals in their fields of expertise, broadened my horizons and helped me grow in the field of community development. And, I believe that during the few years that I spent at St. Christopher's my outreach work within the Portuguese community was beneficial both to the people within the community and the overall work of the agency. This new work environment also introduced me to people outside of a religious setting, to people who were motivated to help create conditions for a dignified life for all. I became sensitized, too, to the many problems facing minorities in adapting to a cultural change in their lives in a large urban setting. I was able to sympathize with them as I drew on my own process of adaptation. I remain grateful for the experience at St. Christopher House during my four years with the agency.

These were precious years for both of us as we came to experience life outside the perimeters of religious structures. Our lives together continue to grow in maturity and love. We have gained new perspectives and have been able to meet people without the status of our former lives.

Throughout this new phase in our lives we met new friends, and maintained our contacts with old ones. We joined several groups interested in reform and renewal, and attended faith groups for prayer and reflection. Justice and development issues remain predominant in my life. I worked for seven years, as a volunteer on the Projects Committee for Latin America with Development and Peace, a Catholic lay organization. In this way I maintained my contacts and study with the Brazilian and Latin American churches. I felt that in this way I was able to support and continue the mission vision of the Brazilian church, and the work of my close friend Jorge Marskell in the Amazon. Work with Development and Peace kept me in contact with like-minded colleagues committed to the cause of social justice.

In October of 1988 we discovered, quite by chance, an old home in the town of Hillsdale, north of Barrie. A weekend excursion to take in the fall colours of the maple forests would accidentally offer a new direction to our lives. Within two weeks we had become mortgaged homeowners. Over the next four years we spent holidays and weekends renovating our new home, as we continued with our life and work in Toronto. During this time we rented the house to a young couple who worked with us in making renovations to the old home.

The time of our decision making and planned marriage had involved a lot of emotional and personal trauma. Some incidents are well worth recounting.

Sheila Coe, Carol's twin sister is direct and down to earth. Visiting with her one evening to disclose our planned marriage, she made a pointed remark, "Well, Carol and Mike, welcome to the world! Your leaving will have lots of tongues wagging for a couple of days, and maybe you will shock a few people, but it will all be *passé* within a week."

As the months went by following our marriage, Carol's mother recounted a conversation with an old and close friend from the Catholic community in North Bay. "Well Margaret, it's big news in North Bay at the moment, and I know that it is an adjustment certainly for you. But my dear, their many years of service to the Lord must certainly carry his blessings in their decision and new life. Is not that what our faith would tell us?"

Margaret Casey, a staunch Catholic of the old Irish tradition, was in her eighties. She had been like an aunt to me, and a close friend of my mother's. About six months after our marriage, I received a call from her daughter Joan asking me to contact her mother.

Margaret wanted Carol and I to visit her. So off to Marmora we went to visit with Margaret on the planned weekend. Margaret greeted us at the door of her home and ushered us in. She gave us both a kiss and remarked, "It's nice to see the two of you looking so happy and well. And I want you to know Carol, that I made coats for you and your sister when you were two years of age." With that she settled us in, and served tea and our visit began. At an appropriate moment she indicated to Carol that she had a nice garden that Carol should have a look at, as she wanted to say a few words to me privately. When Carol closed the front door, Margaret put down her teacup and began, "Now young man we can have our talk, and I just want you to know that the news of your leaving the priesthood was not easy for me to accept. If the pope had left to marry, it would not have been a greater shock. But a close friend has been a great support to me. We prayed together for a few days, and that creation story in the Bible kept popping out at me. The Lord himself said it's not good for man to be alone. So Michael I am at peace and happy for the both of you, and you will have Carol to darn your socks and care for you in old age."

In 1996, when I had occasion to visit Itacoatiara again – the place where I had given so much of myself – I had many interesting encounters with old friends. Three of them will always stand out for me.

Eustachio Lobato was an old friend from my Urucara days, and was now living in Itacoatiara. On a visit to his home he and his wife received me warmly. "Miguel, its good to have you back, looking so well and happy. Is your wife with you? When can we meet her, We hope that you are here to live and work with us."

The *Assembleia do povo*, the meeting of the community leaders was held in the little town of Silves on that occasion. This was the parish where I had worked prior to my leaving Brazil. Over two hundred delegates were meeting with their bishop and the pastoral teams that worked with them. As the week's assembly came to a close, I met an old friend from Itacoatiara, Dona Constanca. She was the niece of the former pastor, Father Alcides, whom we had replaced. Constanca had been very involved in church work when we had arrived in the early 1960s. But as our pastoral work evolved over the years she had distanced herself from the church's involvement in justice issues, and was uncomfortable with our frequent conflicts with civil authorities. Protecting her livelihood had influenced her decision. Now retired, she was attending her first assembly meeting as a delegate from Itacoatiara. The meeting had been a revelation to her. "Miguel, I am so happy for you in your marriage, but this week has been such revelation and grace for me. I never would have believed such a meeting possible. I have been humbled by the wisdom and the decisions of these dedicated lay leaders during this assembly. So, both of us have been lately blessed." In her own way Dona Constanca was telling me of her conversion to the vision of the church of the people. She was affirming the work of Dom Jorge, and his belief and conviction that these people were very capable of being masters of their own destiny.

The third incident was an intimate visit with Jorge, the bishop and my long-time friend. Jorge had just returned from his required visit to Rome. He had succeeded in getting my laicization papers while in Rome. As he gave the document to me and told me the story connected with his visit to this Curial Office he voiced his sentiments as well. "Miguel' he said, "you know I've always supported your decision, and I'm happy for you and Carol. I know this is just a piece of paper but it will mean a lot for Carol's mom, and for that I'm happy. But damn it, it puts such finality to your presence here, and you are missed."

There were many other such incidents. Each one conveyed the feelings of loss and grief I experienced in being separated from both my close friends and our shared vision of the church that might have been.

As 1992 approached, the canoe that Carol and I were journeying in was getting ready to explore another river. Attuned as we were to the Latin American scene, and with the 500th anniversary of the discovery of the Americas imminent, we made the decision to make a pilgrimage by truck to Central America. This meant leaving our work. We had also planned a move to Hillsdale when we returned. By mid-January of 1992 our plans had come together and we set out on another adventure.

The trip was to be a pilgrimage to pay homage to the women and men who had given their lives in the last thirty years in attempting to realize the shared vision of a new church and a new society. We would also be showing our solidarity with those who continued to work for that vision in Latin America. It was motivated as well by a strong desire to touch once more our roots as missionaries, roots that had shaped our personal lives, marked our faith, and made us what we are today.

Our pilgrimage journey would take us through the United States and six countries in Central America, south as far as Costa Rica. We travelled 27,359 kilometers. As well as visiting the historical sites of pre-colonial times, we also spent time with priests, religious and laity. We spent nine days in the diocese of Bishop Samuel Ruiz Garcia in Chiapas, Mexico; with the Sisters of Providence (from Kingston, Ontario) in Guatemala; with the Pont Viau Fathers (from Quebec) in Honduras; and with the Jesuits in El Salvador. In Nicarauga we spent Holy Week with Fr. Buddy Smith, my close friend and Scarboro colleague.

The significance of our pilgrimage was highlighted by our time in San Cristobal de las Casas and the villages in Chiapas, Mexico where the church of Bishop Samuel Ruiz was under siege both from the Mexican government and the Roman Curia. We prayed at the graves of Fr. Ignacio Ellacuria and his Jesuit confreres, and the scene of Archbishop Oscar Romero's death in San Salvador. It was our time to speak and to commune with those who had given their lives for justice, and to create a church of the poor. Spending Holy Week with Fr. Buddy Smith on the isle of Ometepe in Nicarauga, reminded me of all that my Society, Scarboro Missions, had understood to be the flowering of the vision of Vatican II and the Medellin Conference of Bishops. It was an example of what, I believe, the Society's mission to Latin America should be.

Our journey was the inner search of two pilgrims; renewing, strengthening and deepening our hope and our faith in the Christ who lives amongst the poor and the dispossessed. It was also an adventure that is a story in itself. We returned home to Canada to begin a new phase in our lives at our home in the little town of Hillsdale, Ontario.

CHAPTER 31

The Question of Celibacy

The psychological and emotional trauma of leaving the active priesthood weighs heavily on most priests who make such a major decision. Such a change affects not only the individual concerned, but also the faith community he has served, his family and the church at large. Although not explicitly stated, in some circles there remains an undercurrent that judges the decision to leave the priesthood as wrong. Certainly the questions involved in the laicization process imply that the person has abandoned his priesthood, that sex has lured him away, and that he is a disobedient son of the church.

The Roman Curia and the Vatican also look upon such a decision as scandalous to the faithful. It gives little credence to the sacredness of the person's individual conscience. The question is seldom asked whether or not the structures of the church are at fault. Yet, more and more ordinary Catholics appreciate the difficulty a person endures when making such a decision of conscience. They recognize that the discipline of celibacy is not integrally connected to the priesthood, that for centuries the Roman Church had married priests (St. Peter was one himself), and that even now the church accepts married Anglican priests into the ministry. Ordinary Catholics are ready for a change; it is Rome who refuses to look at it.

Priests who choose to leave must comply with the Canon Law of the church. Like any institution, the church has its rules and regulations defining membership in the church and the clerical state. Only by going through the process of laicization, and being duly dispensed from Sacred Orders, can a priest continue as a member of the faithful in good standing.

Prior to the 1960s few petitions for laicization were even considered. There was no law that dealt with such a request. In dealing with Sacred Orders or priesthood, Canon Law covers instances where clerics, because of serious crimes can be dismissed, defrocked, or lose their rights to function as clerics. These laws are to safeguard the state of Holy Orders (i.e. the priesthood), the faithful, and the church. Sacred Orders has traditionally been seen by the church as an irrevocable state of life, one is ordained "as a priest forever, according to the order of Melchizedek."

A priest abandoning or leaving his state of life was looked upon as a Judas. I can remember our Canon Law professor stating that the only answer one would receive from Rome if such a petition were made, would be *pereat* that is "let him perish." This was the mindset of the church for many years. It was never ever considered that someone might leave the active priesthood for reasons of conscience. Leaving Sacred Orders meant the person would not be acceptable in the Catholic community, and so he was barred from active membership in the church, in effect, he was excommunicated.

During the pontificate of Pope Paul VI, following Vatican II, when thousands of priests were leaving the ministry, it became apparent that some type of legislation had to be enacted so that these petitions could be dealt with in a more humane and compassionate manner. From the early 1960s to the 1980s over 110,000 priests left the active ministry. With this new legislation, called laicization, a priest (in good conscience as determined by Rome) could be dispensed from the priesthood and returned to the lay state. Having fulfilled this requirement, he could still be in communion with the church. It was clear that the granting of the laicization was not a right of the individual, but an exception to the rule, a dispensation from that rule which was granted by the lawgiver.

The process, even today, is premised on the assumption that the person is denying Sacred Orders or was unfit for ordination in the first place and should not have been ordained. The process has been modified somewhat in these last years, but the bottom line is that there is something seriously wrong morally and psychologically with the individual involved.

In order for the petition to be presented to the proper authorities, the bishop or superior of the individual had to officially make the request. A long, detailed and somewhat offensive questionnaire had to be answered by the priest petitioning for laicization. This had to be accompanied by a letter stating the reasons of conscience for leaving the priesthood. These documents were then sent on to Rome, and one then waited for a reply. The time involved could be anywhere from one to five years, but was normally about eighteen months.

Sensitive to the individual "conscience" in the petitions, many bishops and superiors included the professional testimony of a psychologist or psychiatrist to strengthen the case. These professionals became adept at satisfying the Roman office for such dispensations. In effect they helped the applicant give the answers Rome wanted to hear. These professionals facilitated both an affirmative and a more speedy reply. Of course, there were times when the petitioner compromised his integrity and conscience by signing such documents. But it became the only way to have petitions granted. The church made no distinction between the sacrament of Holy Orders and the discipline of celibacy. This put many priests in the awkward position of having to deny their priestly vocations in order to marry. For this reason, many that leave the priesthood today simply ignore the whole process on the grounds that it is both a violation of their conscience, and bureaucracy at its worst.

I have never denied my priesthood, and continue to reverence and live it in the married state. The superior at Scarboro Missions at the time of my leaving, urged me to apply for laicization. He was also most sensitive and flexible enough to give me the freedom to respond to the questionnaire in the manner that my conscience dictated. I stated in no uncertain terms that I had fully embraced my priesthood, and reverenced the years I spent in active priesthood and mission. I further stated both in the questionnaire and a letter to the pope that my conscience no longer permitted me to represent the church as an active minister because of the direction the hierarchy was taking against the spirit of Vatican II.

In that letter I wrote the following:

> "As a priest and missionary for 33 years, I served the Gospel and the church in mission with fidelity and dedication. My history and experience in mission have led me to request laicization at this stage of my life's journey. As outlined in the enclosed documents, for me to remain in the active priesthood was personally destructive to my faith. For me personally, the right-wing faction and forces of the church, both in the national churches and the Roman Curia, have successfully negated the spirit and directives of the Second Vatican Council. It seems to me that the institution takes precedence over the working of the Spirit and the Gospel imperatives of the Lord Jesus.

> "With renewed zeal and enthusiasm to the challenges of Vatican II, and the future church, I worked with my Society colleagues, the Canadian hierarchy, and the basic Christian communities in the prelacy of Itacoatiara, Amazonas, in Brazil, to make this vision of church a reality. I believe that vision is contained in the concluding statement of the Amazonian bishops' regional meeting of September 1987."

> "REASON FOR BEING CHURCH: We are a church in the midst of a people, martyred and enslaved in a thousand ways. Suffice to reflect on the afflictions, caused by the problems of migration, the problem of land, the indigenous question, problems of youth, the fish problem, ... add to this the uncontrolled manipulation and misuse in the field of communications, ... of

propaganda, of business, of education, and even of religion! What should be the instruments to help the poor raise their heads, are often used to massacre them even more, and to prevent them from organizing, of taking stock of their situation and their rights. Salvation (the project of God) means liberation from all this slavery and a reaching for the Promised Land; a different society, one of justice, love and peace, … with the opportunity of LIFE for all, a sign of the everlasting kingdom." (Excerpt *Documento Final* CNBB norte 1, Manaus, Amazonas 24/09/87.)

In the presentation of my request I was also aware that my status as a former major superior would further complicate matters. Rome was reluctant to grant such dispensations to major superiors. As I sent off my documentation I was aware that it would be a long and slow process. The first petition was sent in early February 1988, another petition followed in May of 1989. I finally received the laicization papers from Rome in July 1996 eight years after the first request had been made.

There are movements in the church today for a married clergy; one of these, a strong world-wide group of married priests called CORPUS advocates that married priests be reinstated in ministry. I still believe strongly in my priesthood and on certain occasions celebrate Eucharist with a faith community. I reverence my priesthood but in no way would I return to active ministry within the church. If the church opened her doors to a married clergy, I still would not return because of the dysfunctional clericalism I see.

♌ ♌

Mark Twain once remarked: "Marriage gives two questioning natures a reason for living, and something to live for; it will give a new gladness to the sunshine, a new fragrance to the flowers, a new beauty to the earth, and a new mystery to life." So in the month of July 1992, back from our pilgrimage to Latin America, we settled into our new home in Hillsdale. Carol and I were now here to stay, to put down roots in the community. We were like two young children, delighted with each other, and with each tiny improvement! Over the next twelve months we tackled each room, cleaning, painting, tiling and wall-papering, making a house our home. As amateur carpenters and renovators each step became a labour of love. During a visit with family one day Carol expressed her excitement at the outcome of our labour. Her brother-in-law Michael teasingly asked, "Well what's so special about the place, its only a house to live in." Carol immediately replied, "No, no it's not; it's our home!"

Our home continues to be special in so many ways. In the Fall of 1992 we officially opened *O'Kanes Bed and Breakfast*. Since that time we have welcomed visitors from near and far. They have been received as sojourners, as pilgrims on a journey like ourselves. They have been embraced in Brazilian fashion – our home is yours, come in and be family! It is aptly put in the New Testament, "Make hospitality your special care." (Romans 12:13)

I have often remarked, with tongue in cheek, that Nicky Hilton won't have many sleepless nights over our business, but it has been a source of income that helps pay bills. We also consider it as a mission, a safe place where people can share their lives with us, and we can share with them. Sharing and caring has in a sense been our motto. And I believe that in this way we have helped and been helped by the many people who come as guests and leave as friends.

Leaving our secure jobs in Toronto was a risk. But where one door closes another opens. Soon Carol was doing supply teaching in the Barrie-Orillia-Midland area. I got work as a Court interpreter in the courts in Bradford and Barrie. Our income was sufficient for our needs. Someone has certainly been looking out for us. We have been blessed in so many ways! Carol and I never cease to be amazed at how our lives have been fulfilled in this little home that has become our refuge and our sanctuary. It is our place where we can express our thanks to the mysterious ways of the divine.

Our property is small, but over the years we have built flower gardens and beautified the exterior of our home. It has been done with a sense of pride, but more importantly it has been to make our home an inviting place for the stranger who comes to our door. When my colleague Dom Jorge Marskell was in the last stages of cancer, far away in distant Itacoatiara, I kept in communion with him by planting and creating a special garden, Jorge's garden! So Jorge and I have our special spot to spiritually commune with each other among his favourite flowers and shrubs.

In 1986 one of the secretaries at the Barrie courthouse, where I served as an interpreter, asked if my marriage registration number was still valid. She encouraged me to have it renewed; there would be a need for marriage officers. Court officials would not be available for this work because of financial cutbacks. So performing non-denominational marriages has become a new mission. I had always thought that the majority of marriage ceremonies took place in a church, synagogue or religious temple. In this work I have discovered that more than a third of marriages now take place outside the traditional religious locale. We have also discovered that many couples have little or no connection with any religious denomination or group.

While we are just marriage officiants, (Carol also obtained her marriage registration in 1998), it is an opportunity to share with couples the spirituality that is part of our lives. At such an important time in their lives couples are often open to speaking of their core beliefs and of their spiritual needs. In this mission we feel that we have been able to help and encourage couples to develop their spiritual lives as individuals, and as a married couple. We are convinced that we reach out to a population that has little or no contact with any church or organized religion.

Our outreach to these couples is limited because they come to us for a marriage ceremony outside of the traditional religious boundaries. At such an intimate and sacred time in the lives of two people, however, we believe that we have the privilege of leaving with them gentle reminders that their lives have a deeper spiritual meaning and purpose.

Our marriage has been a sacred bond and relationship that has helps us grow both as individuals and as a couple. Our intimate friendship has brought a serenity and peace to my restless journeying. Margaret Casey has departed this earthly scene, but I am sure she smiles on both of us. My soul friends, the Devines and their children, feel the 'Padre' is in good hands, so our journey goes on.

Our lives are full and active. We are both able to contribute to the holistic well being of our community by our outreach in several areas. Our faith life is very important to us. We participate in the Eucharistic celebrations at our local parish and we have a small faith community that meets on a monthly basis. My interest in the Latin American church and its struggles is ongoing. And as I look at the 'bark of Peter' and its direction, I keep asking the question, "Peter, is there no longer any place for Paul?"

The quest or crusade for social justice, inspired by faith, has fashioned my life and my journey up the Amazon River of life. My story of that crusade, and the insignificant role I have played, is a very personal story. But it is most importantly the story of the struggle of the marginalized and the poor of Latin America. It is the story of principalities and powers, and the role of religious belief and faith in that struggle.

Each morning as I awake to a new day, I thank my God for life and I wonder why! I know that I still count, that I have our home, that I have my name, and a certain social peace. But what of countless others who do not have these things? With Bishop Pedro Casaldaliga, I ask, "Did God miscalculate when he decided to sow the seed of humanity in one of the planets of his universe; that today 80 percent of his sons and daughters on this beautiful ravaged Earth are superfluous?"

My prayer and my hope is that by sharing my simple story and struggles in these pages, we will never forget the blood of the many martyrs whose lives were given to prevent greater tragedies. We hold the future of the millennium in our hands. Will we passively listen to the God of the global market? Or will each of us who believes in the equality and dignity of each human person, by our personal lives and by our active voice and involvement, make a better world for all God's children and creation! And where will the church of Peter be in all of this?

CHAPTER 32

Latin America and the Vatican

I can remember my enthusiasm and hopes for the Latin American church and the universal church when John Paul II was elected pope in 1979. His life had been deeply influenced and marked by the "mystical" Poland that had lived under the iron hand of communism for so many years. Many felt that this man who had endured such oppression would have an affinity to the plight of Latin Americans. The tragedy and bloodshed, the poverty and marginalization of the people on the Latin American continent, was so similar to the sad tragedy of Polish history; surely this would provide John Paul II with an understanding and openness to the vision of the Council of Medellin, and the pastoral plan of the progressive bishops of Latin America.

The Puebla Conference of the Latin American Bishops had been rescheduled for January of 1979 to coincide with the new pope's visit to the Dominican Republic and Mexico. This meeting between the Vatican Curia and the progressive church of Latin America would provide signals as to the direction of this new Papacy.

Although the progressives put on a brave front, and interpreted both the Puebla documents and the words of Pope John Paul in the most favourable light, the Medellin documents were being rejected or at best ignored. In his book *John Paul II*, (Scribner, 1995), Tad Szula writes of the Puebla meeting and remarks that, "it was a conference of compromise and the vagueness of its documents strengthened the position of Cardinals Baggio and Lopez Trujillo, both adversaries of liberation theology and the conclusions of Medellin." Szula makes the point that in his talks at Puebla the pope never once alluded to the widespread murders and torture so prevalent in Latin American countries.

A concerted effort by a group of conservative forces and their allies in Europe, the Vatican, and the intelligence services of the United States, had launched a successful and vicious propaganda campaign against liberation theology, its theologians and the progressive bishops. They were using the same slogans and propaganda that the power elite and military had used within their respective countries. Gustavo Gutierrez of Peru, the father of liberation theology, was labelled as "an ecclesiastical excuse for violence." Archbishop Oscar Romero was called a "dupe for the communists', just as Archbishop Helder Camara had been before him. Basic Christian communities were "nothing more than cells of communism."

After Pope John Paul II returned to Rome, the progressive bishops and leaders of the Latin American church returned to their respective countries to assess the outcome of the conference. While the conservative forces and the Curia had controlled the agenda, the compromises worked out appeared to offer future opportunity for dialogue and discussion. The pope and Curial officials had refrained from any outright condemnation of liberation theology. That was to come later.

Looking back over the eleven years since the Medellin Conference, most of these church leaders who assembled at Puebla had been the voice of the marginalized masses. They had taken political stands against oppression and tyranny. They had brought the church to the poor. Would this new pope, so familiar with political tyranny, give them their rightful hearing? Even in their cautious optimism and hope, most clearly began to read the handwriting on the wall.

Back in Rome, the Vatican began plans for John Paul II's visit to his Polish homeland. This fiercely anti-Communist pope had suffered personally under communism, and witnessed the years that his people and homeland had been under the yoke of a totalitarian communist regime. He was determined to set Poland free; and as the leader of the Catholic world he would launch a religious and political crusade that would see Karol Wotyla emerge as the undisputed voice and power of the Polish people. Unable to prevent his homecoming, the Polish government acceded to the Vatican plan for a June visit. John Paul II returned to his beloved land and to his brothers and sisters in triumph. Tens of thousands turned out to greet him at every city and town he visited and at every staged event. The country was brought to a standstill. The communist leaders of both Poland and the Soviet Union could only watch in silence as they witnessed the power of the state being transferred to the person of the pope. It was the beginning of the end of communism's stranglehold on Poland. As this historic saga unfolded, Washington's political leaders recognized very quickly that they must make an ally of this political powerhouse who sat on the throne of Peter.

As the world has witnessed, the struggle for freedom and democracy in Poland would be launched by John Paul and his church. It would take eleven years of relentless political and moral pressure by the Vatican and another powerful ally. In late 1990, Lech Walesa, leader of the Solidarity Workers' Movement would be elected President of a free Poland. Pope John Paul II, a loyal son of Poland, had succeeded in his mission. It was a victory for the 'free world' and certainly a laudatory one. But it was also undeniably one that came about through the expressed co-operation between the Vatican and the United States of America. And here is where an inherent contradiction in the personality of John Paul II is so conspicuous. Social analysts, as well as theologians and Vatican watchers, have raised serious questions about this "holy alliance" between the Papacy and the United States government.

Long before Carl Bernstein's sensational article "The Holy Alliance" appeared in the February 24, 1992 issue of *Time* magazine, a courageous lady by the name of Penny Lernoux had written about the issue in her books *Cry of the People* and *The People of God*. Lernoux, as the Bogota-based correspondent for the *National Catholic Reporter*, had been covering the political and church scene in Latin America for many years. Bernstein's article covers in detail the collusion between the Vatican and the Reagan administrations to bring about the freedom of Eastern Europe from the communists. Bernstein's article and his book *His Holiness: John Paul II and the History of Our Time* (Doubleday Publishing, New York, 1996), clearly exposes in great detail this alliance between the papacy and the American government.

According to Bernstein's *Time* magazine article, it all began when President Ronald Reagan met with the pope in the Vatican library on June 7, 1992. In this "Alliance", Washington and the Vatican would join hands to keep the Solidarity Movement alive in Poland. Solidarity was a labour movement that had been outlawed by the Polish government. Over the next seven years the CIA would back the movement with financial aid ($50 million), with equipment and intelligence reports, and with ongoing advice. In his report, Bernstein quotes Ronald Reagan as saying, "Solidarity was the very weapon for bringing this about because it was an organization of labourers in Poland."

According to Bernstein, "the key (US) administration officials were all devout Roman Catholics, CIA chief William Casey, Richard Allen, Judge William Clark, Alexander Haig, Vernon Walters, and William Wilson". All of these men were also heavily involved in USA operations in Latin America.

In the following years Vernon Walters and William Casey would visit the pope, and/or his advisers fifteen times. In Washington, both William Casey and William Clark would be frequent visitors at the residence of Cardinal Pio Laghi, the Apostolic delegate to the United States, and former Nuncio to Argentina during the "Dirty War." And the back door of the White House was always open for Laghi's visits. Richard Allen was quoted as saying, "the Reagan/Vatican relationship was one of the greatest recent alliances of all time." Ronald Reagan had achieved what he had set out to do on hearing of John Paul II's election to the Papacy, to "make an ally of the church."

William Casey was to become the principal policy architect as the Solidarity Movement went underground. According to Tad Sula, the CIA's code name in this Vatican relationship was the *Entity*. Casey was the principal kingpin as well in CIA operations in Latin America. By 1981 the CIA under Colonel Oliver North was secretly funding the established church. Funding and training were also being provided for 4,000 ex-Somoza soldiers as Contras. Casey was also active in promoting the pope's visit to Nicaragua, that the Reagan administration favoured. They wanted to embarrass the progressive church leaders as well as the Sandinistas. And, as the plan took shape for the pope's visit, both Vice President Bush and Secretary of State William Schultz spoke publicly about what they described as Catholic support for Marxist revolutionary movements in Central America (Bernstein and Politi, *His Holiness John Paul II*, Doubleday, 1996.)

In the pursuit of this "Holy Alliance" *Time* magazine reported that the Reagan administration, in response to concerns of the Vatican, altered its foreign aid program to comply with church teaching on birth control. American aid funds to international health organizations or countries that promoted birth control were cut off.

There are several incidents that reveal the Vatican's campaign against the church of Medellin, following the Puebla conference.

The first incident involved the treatment of Archbishop Oscar Romero by the Roman Curia. In May of 1979 Cardinal Edward Cassidy had met Romero briefly in Rome. He found Romero depressed and realized that he was under suspicion and not trusted by Rome. Romero had been made to wait six weeks before he got in to see the pope. (Edward Stourton, *Absolute Truth*, Penguin Books, 1998, p.127.) As Jesuit theologian and fellow Salvadoran Jon Sobrino tells us "he (Romero) did not find understanding with the pope; with no support he was an outsider. Rome takes life for granted, but here in Latin America that is not the case."

A few months later a Roman *visitator* was appointed to investigate the Archdiocese of San Salvador and its Archbishop. Oscar Romero was shot to death on March 24, 1980. His funeral on March 28 witnessed the largest religious gathering in El Salvador's history. The army that had betrayed him in life, shamefully disrupted his funeral, by shooting off guns that terrorized the people present at the funeral of their slain pastor. On the first anniversary of his death, thousands of people throughout the world gathered in their churches and public places to remember Oscar Romero, but Rome and the pope were silent. A few short years ago, the current Archbishop, Fernando Saenz, accepted the rank of Chaplain General of the very army that had ignored a man crying for peace.

As Leonardo Boff said regarding his experience with Roman authorities, "My personal experience of dealings over the last twenty years with doctrinal power is this: it is cruel and without pity. It forgets nothing, forgives nothing, it exacts a price for everything...." (Penny Lernoux, *People of God*, Penguin Books, 1990, pp.107-110.)

Then in the early 1980s, the Vatican began to focus on the Jesuit Order. Throughout the years following Vatican II and the Conference of Medellin, the Jesuits had enthusiastically embraced the new vision of church and the "preferential option for the poor." Leaving their historical role as educators of the Christian elite of Latin America, their resources and expertise were redirected to their local churches. Their priests and brothers were on the front lines of pastoral and basic Christian communities. Endorsing liberation theology, Fr. Pedro Arrupe, their Superior General, strongly supported his colleagues' involvement in this church of the poor. In each of the countries of Latin America during the 1960s to the 1980s the Jesuits worked hand-in-hand with the local bishops, priests and other religious of this progressive church.

During the mid-1970s they were the subject of investigation by Archbishop Lopes Trujillo, later the Cardinal of Medellin, Colombia. With allies like Cardinal Sebastiao Baggio in Rome, President of the Pontifical Commission for Latin America, Trujillo wanted the Social Research centres of the Jesuits closed down. By 1981 the Jesuit centre in Bogota and its chief publication was condemned by the bishops of Colombia.

The use of Marxist analysis was the underlying cause of the dispute. Arrupe, after consulting with sixty-eight Jesuit experts on the issue, wrote his famous letter "On Marxist Analysis." Arrupe was firm in his rejection of Marxism as a doctrine, and even as an exclusive method of analysis. "To adopt therefore not just some elements or some methodological insights, but Marxist analysis as a whole, is something we cannot accept." This was not good enough for Lopes Trujillo, who perhaps was stung by Arrupe's rhetorical question: "Have we not often seen the forms of anti-communism that are nothing but means for concealing injustice?"

In June 1981, at a meeting of the Pontifical Commission for Latin America, the Jesuits were accused of being Marxist, and Fr. Jon Sobrino, the Salvadoran theologian, was personally blamed for inventing the term the "Popular church" which was at odds with the hierarchy. Arrupe defended his men as he always did. Two months later Pedro Arrupe suffered a stroke that left him paralyzed and unable to talk. (Peter Hebblethwaite, *National Catholic Reporter*, 15/01/91.)

Arrupe had earlier offered his resignation to the pope so that a new superior general could be elected, but John Paul II had turned him down. No official explanation had been given at the time, but many Vatican watchers felt that John Paul II did not want a couple of hundred Jesuits in Rome offering a different analysis of the needs of the church from his own. And he did not want another Arrupe as head of the Jesuits. Now that Arrupe was unable to continue as General of the Order, John Paul II accepted his resignation. Fr. Vincent O'Keefe became Vicar general until a congregation chapter and elections could elect a successor to Arrupe.

In an unprecedented move, John Paul II suspended the Jesuit Constitution, sacked Fr. Vincent O'Keefe, and appointed Fr. Paolo Dezza, an eighty year old Jesuit, as his personal representative to run the Society. Dezza was assisted by Fr. Giuseppe Pittau, a provincial superior from Japan. Rome's contention was that the Jesuits were "causing confusion among the people of God." As Tad Szula noted, "they had crossed over into the social and political order."

Not long before his stroke Pedro Arrupe had said: "We are about to offer yesterday's answer to address tomorrow's problems, ... that we are talking in such a way that people no longer understand us, using a language that does not go to the heart of men and women. If that is the case then we will talk a great deal, but only to ourselves.... No one will be listening anymore, no one will grasp what we are trying to say." (Bernstein & Politi, *His Holiness John Paul II*)

On October 6th, 1981 Cardinal Agostino Casaroli, Secretary of State, arrived at the Jesuit residence, went straight to Arrupe's sickroom, and read the papal letter informing him he was no longer Superior General. This news, communicated in such an uncharacteristic way by Casaroli, so apparently brutal and unnecessary, left Arrupe in tears. This was Arrupe's darkest hour; it was a judgement on his leadership, his policies, and the team of Jesuits he had gathered about him. On October 31st, the official changeover took place.

Two years later in 1983 at their 33rd chapter, Fr. Peter Hans Kolvenbach was elected to succeed Arrupe. Kolvenbach was to prove a worthy successor of Arrupe and to continue his policies. Rome had apparently underestimated the Jesuits. Paolo Dezza and Giuseppe Pittau had successfully filled the void left by the absence of Arrupe and O'Keefe. The Jesuits had simply got on with their work without protest or mass resignations. Fr. Pedro Arrupe died on February 5th, 1991. (Peter Hebblethwaite, *National Catholic Reporter*, 15/02/91.)

∞∞

The Jesuits marked the tenth anniversary of their six Jesuit confreres who had been murdered in El Salvador in 1989 along with their housekeeper and her daughter, with commemoration ceremonies at Jesuit colleges and campuses. Fr. Jon Sobrino offered a sombre analysis of developments in those last ten years, at the University of Notre Dame on October 12,1999.

"The dominant impression today is that the majority of churches, both pastors and faithful, are turning back to the past. This church no longer hears the voice of the poor majorities, listening rather to that of its traditional public, those who go to Mass. Notwithstanding a flood of words and documents, many of them good, we have gone from a church of the poor, dedicated utopianly to their defence, and prophetically to the denunciation of their oppressors, to a church that pendulum-wise, would seek to get back to normality, to harmony with the powers of this world." (*National Catholic Reporter*, 19/11/99.)

Sobrino ended his talk on a hopeful note, quoting his friend, Ignacio Ellacuria, one of the six Jesuits killed: "All the blood of the martyrs shed in El Salvador and in all of Latin America, far from plunging us into discouragement and despair, instils a new spirit of struggle and new hope in our people. In this sense, even if we are not a 'new world' or a 'new continent', we are clearly and verifiably… a continent of hope. This is an extremely important symptom of a future society in contrast with other continents that have no hope, that have only fear."

CHAPTER 33

Brazil and the Vatican

In May of 1981 the Vatican initiated a campaign against the Brazilian Conference of Bishops. A harsh papal letter admonished the bishops to stay out of politics. The Brazilian Conference of Bishops was the largest in all of Latin America. It was also viewed as one of the most progressive. Following the Medellin Conference it became a prophetic voice, reading the "signs of the times" for the poor of the continent. It had become the social conscience of the nation. It had also been involved in a long struggle with the Vatican over recognizing the rights of local churches. Slowly but surely Rome began to dismantle the Brazilian Conference. As Francis McDonagh writes: "The Conference gained international renown as the model for socially aware Conferences. The Bishops' Conference had argued its case from religious and theological terms. The Conference had advocated liberation theology. The theological models coming from the Brazilian church were reaching further around the world, and the Brazilian bishops became one of the most prominent forces fomenting the Vatican II tenets of social commitment and openness." (McDonagh, *National Catholic Reporter*, 02/06/95.)

Within the Brazilian hierarchy there were pockets of opposition to the progressive church led by two staunch conservatives, Cardinal Eugenio Sales of Rio de Janeiro and Cardinal Vincent Scherer of Porto Alegre. They had a strong ally in Rome, the Brazilian Archbishop Lucas Moreira Neves, who served as secretary for the Congregation of Bishops in the 1980s.

In 1984 Dom Helder Camara, the much loved and charismatic bishop of Olinda-Recife in northeast Brazil, reached the mandatory age of retirement. As Gary MacEoin wrote of Camara, "He was a brilliant thinker and one of the Catholic Church's most inspired and charismatic leaders of the 20th century. Under his moral leadership the Catholic Church in Latin America moved from its traditional support of the wealthy landowners and business elite to a preferential option for the poor." (*National Catholic Reporter*, 10/09/99.)

MacEoin quoted some of Camara's observations. Two weeks before the end of Vatican II in 1965, Dom Helder had summed up what he and his fellow bishops had reflected upon.

> "Almost 2000 years after the death of Christ, at a time when the Declaration on Religious Liberty is to be promulgated nearly two-thirds of the human race live in a sub-human condition that makes it impossible for them to understand the true meaning of liberty.... Underdevelopment has plunged Latin America and the whole Third World into a situation unworthy of the human person. It constitutes an insult to creation. A revolt by Latin American Christians against the church is inevitable if the church sins today by omission, in an hour of oppression and slavery."

And again Camara stated,

> "The church must speak clearer and louder to the rich and the powerful. They often mistake a stratified disorder for law and public order....The church should encourage the use of lawful non-violence, a democratic political pressure. The social revolution necessary in Latin America presupposes a social revolution in North America; there is a problem of justice in the relation between a developed and an underdeveloped world....The church should stop thinking that this implies an intrusion into politics, realizing rather that

it is her duty, because it deals with the common good
and relates directly to world peace."

It was ironic that this man of the poor was to be replaced by a Roman canon lawyer, Dom Jose Cardoso Sobrinho, who came to the archdiocese with the mission of "putting the house in order." Cardoso said that his mandate was from Rome. This, it would seem, is what Rome thought of Archbishop Helder Camara and his life's work for the poor! It was also a direct and blunt message to the Brazilian Conference of bishops.

Fr. Tony Terry, an Irish missionary and colleague who worked in Camara's Archdiocese commented on Cardoso's first years in Recife; "I feel the man has not the ability to deal with priests (72 of the 98 priests in Recife had written to Rome asking for Cardoso's removal)...We feel that he is a forerunner of a line that the Vatican is trying to impose on the Latin American church. He is one of 38 bishops appointed recently who are following a line laid down in the Vatican, of a church without any preferential option for the poor." (Edward Stourton, *Absolute Truth*, Penguin Books, 1999, p. 146.)

Archbishop Helder Camara died on August 27, 1999 at the age of ninety. During the years of the military dictatorship he was forbidden to speak in public; in retirement he had been forbidden by the church to speak. In silence, he looked on as his pastoral plan for the poor was systematically destroyed, as various pastoral groups were disbanded, and his seminary and various pastoral institutes shut down.

As well as the other conservative appointment to dioceses in Brazil mentioned by Terry, the Vatican in 1987 appointed Lucas Moreira Neves as Archbishop of Salvador in Bahia State, and primate of Brazil. Neves had Roman credentials, 13 years in Rome as vice president of the Pontifical Council for the laity, and as secretary of the powerful Congregation for bishops. He became "the pope's man in Brazil." Neves had long been a steadfast opponent to the work of the Brazilian Conference of Bishops, and an ally of Sales and Sherer in their opposition to liberation theology. About the same time Dom Luciano

Mendes de Almeida, the President of the bishops conference, was relegated to the distant diocese of Mariana in the state of Minas Gerais.

Dom Mauro Morelli, the outspoken Bishop of Duque de Caxias, one of the poorest Brazilian dioceses, in southern Rio de Janeiro state, commented on the tense relationship between the Vatican and the church in Brazil at the time.

> "I'm hopeful, at least there is mutual understanding. But the church has some structural problems, and unless these are changed we can expect no real peace in the church. I believe the Vatican state is an obstacle, not just for other churches (national), but for ourselves. Let's face it, it is a world power. For me, the Papal nunciatures are not the expressions of the Gospel. They are the long arm the Vatican uses to control everything. The church cannot compete with the world; it cannot take two positions. It has to be consistent. The church (as state) deals with faith and diplomacy, but the way diplomacy is understood, it is incompatible with the Gospel." (*Latin American Press*, 16/10/86.)

In the Sao Paulo Archdiocese, Cardinal Evaristo Arns, another apostle of the poor, had seen his archdiocese divided into seven autonomous dioceses to lessen his effectiveness. Arns was quoted in the newspaper *Estado de Sao Paulo* as saying, "The pope appears to have placed the destiny of the church with the Curia; my impression is that the curia is governing the church; it has greater autonomy now than under Paul VI." (04/09/96) Arns is quoted as saying that in an audience with John Paul II, he once remarked, "I like you as a person but you give the Curia a free rein", to which the pope replied "You are mistaken, the Curia is the pope."

Awaiting a successor, Arns went on to say, "I would suffer greatly to see the destruction of everything I had worked for these last 25 years, alongside the people and priests of the archdiocese."

Celebrating his last public Mass as Archbishop of Sao Paulo in May of 1998, Cardinal Arns made the following remarks during his homily; "The church must make itself more visible, sometimes taking a political position to aid those in need..... The Catholic Church has not only stagnated, but is in regression."

The break up of the progressive Brazilian conference of bishops had taken Rome less than ten years. Archbishop Lucas Moreira Neves, the pope's man in Brazil became the President of the National Conference of Bishops in 1995; and the curtain came down on the progressive wing of the Brazilian church. The Vatican's assault on the Brazilian church would see the silencing of Fr. Leonardo Boff, and the investigation of his writings on liberation theology and the church. Bishop Pedro Casaldaliga of Sao Felix de Araguai in Mato Grosso de Norte also came under investigation in 1987.

The progressive churches in other Latin American countries met with the same fate. Rome had proclaimed "that the church cannot be exclusively occupied with the poor, pastoral care for the leading sectors of society has been neglected in key areas such as politics, the military, unions, etc.– the evangelization of these leaders is the best antidote to corruption."

Under this shadow of suspicion and distrust the church of the poor labours on in Brazil and the rest of Latin America. The Landless Peasant Movement that was given birth under church auspices has grown nationally, and is a force within the political scene in Brazil. Thousands of basic Christian communities attempt to carry on their work.

In Chiapas, Mexico, in the diocese of San Cristobal de las Casas, Bishop Samuel Ruiz Garcia has worked with the indigenous peoples for thirty-five years. Over the last years he has been a special target of the Mexican government, and the Vatican as well. He has been under investigation by the curia, and the former nuncio to Mexico, Archbishop Prignone, had attempted to have him removed from his diocese. Close to retirement Ruiz had withstood attacks on his pastoral and his orthodoxy.

At a conference in Milwaukee, Wisconsin, Jim Loney from Toronto interviewed Ruiz for the *Catholic New Times* (28/11/99). Loney asked Ruiz to comment on the profound divide in the church, when on the one hand there is a church that accompanies and protects the interests of the rich, and on the other a church that accompanies the poor in their struggles for justice. Before Loney finished his question Ruiz interrupted him and responded, "I cannot accept that we have two churches.... the church that is not for the poor is not for Jesus Christ." Ruiz added: "the only question that one must answer at the end of our lives is this: Were you visiting me when I was in jail? Were you giving me food when I was hungry? The final question is not from orthodoxy, but from practice."

A few years ago, my colleague Dom Jorge Marskell, being interviewed by a team filming the pastoral work of Dom Jorge and the Scarboro Missions in Itacoatiara, expressed his pastoral approach in this way: "The majority of the people in this area of the Amazon live under unjust living and economic conditions. The message of the church must be that you have dignity, you have value as sons and daughters of God."

On basic Christian communities, Marskell commented, " A basic Christian community is not just a pastoral method or an instrument or tactic of the church. It is a way of being church, people living and working together, celebrating their faith together and assuming their mission as Christians; they are the salt of the earth, the ferment that Jesus speaks of, to bring the values of the gospel into all walks of their lives."

"The church's mission is to transform society. Human life is politics. You cannot separate faith from life. The political and economic structures that are evil have to be addressed. My role as bishop", Marskell observed, "is to animate these people in their faith, to walk with them in their joys and their difficulties. I hope to see the day when people have enough to eat, just salaries, better working conditions, title to their lands; because that is what God wants, fullness of life for all people."

Jorge Marskell died of cancer on July 2nd,1998, having spent thirty-one years living and working with his people in the Itacoatiara region of the Amazon. He was a true bishop of his people, a shepherd who walked with them. His pastoral commitment and his life as a missionary and bishop had taken on "the preferential option for the poor." But that pastoral stance never excluded anyone from his embrace! Eighteen months after the death of Dom Jorge Marskell his successor arrived in Itacoatiara. As happened in Olinda-Recife, the dismantling of this church of the Poor began immediately. The pastoral plan and vision of the prelacy was dismantled and abandoned. Pastoral agents, priests, religious and lay, were summarily dismissed. *Centrepi*, the training centre was closed. The actions of the new bishop and clergy, who came to the prelacy with him, were scandalous, yet not surprising.

The following is a summary of a critical analysis of the Vatican's policies in Brazil under John Paul II, that appeared in the *National Catholic Reporter* newspaper in July, 2003. The author, Father Jose Comblin, is a theologian of international repute. He resides in Joao Pessoa, Paraiba, Brazil.

> "For Latin America, the pontificate of John Paul II, began under the seal of restoration. From Rome's point of view, the church in Latin America had to be freed from two evils: liberation theology and basic Christian communities with their new way of reading the Bible. Liberation theology was treated as if it were the synthesis of all heresies. Basic Christian communities were discredited, treated with suspicion and finally suppressed in most dioceses.

> "The basic goal of this restoration was a return to the Council of Trent, limiting the role of the laity and restoring full authority to the clergy, a return to clericalism. To complete this restoration program, Rome had to repress and control the institutions and groups that were the bearers of a new message based

on Vatican II. This program has succeeded by making both the Latin American Bishops' Conference and the Religious Conference irrelevant and ineffective bodies.

- All appointees as bishops have been completely submissive to the authority of the Holy See, and have no social commitment or option for the poor.

- New appointees had as their mission, to destroy anything their predecessors had accomplished. One can only imagine how many human and pastoral dramas were the result of these destructive successions.

- All conservative lay movements now endorsed by Rome (such as Folkolare, Comunione e liberatione, Opus Dei, etc.), have been efficient in the restoration of clericalism, because they are based on a personality cult, the cult of the priest.

- Priests today are more concerned with their priestly identity. This identity has to be affirmed and strengthened constantly.

- Whereas there was one priest for every 10,000 Catholics 50 years ago, despite all the vocation drives, today there is one priest for every 11,000; and this new breed of priests are completely ignorant of what the church was, and did in the 1960s and 1970s.

- The supplanted social vision of the Medellin church by this Vatican process, explains the passivity of the church as it faces social and human disasters caused by the neo-liberal system adopted in all of Latin America. The poor in Latin America now face a crisis worse than we have ever seen.

- The church is greatly responsible for the increase in social inequalities, for unemployment, for the misery that the majority live in, for the unjust distribution of wealth among workers, and for the progressive disappearance of all the socially positive laws passed in the last half century." (Fr. Jose Comblin, *National Catholic Reporter*, Global Perspectives, on-line edition, 02 and 09/07/2003.)

As well as the church in Latin America, the universal church has been reshaped these last twenty years into a church based on authority, discipline, power and orthodoxy. As an editorial in the *National Catholic Reporter* (17/06/88) points out, "the policy of this pontificate has been increasingly one of restoration; what is being restored is the papal monarchy as conceived by Vatican I, in 1870."

Even closer to home, the Vatican's change of policy on social justice has also had an effect on the Canadian church.

In August of 1987 a classmate and friend, Bishop Adolphe Proulx of Gatineau-Hull died suddenly from diabetic complications. At his funeral, Bishop Bernard Hebert, the president of the Catholic Conference of Canadian Bishops was the homilist. In his homily Hebert spoke of Adolphe being a holy man and a model bishop because he had practised the preferential option for the poor in his pastoral work. Several lay leaders representing various diocesan groups spoke in similar fashion. At the end of the funeral rite, the apostolic delegate to Canada, Archbishop Angelo Palmas, pointedly corrected Hebert by saying that Proulx was a good bishop because he practised "the preferential *love* of the poor." "The church", he said, "loves the poor as well as the rich. Yet the poor whose needs are the greatest, have a prior claim on the church's love. They have the urgent need for the church's help." As the Vatican's representative, he was putting a new and paternalistic interpretation to the intent of Medellin.

In the following years many, if not all the social justice offices in the Catholic dioceses, were closed because of a "lack of funds."

In any human institution, there are a multitude of voices on how that institution best achieves its aims and objectives, often at variance with one another. When that institution is the church, which possesses what it believes is a divine mandate with centuries of tradition, the situation becomes even more complex. There is most certainly a role for Peter as teacher and guide, but there is also a role for Paul who ventures out into new territory. My hope is that both roles are guided by the presence of the Spirit. At times it is easier to perpetuate the false myth that the church has carried the same unchangeable truth down through the centuries. Some truths are unchangeable, but the fact is that not all truths carry the same weight, and how these doctrines and beliefs are understood has often changed throughout the long history of the church.

As I sit here in my canoe at the fork of the river, I cannot help but reflect on "the bark of Peter" as it journeys up a different river. And my reflection brings a host of questions.

- Where is the Spirit of God in all of these latter years of church history?
- Where is the voice of Paul in today's church?
- Was the captain of the "bark of Peter", in the person of Pope John XXIII, completely lost in fog. Did he completely lack navigational skills to plot a new direction for his church?
- Were the lieutenants on the "bark of Peter", with direct approval of their captain, 'lost at sea', in their Latin American crusade for justice and human rights, for the passengers onboard?

As I continue my reflections the following questions cry out for answers.

- Was the thrust and pastoral orientation of the Council of Medellin less gospel-oriented than the political collusion of the Vatican, in its' efforts to rid Poland and the world from the evils of communism?
- Was the Vatican's policy of moving away from the pastoral practice of the Latin American church, motivated only from religious conviction, or was it a political exchange given for another religious option in Eastern Europe?

- Were not the political and military alliances of American foreign policy aligned with the dictatorships and oligarchies of Latin America, every bit as ruthless and anti-gospel as communism?

- Did not the entering into an alliance with American foreign policy, and subsequently rejecting the pastoral practice of the whole Latin American church, indicate the willingness of the Vatican to condone the underhanded methods and bloodshed inflicted on civilian populations that took place in implementing that American policy?

- Were the uprisings of guerrilla forces throughout Latin America not due in large part to the economic exploitation of the continent by American capitalists?

- Did not the church of Medellin in the person of its prophetic leadership not preach an evangelising message to all of its citizens, its politicians, the military, the elite as well as the poor? Was that message not in line with the social encyclicals of the church, and recent papal encyclicals of John XXIII, Paul VI, and even the present pope?

- Did not the prophetic leadership of Medellin, speak to its neighbour to the north regarding the social problems inherent in that Latin American society. "The social revolution necessary in Latin America presupposes a social revolution in North America; there is a problem of justice in the relation between a developed and underdeveloped world" (Dom Helder Camara).

During the papacy of Pope John Paul II a good number of cardinals and bishops who followed the conclusions of the Medellin Conference, have been investigated for orthodoxy, and in many instances totally marginalized by Rome. Yet to this day I have yet to read or hear of those church leaders who collaborated with the leaders of the "dirty war" in Argentina or Chile being subject to any scrutiny or even reprimand.

- Were the poor and the dispossessed of the Latin American continent not betrayed by the universal church and her reactionary leaders?

- Does not the church of John Paul II, and his clerical advisers, resemble in many ways the totalitarian Polish government that John Paul worked to free the Polish people from?

- Does not that church today embrace movements within, such as Opus Dei, Communione e Liberatione, Folkolare, the Neo-Catechumenate and the Legionaries of Christ. All these religious groups are reactionary, secretive, elitist, and are the antithesis of what John XXIII called for when he convened the Second Vatican Council.

As I sit in my canoe in this huge river of the world, I recognize that I am but a small player in this whole historical and religious saga. But I have been a player. Just as tiny Amazonian frogs croak their right to be alive, and contribute to the symphony of frogs around them, so am I called to proclaim the truth as I see it! After all, it is my church too. In fact, it is our church – the church of the People of God.

I end these pages with a prayer of faith and hope, from a reflection by one of Latin America's most famous martyrs, Archbishop Oscar Romero, who was assassinated in San Salvador, March 24, 1980.

CREATING THE CHURCH (and a World) OF TOMORROW

It helps, now and then, to step back and take a long view.
The kingdom is not only beyond our efforts,
It is even beyond our vision.
We accomplish in our lifetime only a tiny
    fraction of the magnificent enterprise that is God's work.

Nothing we do is complete, which is a way of
Saying that the Kingdom always lies beyond us.
No statement says all that could be said.
No prayer fully expresses our faith.
No confession brings perfection.
No pastoral visit brings wholeness.
No program accomplishes the church's mission.
No set of goals and objectives includes everything.

This is what we are about.
We plant the seeds that one day will grow.
We water seeds already planted,
    knowing that they hold future promise.

We lay foundations that will need further development.
We provide yeast that produces far beyond our capabilities.

We cannot do everything,
    and there is a sense of liberation in realizing that.
This enables us to do something, and to do it very well.
It may be incomplete, but it is a beginning,
    a step along the way,
    an opportunity for the Lord's grace to enter
    and do the rest.

We may never see the end results,
    but that is the difference between
    the master builder and the worker.

We are workers, not master builders;
    ministers not messiahs.

We are prophets of a future not our own.

Amen.

APPENDIX

A Short History of Latin America
and the Church's Involvement in that History

Latin America

In the following pages I want to retell the history of Latin America, which has become so much a part of my life, and show how the church was enmeshed in that history. This was the history that set the course and direction of my journey. In the recounting of this history, my other objective is to provide those who read *Beyond Our Vision* a political and religious context for the book. I invite you, to walk with the poor and the dispossessed of Latin America in the turbulent years of the last half of the 20th century.

Bear in mind that Latin America had been traditionally Catholic since the colonial times of Spain and Portugal. The elite were the sons and daughters of the church, educated in the finest Catholic institutions. Historically, the church had always been aligned with the economic and political powers, and was, for the most part, a church that upheld the status quo.

My personal journey as a missionary priest in Brazil never required of me, the torture, prison or death that hundreds of fellow missionaries endured. This was the plight not only of religious and priests, but also of thousands of lay people. But in my heart, I believe I walked with them in solidarity.

While Latin America has gained her independence from its Spanish and Portuguese colonial masters, the results of colonialization and a new form of tyranny still exist in the lives of some 320 million people. A democratic political and civil life, as we understand and experience them, simply do not exist for the vast majority of its citizens.

At the time that Latin America was "discovered", there were 3 million indigenous people living in Latin America. The Spanish and Portuguese considered these people as less than human. They were used as beasts of burden, mere slaves to their imperial masters with no rights. They were often the victims of mass genocide, tyranny and brutality.

Eight to ten million Africans came to Latin America as slaves to toil in the mines and the sugar fields. The colonial masters were there to exploit the riches, and send them home to Portugal and Spain. When emancipation finally came for these millions of Africans they joined their indigenous brothers and sisters on the margins of Latin American society. Aside from a few hard earned concessions, over the years these peoples and their descendants never became a part of mainstream life that was the automatic birthright of the elite.

Imperial decree created the masters of society as it doled out land grants to the white minority. Justice systems slowly evolved in Latin America, but the 'strongman' and his army kept the masses in subservience through murder, torture, and intimidation. Local or regional strongmen controlled peasant workers and their families for their patrons or overlords. In the northeast of Brazil they were known as the *captains*, made famous in the stories of the Brazilian novelist Jorge Amado. These *captains* and their families emerged over the years into oligarchies and dynasties in many Latin American countries.

Where universal suffrage was introduced in the last century in some of these countries, the uneducated masses became tools for the local, municipal, and state elections. These elections were marked by false promises, intimidation and fear. Populist mayors, governors, and presidents were elected by the poor and uneducated. It was always the poor person's hope to elect a saviour who would look benignly on their plight.

In a general way, in most Latin American countries this is the way the electoral process evolved. Only within the last forty years was the general populace allowed to organize in such a way as to elect their own political leaders; those who would represent the economic realities they faced. But the real power over political leaders, even to this day, resides in the hands of the military. The influx of immigrants from Europe has helped the political process to become more democratic, but immigration also brought new masters with whom the subjugated masses had to contend. When we speak of the masses we speak of 320 million people in the 1960s, living in what has been described as the "dark ages" by Dom Helder Camara.

I would like now to focus on some of the countries of Latin America and their history. This will provide a better understanding of why the Medellin Conference and the progressive church spoke out regarding the economic and social reality of these countries. Another important factor resides in the fact that while all of these countries gained independence from their colonial masters, they came to be the colonies of their superpower neighbour, the United States of America. The presence and power of the American military in Panama, Guatemala, the Dominican Republic, and Nicaragua is not something new. It goes back almost a hundred years. During the Cold War, and with Fidel Castro and the communists in Cuba, the watchdog tactics of the United States became even more obsessive.

While the American presence has been a strong one, we cannot say the same for objective news coverage. Until the signing of the North American Free Trade agreement a few years ago, only a very few newspapers and magazines kept their readership informed as to what was happening south of the border. The facts of the following summary are well documented, and have been reported by a number of reputable foreign correspondents in both the secular and religious press.

The Dominican Republic

Many of my colleagues worked in the Dominican Republic. The Scarboro Mission Society retained an active mission there since 1943. This presence provides a first hand look at life under a Latin American dictatorship.

In these last twenty years, the Dominican Republic has become a mecca for American and Canadian tourists, who mingle in a transitory way with the 3.5 million Dominicans. The island of Hispanola is shared by the Dominicans with their Haitian neighbours. The Dominican coastline from north to south is dotted with luxury hotels, fabulous beaches, and professional first class golf courses. Santo Domingo, its capital, is the reputed burial place of Christopher Columbus who sailed to the island in 1492. The old city, the first in the New World, still has that ancient Spanish aura, history and architecture.

The Dominican people have charmed their holiday seekers from North America with their hospitality and friendliness. To the average Canadian the Republic is known as the home of many baseball stars. It is looked upon as an exotic winter holiday island, a tropical paradise of swaying palm trees and sun soaked beaches. Many Canadians would be unaware that this beautiful haven for tourists was a living hell for the majority of Dominicans up until a few short years ago.

In 1918, the United States Marines who were present on the island to ensure social stability, recruited a quick-witted young hoodlum by the name of Raphael Leonidas Trujillo Molinas into the National Guard. By the time the U.S. Marines had left the island in 1924 Trujillo had taken over the military. In 1930 Trujillo led a coup that overthrew the President, Horacio Vasquez, and installed himself as President. For the next 31 years Trujillo was to reign as one of the bloodiest dictators in the Southern Hemisphere. He was aided and abetted in his absolute control of the Dominican people by the United States of America. Cordell Hull, a former American Secretary of State was to refer to Trujillo as "that son of a bitch, but he is our son of a bitch."

Trujillo created a culture of political and civil tyranny and violence. He spent between $5 and $7 million annually on security. He ruled as a despot instilling fear and terror in the lives of Dominicans. *La Victoria* and *La Quarenta*, his prisons, became infamous as his private torture chambers. In 1937 he massacred 20,000 Haitian cane workers; it was simply the cheapest and most efficient way to get rid of them. From his well-equipped and trained army he selected an elite core of trainees to form his Secret Service. His most famous hit man and Secret Service agent was one Johnny Abbes Garcia. Garcia upgraded *La Victoria* and *La Quarenta* jails with the latest and most sophisticated torture devices. The Dominican Republic became a police state ruled by torture, murder, and fear. Trujillo's three decades of rule have often been described as an "extravagance of tyranny." Bernard Diedrich, a biographer of Trujillo, wrote that "like the Roman Emperor Caligula, he cared more for his horses than for humans."

Once the National Treasury became family property, Trujillo embarked upon a cult of adulation. He was the great benefactor. Every town and village was beholden to him, through his bestowal of a hospital, a church, a civic building, or a water system. The basics of any civic life were gifts bestowed on unworthy citizens.

Trujillo maintained his grip on power by means of a powerful propaganda machine at home and abroad. He was the great leader who brought order and civic pride to the masses. He was the man who stood as a Christian bulwark against anarchy, and most of all, atheistic communism. Cardinal Francis Spellman of New York, as well as the U.S. Congress and many American Presidents, honoured him for fighting communism. He maintained a permanent lobby in Washington with many Congressmen on his payroll.

As long as Trujillo served American interests the United States was his friend and defender. America chose to look the other way from his atrocities, and the poverty stricken condition of the Dominican people.

Needless to say, the economy of the country, the control of the sugar industry, cement factories, import and export businesses, and mining interests were either owned by the Trujillo family or beholden to them financially. The country was run as a private fiefdom or enterprise.

But something happened that changed things. In early 1956 Jesus Galindez, a well-known critic of the dictator, was kidnapped in Manhattan, New York. He was flown back to the Dominican Republic and tortured personally by Trujillo, and then killed. His crime was insulting the honour of Trujillo by publishing a dissertation on the 25 year dictatorship of Rafael Trujillo at Colombia University on Dominican Independence Day, February 27 – the ultimate insult to the Father of the Nation.

With world-wide attention surrounding the Galindez kidnapping and murder, Trujillo became a political liability to the American government. Not all of Congress was on his payroll and his brutal excesses and complete disregard for human rights was finally debated in the American Congress. His blundered attempt to assassinate President Betancourt of Venezuela was the final straw. Betancourt had financially backed a group of Dominican dissidents, known as the *Fourteenth of June Group*, in a failed invasion of the Dominican Republic. American policy could no longer tolerate such an embarrassment.

In addition to his problems with his Latin neighbours, and his former sponsor, the American Government, internal dissension gained momentum and strength. Trujillo and his 20,000-man Army had liquidated another Anti-Trujillo Group in 1959. The group had been supported and backed by Cuba and Fidel Castro. Trujillo proceeded to torture and slaughter imprisoned members of the 14th of June Group.

By 1958 the Eisenhower Administration became sick and tired of "their son of a bitch." The CIA sent regular reports to Washington from within the country. Diplomatic and economic sanctions against Trujillo were enacted by his Latin neighbour members of the Organization of American States (O.A.S). As well, world opinion helped to mobilize a strong case against the dictator. Washington finally gave the CIA within the country the green light to help dissidents overthrow the regime of Raphael Trujillo.

The relationship of the Catholic Church and Trujillo had also reached an impasse. In February of 1961 the six bishops of the country issued a joint pastoral that demanded basic human rights for its long suffering people. The church had finally recognized its silent complicity to the unjust regime.

On the night of May 30, 1961, Rafael Trujillo was gunned down on a lonely road leading out of the capital. This group of 13 or15 poorly organized dissidents, with little help from the Americans, and no recognizable political ties had killed Trujillo, fuelled only by hatred and contempt for the man.

Although brought to its knees, the dynasty was still alive in the Trujillo family and sycophants of the regime. The following day, Trujillo's son, Ramfis, an international playboy, assumed the Presidency. There was no organized leadership to thwart the long years of repression, and the Army was loyal to the Trujillos. Ramfis precariously held onto power for a few months. He hunted down, tortured, and killed all but one of the conspirators – the men who had rid the country of its despotic leader. By mid-November, 1961 the U.S. Atlantic fleet was riding anchor off the Dominican coast. Ramfis fled the country for exile in Spain. Under a military U.S. guard the rest of the Trujillo clan and entourage left the country for exile in the United States and Europe.

With the end of the Trujillo regime the country was in a political vacuum and disarray. Leaders returned from exile and from within the country. Slowly, political life and parties emerged, the electorate were more or less organized – all under the watchful eye of the United States. By 1962, Juan Bosch of the Dominican Revolutionary Party had been elected President, in the first free elections in Dominican history. Within a year Bosch was overthrown after attempting a few mild reforms. At that time, the *Wall Street Journal* reported; "the United States embassy has done nothing publicly to dissociate itself from terror. The United States continues to provide substantial aid, including training equipment and arms to the Dominican Army and Police."

In 1965, the U.S. Marines invaded the Dominican Republic in order "to quell unrest and political instability", a situation that had been instigated by the United States itself. The police and military adopted terror tactics once again, aided and encouraged by the American embassy. A group of police called *La Banda* spread more terror and death throughout the island. They rounded up mostly apolitical people, torturing and killing many of them. It was in the midst of this political unrest that Scarboro's Padre Arthur MacKinnon, who socially and spiritually desired to help the poor, was shot to death in El Seibo in 1965.

How was it that Padre Arturo came to be shot down in cold blood? He was lured from his residence by a group of men, calling him to visit a sick parishioner. Was it because he was devoted to the care of the sick, or his involvement in social justice issues? And who were his assassins? Members of *La Banda* or a rogue gunmen? The answers to these questions where never answered satisfactorily.

Joaquim Balaguer, a longtime confidant and associate of Trujillo, then came to the Presidency in 1967. Balaguer was also favoured by the American government. Once again the country reverted to a police state. Any political activity was suppressed with the familiar tactics of violence, torture, kidnapping and disappearances. The suppression of basic rights was justified as a legitimate campaign against communism. Save for one brief term of office, when a socialist Juan Guzman took over the Presidency, Balaguer was the perennial President of the country until the early 1990s.

According to many, Joaquim Balaguer brought stability to the Dominican Republic. It is said that he had the interests of the people at heart. He was intelligent and articulate. Others considered him a despot, who sold out Dominican sovereignty to Gulf and Western, a large multinational American company. His detractors claim he closed his eyes to terror and the killings by the military, in order to create a

Free Zone within the country for U.S. companies, providing many concessions for Gulf and Western. What were these dealings or concessions to Gulf and Western?

The Gulf and Western Corporation and Rosario Industries (a subsidiary of Gulf), became the largest landowners in the Dominican Republic (109,642 acres), and the largest foreign investor in the Republic. Its plantations for sugar cane were in the southeast of the country where the land is most arable. According to 1972 statistics, of the 4.5 million population, only 1.2 percent controlled the majority of arable land on the island.

Sugar cane occupies 25 percent of the cultivated lands. During the 1970s, such concentration of land control aggravated both the social and economic divisions in the countryside. Within a period of ten years, food produced for local consumption had declined by 60 percent. Over 60 percent of food production was being exported principally to the United States. The average monthly salary for a Dominican family of five was less than $50.00, and two-thirds of the population remained outside the mainstream of the country's social, cultural and economic life. In those years 400,000 Dominicans fled the country for better lives in New York and New Jersey.

Powerful allies aided the corporate invasion by Gulf and Western into the Republic. The Chase Manhattan Bank financially backed the development plans; the Wall Street Law firm of Simpson, Thecker and Bartlett were the legal experts representing Gulf and Western. Cyrus Vance, who had begun his career with this law firm, had become Secretary of State, under President Lyndon Johnson. As Assistant Secretary in 1964, Vance had helped plan the U.S. invasion of the Dominican Republic. He had also been involved in setting up a provisional government. While the Dominican Republic was in a destabilized state politically and economically, U.S. financial interests took advantage of this situation like vultures.

Under Balaguer, Gulf and Western was granted 20 more years of tax exemption on the La Romana Free Port enterprise. This setup at La

Romana attracted U.S. companies, where wages were 30 cents an hour. Even the Dominican Constitution was changed to allow Gulf and Western to operate. At about the same period Rosario Mines were granted exclusive access and mining rights for 75 years at Pueblo Viejo, along with the exclusive right to market gold.

The political and economic ramifications on the country by Gulf and Western, is well documented in an audio-visual presentation produced by Packard Manse in 1976, entitled *Guess Who's Coming to Dinner*. Packard Manse belonged to an ecumenical intentional Christian community that worked out of Stoughton, Massachusetts, and was involved in justice issues. Patrick Hughes, a former Paulist priest and member of Packard Manse was involved in the production of the documentary. Scarboro Missions became the Canadian distributor of this audio-visual, and another entitled *Banking in South Africa*. Scarboro Missions used these documentaries in its Justice Educational program.

The documentary paints the following tragic scenario. Gulf and Western tightened its control on the Dominican sugar industry by bringing in a team of union busters who labelled it as communist.. Two prominent union leaders, Guido Gil and Miguel Fortuna, were murdered. Eighty-three union leaders were fired from their jobs with the complicity of the Balaguer government. After many bitter struggles the strength of the union was broken. In 1975 a cane cutter earned less than he had in 1964. Haitian cutters were paid $200 for their seven months of cane cutting. Gulf and Western had become a "state within a state, stronger than the government itself," critics claimed.

Rosario Enterprises operated in similar fashion. The land area around Puebla Viejo where its mines were located, was formerly made up of small landowners and farmers. These lands were expropriated by Rosario; rivers were polluted with cyanide and mercury, and very little compensation was paid out to the farmers involved.

Church leaders such as Bishops Juan Flores of La Vega, Roque Adames of Santiago, and Juan Pepen and Hugo Polanco of Higuey, and some of their priests and religious were involved with the farmers and the cane workers. They supported the rights for indemnification of the small farmers, and just pay and better working conditions for the cane cutters. When the peasants reacted and vigorously protested the brutal tactics of Rosario Mines, Balaguer ignored their protests. Bishops Flores and Adames stood with the peasants; they demanded the agrarian reform long promised by the government. The church supported radio schools and education programs to promote social awareness among the peasants. They criticized Balaguer's repressive tactics. During the long bitter struggle, priests and religious were expelled from the country. Bishop Flores was transferred from Higuey. But, inspired by Medellin the Dominican church had mobilized to some degree, to hear the cry of the poor and work with the poor for recognition and equality, both as human beings and as Dominican citizens.

Joaquim Balaguer's early political platform had been for mild reform, orderly change, moderation and peace. In the last 25 years one can say that most of those goals have been achieved, but at what cost? The tourist industry, aided by stability and relatively peaceful conditions, has certainly improved the overall economy.

Today only a handful of Scarboro Missionaries are present in the country pursuing their pastoral work. Amongst them, Padre Luis Quinn, continues his labours and involvement with the peasant farmers in the hill country of San Jose de Ocoa. He has been working with the poor these last forty years. His particular philosophical and practical brand of development has brought him national recognition. His organizational talents and drive have given a decent life to hundreds of peasant farmers, built up their health and educational systems, and brought hope and determination to a people long exploited and manipulated.

Today the social climate in the Dominican Republic appears calm and stable. But what of its future in the new world order of neo-liberal economics? The Dominican church's social activity is not quite as visible today, whether due to respectful social and economic advances for the masses, or because of a new agenda emanating from the Vatican!

Sources
Life Magazine, "The Galindez Case", 1957-58.
Bernard Diedrich, *Trujillo, Death of the Goat*, Little, Brown, New York, 1978.
Penny Lernoux, *Cry of the People*, Doubleday, 1980.
Conversations with fellow missionaries

∽∾

Nicaragua

Until a few short years ago Managua, the capital of Nicaragua, still had the look of a bombed-out city in its core, a reminder of the earthquake that destroyed so much of the city in 1972.

This is the country of Somoza and of the Sandinista Revolution. America has been heavily involved in Nicaragua for more than a hundred years. The U.S. marines invaded the country in 1912. This occupation came about after the ousting of the Zelaya liberal government and was engineered by the U.S. embassy. During this first American occupation, the country was ruled by a series of U.S.-backed conservative presidents. It was during this period that the United States imposed the so-called Bryan-Camorro treaty on Nicaragua. This agreement, signed in 1914, and ratified in 1916, gave the U.S. exclusive rights over the building of any trans-oceanic canal in Nicaragua.

The United States attempted to end its occupation in 1925, but this withdrawal was followed almost immediately by armed strife between the liberal and conservative forces. Thus, Washington again occupied the country from 1926 to 1933.

It was during this period that Augusto Cesar Sandino (who had been in the liberal camp) led a peasant-based rebellion against the American occupation. Sandino did succeed in driving American forces from the country, but fell victim to a plot by Anastacio Somoza to assassinate him and his followers. As in the Dominican Republic, the Americans had named Anastacio Somoza, an army man, to head the army police forces. It has been said that Somoza measured up for the Americans because he could speak English. This was the beginning of a dictatorial dynasty, which controlled the lives of 2.5 million Nicaraguans for forty years.

The Somoza family ruled Nicaragua according to their fancy, aided by successive American administrations. Nicaragua interested the Americans as a back up country for another canal, just in case the Panamanians decided to blowup the Panama Canal. Deceit and treachery would be the trademark of the Somozas. Thirty thousand Nicaraguans would die at their hands in the ensuing years.

Dissenting voices that survived the Somoza ruthlessness had to be bought off, forced into exile, or allowed to function within the web of economic control of the Somoza family. In the 1950s, when Nicaragua had a population of 2.2 million, there was plenty of land for all. Yet 20,000 peasants were landless, while the Somoza family had land holdings of 13,293 square kilometers (8,260 square miles); an area as large as neighbouring El Salvador.

As in the Dominican Republic, control of the masses by father Anastacio and sons Luis and Anastacio Jr. was through the creation of the National Guard, an elite force, armed and trained by the United States. Somoza Sr. assumed the Presidency of the country in 1937, after an army coup.

Attending the inauguration of a new educational complex in neighbouring Costa Rica in his early years, Somoza Sr. was heard to remark: "I don't want educated people, I just want oxen." Any movement to better the economic or social life of the people was met by the now familiar tactics employed by dictators – repression, torture, imprisonment and death. A teacher in the 1970s remarked that "teaching people to think is the worst crime you can commit under a Somoza

Government." The Somoza control of civic life extended to an elaborate spy system that kept the National Guard abreast of any opposition.

Many of the massacres perpetuated by the National Guard were motivated by greed for land, cattle and women. In 1972, the United States granted $76.7 million for the reconstruction of Managua, the nation's capital, after the terrible earthquake that had killed more than 10,000 people and left 200,000 homeless. No reconstruction was ever done until the Sandinistas came to power.

As in other Latin American countries that are controlled by despotic leaders, the Somozas and their hierarchy dominated and owned the national economy. Their financial interests, as well as their land holdings, extended to the media, breweries, distilleries, cement and metal plants. While their annual income was in the millions, the average annual per capita income was $300.

The United States in the 1970s continued to financially support and back the Somozas. The guerrilla movement that came to life against the rampant corruption and abuse of power in those years, was a legitimate revolt against the Somozas and the policy of the United States[1]

In 1977, Pedro Joaquim Chamorro, editor of the *La Prensa* newspaper, was murdered by the Somozas. Chamorro was from an influential

---

1. Most of the original leaders of the Frente Sandinista, including the main founder, Carlos Fonseca Amador, considered themselves to be Marxists and looked to the Cuban revolution as their inspiration. But, in founding the Frente Sandinista, they broke from the Stalinist (Nicaraguan Socialist Party) tradition, to move closer to the orientation and example of Ernest Che Guevara. So the Frente had a lot to do with Cuba, including the military and political training of many leaders in Cuba, and arms and logistical support from Cuba. This does not contradict the notion that the Sandinistas were a legitimate and authentic national expression of Nicaragua's nationalist and anti-imperialist tradition – this why they looked to Sandino for their inspiration. Much later, liberation theology came to play an important role among a layer of Sandinista activists and leaders. (Matilde Zimmermann, *In the Footsteps of Che and Sandino: The Life of Carlos Fonseca Amador of Nicaragua*, Duke University Press, 1999.)

family in Nicaragua, and a leading critic of the regime. His death fuelled the growing unrest in the country. Landowners and the business elite sided with the Sandinista guerrillas.

In retaliation against the guerrilla movement, there was indiscriminate bombing, shelling and strafing of the civilian population by the National Guard, aided by American mercenaries. The towns of Esteli, Condega, Masaya, and Leon were left in ashes. The Red Cross estimated that this slaughter by Somoza in 1978 left 5,000 dead, 10,000 missing, 15,000 injured and 25,000 homeless. In view of international opinion, the Carter Administration cut off the $3.1 million allocation. Carter did this in spite of a very strong lobby by right wing factions in the United States. Israel came to the aid of the Somozas when America faltered.

"It was beyond the capacity of the Pentagon to grasp the real causes of popular discontent in Latin America," writes Penny Lernoux in her book *Cry of the People*. "And because Washington would not have sanctioned meaningful social change if they had, every potential disturbance had to be met with military and police tactics." It was much easier to explain the appearance of Marxist guerrillas in Latin American countries, as part of an international communist conspiracy.

In 1979 the Sandinista guerrillas were victorious and Anastacio Somoza Jr. fled to Paraguay, where he was assassinated a year later. By 1983 the Contras, a guerrilla movement funded and trained by the Americans, invaded north-eastern Nicaragua. This was the beginning of a five-year Civil War that devastated the country.

Daniel Ortega, as leader of the Frente Sandinista had assumed the Presidency. The Sandinista guerrilla movement was Marxist-oriented. Many of their leaders were hard core communists. But the revolution to oust the Somozas was a popular movement of all Nicaraguans. Many church people were strong supporters of the Sandinistas. Gradually, their hard line propaganda gave way, and the Frente adopted a more socialist approach. Several prominent priests, Fernando Cardenal, a Jesuit, his brother Ernesto, a priest-monk who had a peasant community called Solentiname on Lake Nicaragua, and Miguel D'Escoto, a Maryknoll missionary, assumed important government posts. Their objective was to build a civil society that respected the rights of its citizens, and move away from American bondage that had supported the Somozas.

But as the Godfather of Nicaragua, the United States, remained determined to overthrow the Sandinistas. The U.S. set up an embargo against Nicaragua and mined their harbours. They installed American bases in neighbouring Honduras, to train, supply and send the Contras to battle against their fellow Nicaraguans. As Fr. Robert Drinan, a Jesuit, former member of Congress, and professor at Georgetown University Law Center wrote recently in the *National Catholic Reporter*, in an article on U.S. Foreign policy, (April 9, 1999) "During the 40 years of the Cold War, the United States became accustomed to insisting on its own way in foreign affairs. It helped remove indigenous leaders who did not conform to America's dictates. These include Arbenz Guzman in Guatemala, Ngo Dinh Diem in South Vietnam, Salvador Allende in Chile, Daniel Ortega in Nicaragua, and Manuel Noriega in Panama."

"The White House and the CIA had acted in those cases without the knowledge or consent of the American people." Senator Patrick Moynihan has made this clear in his recent book on secrecy. "The icon of *threats to the national security* was the essence of the cult of secrecy that was maintained so assiduously during the entire Cold War. The struggle against the *Evil Empire* justified these events in the eyes of millions."

In 1984 Daniel Ortega was elected as President, as Nicaraguans returned the Sandinistas to power. But their chances of effectively governing or rebuilding the economy, and reforming Nicaraguan society were doomed to failure. They made serious internal mistakes. They antagonized the conservative element in the Catholic Church; and American might was against them. The Iran-Contra scandal that came before the United States Congress brought before American and Canadian television viewers the extent of American involvement in the Contra War and the internal affairs of Nicaragua. The World Court condemned the United States for "terrorist activities" and extreme violence against Nicaragua. The obvious involvement of high government officials, including President Ronald Reagan, and their coverup, brought the rogue activities of Colonel Oliver North out into the open. By 1988 a cease fire between the Contras and the Sandinistas was worked out.[2]

But the dream was over, and in the 1990 elections, with continuing pressure from the U.S., Violeta Chamorro defeated Ortega and became President. President George Bush Sr. had promised billions in aid and 1.5 billion in grants that bolstered the faltering economy.

The Chamorro government had its work to do. The Nicaraguan economy was crushed under a $10 billion foreign debt. The country was the second poorest in Latin America, next to Haiti. There was 50 percent unemployment in the cities and 80 percent in the countryside. Squatter's camps of unemployed and homeless came to dot the countryside. A middle class monthly family salary of $155 was inadequate to feed a family of four. Thousands of families could not afford school for their children. There were no resources for education or health.

The country suffered another major setback with the devastation wrought by Hurricane Mitch in early 1999. Thousands lost their homes to mudslides and their meagre crops were wiped out. The government of Arnoldo Aleman Lacayo that had succeeded Chamorro did little for those areas of the country that had supported the Sandinistas. Arnoldo Aleman Lacayo had been mayor of Managua during the Chamorro government. He comes from that breed of politician close to the Somozas. He promised

---

2. In the book, *9-11* by Noam Chomsky, an interviewer asks the question, "You said that the main practioners of terrorism are countries like the U.S. that use violence for political motives. When and where?" Chomsky replies, "I find the question baffling. As I've said elsewhere, the U.S. is, after all, the only country condemned by the World Court for international terrorism, – for 'the unlawful use of force' for political ends, as the Court puts it – ordering the U.S. to terminate these crimes and pay substantial reparations. The U.S. of course dismissed the Court's judgment with contempt, reacting by escalating the terrorist war against Nicaragua and vetoing a Security Council resolution calling on all states to observe international law. (Noam Chomsky, *9-11*, Seven Stories Press, N.Y., 2001, p. 84.)

to fully comply with the draconian economic conditions of the International Monetary Fund (IMF) and the World Bank.

As the millennium unfolded, those in the know say Nicaragua is regaining its reputation as one of the most corrupt countries in Central America. One of the saddest signs of that corruption was an apparent pact between Aleman and Daniel Ortega.. The pact ensured Ortega, as a Deputy, immunity from prosecution on charges of sexual molestation of his step-daughter. Ortega and a few other Sandinistas also held onto certain properties they confiscated during the Revolution. Fernando and Ernesto Cardenal have resigned along with others leaders prominent in the Frente Sandinista. "The corrupt acts of a small group broke the tradition of Sandinista honesty; it constitutes the greatest damage in all its history to the Frente", says Fernando Cardenal. "I end my political activity, but shall continue faithful to my original commitment, the poor."

Many Nicaraguans were unhappy with the Presidency of Arnoldo Aleman. But he had the support of the United States, the World Bank and the IMF. The Aleman government was defeated at the polls in 2002, and the new President is Henrique Bolanos. Arnoldo Aleman has been accused of mass fraud and the embezzlement of millions of dollars. So what future lies in store for the majority of Nicaraguans?

The Sandinista Revolution overthrew a bloody and despotic dictatorship. It gained wide support amongst the Nicaraguan people with its objective of building a more just society for Nicaraguans. Yet it was also the cause for serious division within the Catholic Church, one sector being for the Frente Sandinista, and the other violently opposed. This tragic split could be partially blamed on the Sandinistas themselves, but Vatican policy was the main factor. Miguel Obando y Bravo, the Archbishop of Managua, was rewarded by being named a Cardinal for his steadfast opposition to the Sandinistas, while Ernesto Cardenal received the Papal stare and public chiding when the pope visited Nicaragua. In the unfolding of the Nicaraguan tragedy, Jesse Helms, and his right wing allies in the Republican Party, were aided by another powerful ally – the tremendous power, financial input and political persuasion and lobbying that was held by right wing Catholic conservative American organizations.

One such organization, the Knights of Malta, are an age-old Catholic group founded for the elite of Europe. It was to be the aristocracy's institution to perform charitable acts of mercy. But with its power and financial influence various sectors of the Knights of Malta have long marched to their own political agenda.

The New York chapter of the Knights of Malta have long been powerful lobbies in Washington. Led by Peter Grace, of W.R. Grace and Company, the Knights were more than active in bringing about the downfall of the Sandinistas. With a loathing for communism that had certainly wrought havoc on his business dealings in Central America, Peter Grace led a Team of Knights on this holy crusade. Amongst his followers were fellow Knights, William Casey, and John McCone, both former CIA directors, and General Alexander Haig, who was also involved in the U.S. plot to overthrow Allende in Chile. Others were William Buckley, owner and writer for the conservative *National Review*, his brother James, a former Senator, William Simon, treasurer-secretary under Nixon and Ford, Clair Booth Luce of *Time* magazine, and Lewis E. Lehrman of New York. In addition to their political campaign and propaganda war against the Sandinistas, and financing the Contras, one can be sure they brought effective pressure on church policy.

Life goes on in Nicaragua, and reconstruction has taken place in Managua. Thomas Monaghan, owner of Domino Pizza, completed a $3.5 million cathedral for Miguel Obando. The government built a $4 million John Paul II Plaza, and Cardinal Miguel Obando had a statue of John Paul sculptured at the cost of $150,000 for the plaza.

All of this must be of tremendous comfort to the victims of Hurricane Mitch, and the thousands of unemployed in Managua, and the country's impoverished masses. All of these poor are daily devastated by the hurricane effects of the IMF, the World Bank, and globalization.

Sources
Latin American Press
Central America, Life World Library, Lavine p. 64-68.
Penny Lernoux, *Cry of the People*, Doubleday, 1980,
Conversations with missionaries

Honduras

The Honduran economy has been in shambles since the United States pulled up stakes following the peace accord in Nicaragua in 1988. The largest employers in Honduras operate in the Free Zone areas set up by American companies in the San Pedro Sula district of the country. Chronic unemployment is prevalent throughout the rest of the country.

Honduras was often referred to as "USA Honduras" because of the American involvement and presence in the country during the Contra War. Their 26,000 person army and 2,000 strong Special Police Force was set up during the American presence. Seventy percent of the Honduran economy, $580 million, was spent on military readiness. Five major U.S. military bases, plus other military installations had been set up in the country. There were constant U.S. military manoeuvres with Salvadoran and Honduran forces. There was a campaign of selective disappearance carried out by Honduran death squads with CIA/U.S. army support against Hondurans opposing the American presence in the country.

El Salvador

Archbishop Oscar Romero once proclaimed "To the Armed Forces I say, stop the killing, I beg you, I urge you, I command you, stop the killing of innocent people."

This powerful message of the Archbishop was delivered to the Salvadoran nation on Sunday February 17, 1980. In that same message to his people Romero had told them that he had written to President Jimmy Carter to stop U.S. aid to El Salvador because it was being used to kill innocent people. One might say that Romero had sealed his own fate. A month later, Oscar Romero was gunned down as he celebrated Mass in a cancer hospital run by the Sisters of Charity. He had been Archbishop for only three short, tragic years.

His pastoral leadership was one of profound courage and conviction in attempting to bring peace and justice to his country and her people, – a country engaged in a fratricidal war.

The country of El Salvador is the smallest in Central America. But it has the highest population density, and the lowest per capita income. It has a population today of close to 5.5 million, of whom 89 percent are *mestizo*, persons of mixed-blood. During the 1960s and 1970s the military, or a civilian President selected by the military and the elite, ruled the country.

For many years El Salvador professed to have a democratic government, at least on paper, but in reality it was an alliance of the military with the conservative families that owned the country. This oligarchy of 14 families made their wealth in cotton, coffee and indigo, as well as politics. Since independence from Spain in 1821, El Salvador has functioned like a collection of small vassal states. Most of the country's arable land has been in the hands of these powerful families.

This elite group has always resisted and been scornful of social change. It took a military government in 1960 to force these wealthy landowners to pay their workers a minimum of 70 cents a day, to reduce slum rents, and make other reforms necessary so that the country could qualify for the *Alliance for Progress* programs.

The Catorce (fourteen), families have always flaunted their wealth. They maintained lavish homes in San Salvador, and imposing estates in the country. The country club was the centre for their social life as well as tennis, polo and swimming. The men worked in first class air-conditioned offices and drove flashy sport cars. Their women wore the latest styles and fashions, acquired on their shopping tours in Rome, Paris and New York. Again, as we have noted in other Latin American countries, their disdain for the peasant is best illustrated by the following story. A banker's wife in San Salvador, upon hearing that John F. Kennedy was launching the *Alliance for Progress* program remarked to an American visitor that "she always suspected Kennedy of being a communist, and now, he is going to feed those dirty animals that have names."

At times in the recent past any uprising by the peasantry working the fields was put down by simply staging a massacre; then 'order' was restored. Maximiliano Hernandez, whose government was responsible for the massacre of 30,000 peasants, set a 'record massacre' in 1932. Such arrogance and utter disdain for any attempts at reform provided a natural setting for revolution, and by the end of the 1970s guerrilla activity was becoming widespread. "Communist subversion, a communist conspiracy", this was the regular reaction to any attempts at reform, or better working and living conditions of the poor. Now the wolf cry was a reality.

Again, instead of any honest effort at reform, the power elite reacted in their usual manner. According to the Archdiocese of San Salvador, 46,000 civilians had died by the end of 1983. Paramilitary death squads perpetuated most of the killings.

There was an indiscriminate killing of teachers, university students, labour organizers and Catholic catechists. By 1985, 500,000 Salvadorans had fled to the United States. There were 21,000 Salvadorans in refugee camps in Honduras, while another 300,000 subsisted in miserable conditions in Salvadoran cities.

Two days prior to Archbishop Romero's installation in February of 1977, Carlos Humberto Romero had been elected as the new President despite evidence of massive fraud. Humberto Romero was a friend and confidant of the landowners and close ally of Anastacio Somoza of Nicarauga. He had a reputation for ruthless repression of any opposition. Protests followed his election. On February 28 the army and police surrounded a peaceful demonstration of 6,000 people in the Plaza Liberdad in San Salvador. One hundred were killed, 220 wounded, and 500 were arrested. Humberto Romero organized a spy system called ORDEM with 50,000 armed members. Committees were established in every town and city, so now neighbour spied on neighbour.

Archbishop Luis Chavez e Gonzalez, San Salvador's elderly prelate and Oscar Romeros' predecessor, had turned the church in the direction of the poor. The church spoke out for land reform and social change. Supported by some of the hierarchy and the Medellin documents, priests and religious became ever more actively involved in the cause of the poor. In so doing the church felt the wrath of the oligarchy. Priests and religious were expelled from the country, others were tortured and killed. Lay leaders and their families suffered the same fate. The church was branded as subversive, a tool of the communists. The shadow of communism continued to be the mask for violent opposition to change. "Kill a priest, be a patriot", was the slogan of many paramilitary groups, as they roamed the countryside terrorizing and killing any suspected reformers.

Archbishop Oscar Romero's nomination and installation as the new Archbishop of San Salvador was greeted by the wealthy and powerful as sign of better days for their cause. Although a charismatic preacher, Romero was looked upon as a bookworm and an introvert. He had not been involved in justice issues. The progressive clergy had been disappointed when Bishop Arturo y Damas had not been chosen for the post.

Following Archbishop Romero's installation, events unfolded in a turbulent manner. There was the brutal Monday Massacre in the Plaza

Liberdad. And within the month Fr. Rutilio Grande, a close friend of Romero and a priest he admired, was brutally murdered. Grande, with an elderly peasant and a young teenager, was on his way to the mission station of Aguilares, where he was to celebrate Mass. A death squad terminated the lives of all three of them.

Rutilio Grande had predicted his death. At a peasant march, protesting the expulsion of a fellow priest from the country, Grande had spoken. "The real issue facing us today in this country and on the continent is how to be an authentic Christian. We are suffering our hour of martyrdom. Very soon I fear the Bible and the Gospel will not be allowed.... And if Jesus were to cross the border they would crucify him again, because they prefer a Christ of the sacristy or the cemetery, a silent Christ with a muzzle in his mouth."

On the Sunday of Rutilio Grande's funeral the Archbishop and seven other bishops and 400 priests celebrated the only Mass in the country. Against the government-declared state of siege, 100,000 people attended his Mass of burial. The slain Grande, a giant amongst the poor with whom he laboured, became a national hero in death.

Rutilio Grande was a Jesuit, and his Jesuit colleagues became targets for the right wing militia. The Jesuit University in San Salvador was bombed six times. Students were warned to stay away from Jesuit schools or be killed. The Jesuits were warned with threats to leave the country or face the same fate. Aguilares, where Grande worked as pastor was under siege, and *Operation Rutilio* became an attempt to destroy peasant organizations set up by the Jesuits. In Rome, Fr. Pedro Arrupe, the Superior General of the Jesuits responded to the threats by declaring, "They may end up as martyrs, but my priests are not going to leave El Salvador because they are with the people."

Another diocesan priest, Fr. Alfonso Navarro Oviedo suffered the same fate as Grande for his work amongst the poor. But priests were not the only targets. Hundreds of lay people were persecuted, tortured and harassed for their work in peasant organizations. As the climate of violence grew, the Popular Forces of Liberation, one of the four guerrilla groups active in the country since 1971, kidnapped and murdered Mauricio Borgonovo, the country's Foreign Minister, and a member of the *Catorce* families.

Under such deplorable conditions Archbishop Oscar Romero became the country's leading churchman. He spoke out against all violence, and pleaded with both sides in the conflict to give up their tactics of war, and to stop the killing of innocent lives. His attempts at peacemaking met with more blood letting on both sides.

Romero traversed the countryside to show his support of the poor, and he continuously reasoned with all factions. He used his preaching skills to reach out to his people as their Pastor. His weekly Sunday radio broadcasts, which included his sermon along with a report to the people about what was happenings in the country, were listened to by 73 percent of the rural population and 47 percent of those in San Salvador. The radio station of the Archdiocese was twice bombed and forced off the air.

Bishop Romero met weekly with a variety of lay and clerical groups to keep abreast of the ever-worsening national situation, to plan how best to respond to the rampant persecution, and to consider how to be more effective in his role as pacifier. He maintained a disciplined schedule, attending to the spiritual needs of his people, celebrating Mass and administering the sacraments. He visited his priests, gave spiritual counselling at his seminary, and visited the sick. It was a hectic schedule, but each night he wrote his journal of the day's events. He devoted special times to solitary prayer and reflection.

All his fellow bishops did not share the direction of his pastoral practice. The Nuncio took exception to much of what he was doing. Only bishops Arturo Riveira y Damas and Rosa Chavez supported his work. Aside from a few close confidants, Romero felt isolation and lack of support. This lack of support was not just from his fellow bishops within the country, but from across the sea in Rome. Fr. Jon Sobrino, a Latin American theologian, said that Romero "did not find understanding with the pope." He felt like an outsider with little support. On a visit to Rome in 1979, Cardinal Edward Cassidy related that "Romero was depressed. He felt that he was not trusted by Rome, and was under suspicion."

Shortly before his death Oscar Romero wrote the following in his journal; "Let my death, if it is accepted by God, be for the liberation of my people, and a witness of hope in the future. You can say, if they do kill me, that I forgive and bless those who do it. I wish they would realize that they are wasting their time. A bishop will die, but the Church of God, which is the people will never perish."

"Because the church has opted for the truly poor, not for the fictiously poor, because it has opted for those who are really oppressed and repressed, the church lives in a political world, and politics is one way in which it fulfils itself as church. It cannot be otherwise, if the church like Jesus, is to turn itself toward the poor."

Archbishop Oscar Romero was shot to death on March 24, 1980 by a lone gunman. Roberto D'Aubuisson, one of the powerhouses in the ARENA Party that ruled El Salvador, has long been suspected of masterminding Romero's death.

Following Romero's death, war and violence continued. The rape and murder of three American Maryknoll Sisters and a lay worker in 1981 brought the American church into confrontation with the American government. The confrontation forced the United States State Department to back off from its longstanding support of the Salvadorean government. Leadership in the Archdiocese of San Salvador had fallen to Arturo Riveira y Damas who was appointed Archbishop. He and his church people continued the pastoral convictions and direction of Romero. Persecution against the church continued. The murder of Fr. Ignacio Ellacuria, and five of his Jesuit colleagues in their residence, along with the housekeeper and her daughter, became international news in 1989.

During the following years, until the United Nations brokered a peace agreement, the United States is estimated to have spent $4 billion propping up right-wing military-backed governments. The Peace Accord, signed between the socialist Faribundo Marti and the National Liberation Front (FMLN) took place in December of 1990.

El Salvadorans continue to try to bury the ghosts of the past, and to build a new country. Integrating 50,000 soldiers into civilian society and the workforce, within a shaky economy, has not been easy. Reconciliation of neighbour with neighbour is an ongoing process. A war weary population continues to hope in the face of neo-liberal policies. According to 2001 statistics, 49.7 percent of the population live in poverty. A deplorable 22 percent of Salvadorans live in extreme poverty unable to satisfy their basic needs.

What of the church and its involvement? With the appointment of Archbishop Fernando Saenz as San Salvador's Archbishop, there has been a radical shift in pastoral direction. One observer remarked that "there are two currents, it's that some are with the people, and with the other ones you have to ask for an appointment." There does not seem to be too much concern with the difficult reality that people confront in their daily lives. Monsignor Ricardo Urioste, the former Vicar General, says that the direction of the Archdiocese reflects "a clear proximity to the structures of economic and political power." Bishop Rosa Chavez speaks of "a tendency in the church to close in on itself, to lean toward a disembodied spirituality, to be absent from the immense problems facing the world." Chavez goes on to say that "we must globalize solidarity against neo-liberalism and its policies. People feel deserted, less protected, less heard."

Sources for El Salvador & Guatemala
Same as above for other Latin American countries
Penny Lernoux, *People of God*, Penguin books, 1990.
New Internationalist, August, 2003.

Guatemala

This short reflection on Guatemala will concentrate on the latter half of this century. But in Guatemala, in such places as Tibal, Palenque, and Bonampack, archeologists and tourists still visit and search the ruins of a bygone civilization for new discoveries. For Guatemala, along with Honduras, Belize, and the Yucatan Peninsula in Mexico, holds the secrets of the Mayan world, one of the most remarkable civilizations our world has ever known. Great architects and engineers, remarkable artists and sculptors, and particularly brilliant astronomers and mathematicians, flourished here through most of the first thousand years of this era.

Today Guatemalans are attempting to adjust to the aftermath of almost fifty years of civil conflict, and atrocious acts of genocide against the Mayan population. A tenuous Peace Accord was signed at the end of December 1996 between the National Guatemalan Revolutionary Union and the government.

Guatemala has one of the largest indigenous populations in Latin America. The Mayans comprise 44 percent of the 10.5 million populations, and speak some 21 Mayan languages. The other 56 percent of the Guatemalan inhabitants are mainly *mestizos*, a mixture of Mayan and Spanish. Like in all of the Americas, those who colonize never fully appreciate, nor understand the traditions, cultures and religious beliefs of the colonized population. The Mayan population of Guatemala have always been treated as 'serfs' in their own land. Their history has been one of marginalization, oppression and racism.

Similar to her neighbours, Guatemala has been ruled by a small elite group that has controlled the financial and the civil power. Seventy percent of the arable land has been in the hands of less than 2.2 percent of the population. Guatemala, along with Honduras, has long been referred to as "the Banana Republics" of American business interests. Certainly these American interests, as well as other foreign investors, supported the traditional social structures of the country, which are dominated by the elite and the military.

In 1954 at the height of the Cold War, when Senator Joseph McCarthy's anti-communist crusade was in full force, President Dwight Eisenhower approved a CIA plot, (Allen Dulles headed the CIA) to assist the Guatemalan military to overthrow the government of Jacobo Arbenz Guzman. Arbenz, who was a leftist and had invited communists into his inner circle, had also initiated reforms to confiscate unused lands and hand them over to landless peasants. Much of this land belonged to an American firm, the United Fruit Company that had large holdings in Guatemala and Honduras. With the overthrow of the Arbenz government, the first Guerrilla movement began in the country.

A long and bloody civil conflict within Guatemala ensued that the outside world largely ignored. Media and world press coverage was practically non-existent, or slanted to favour the military operations. The curtain of anti-communism was used to cover up the atrocities and the scorched earth policy of the Guatemalan military. In 1960, young military officers, dismayed by the corruption and misuse of the military against the civilian population, attempted a coup that failed.

During this genocidal war that went through several distinct phases from 1954 through to 1996, the United States aided and actively participated in operations within Guatemala. A thousand Green Berets worked with the military. Guatemalan officers were trained at the American School of the Americas. America supplied arms and millions of dollars to the Guatemalan government. The CIA operated alongside the Guatemalan military.

Up until the signing of the Peace Accord in December of 1996, more than 200,000 civilians were murdered, 400 villages were wiped out. One million people were displaced, 150,000 taking refuge in Mexico and 200,000 children were orphaned. Clandestine prisons, torture centres, death squads were the order of the day. There were multiple acts of savagery, and the torture and burning of victims including children. In the 1980s there were 626 separate massacres in Mayan villages. Since those brutal years former soldiers have related to the Truth Commission how they were trained in the step by step process for conducting massacres.

President Jimmy Carter suspended military aid to Guatemala in the mid-1970s and publicly condemned the government's human rights abuses. Israel and other countries filled the gap and supplied arms to the military. By the early 1980s, the Reagan Administration had resumed support of the regimes of General Romero Lucas Garcia, and Efrain Rios Montt. During Rios Montt's tenure of office, the slaughter became an ideological right wing crusade. During the decade of the 1980s, violence by the military against the mostly Mayan rural population reached its greatest proportions.

Early in 1999, a United Nations sponsored Truth Commission report was made public. The *National Catholic Reporter* devoted its March 12 edition to a cover story, written by Tom Roberts, with details of the report. The following is a synthesis of the article.

The report, published in nine volumes and titled *Guatemala: Memory of Silence*, was compiled by the Commission for Historical Clarification. The Guatemalan peace process that culminated in the Accord of Oslo, signed in Norway in June of 1994 mandated it.

The report vindicates the religious and human rights groups whose characterizations of the terror and torture were largely dismissed over the years in official American circles.

The report adds additional weight and credibility to the Project to Recover Historic Memory, begun by Guatemala's Catholic Bishops in 1994, and overseen by the late Bishop Juan Gerardi, auxiliary bishop of Guatemala City.

In comments made during a ceremony on February 25, 1999, Christian Tomuschat, a German law professor and co-ordinator of the commission, said the group "has been able to establish that state forces and allied paramilitary groups were responsible for 93 percent of the documented violations." He went on to say that the insurgent forces were responsible for 3 percent, and that the remaining 4 percent of the cases include other authors.

Tomuschat also accused the CIA of "directly and indirectly" conducting "illegal" state operations during the period of conflict. "Until the mid-1980s the United States government and U.S. private companies exercised pressure to maintain the country's archaic and unjust socio-economic structure", said Tomuschat.

The report mentions the support Cuba provided to the insurgency and its support of armed struggle as a contributing factor to the violence. The insurgency, however, developed "as a response... to the country's diverse structural problems. Faced with injustice, exclusion, poverty, and discrimination, it proclaimed the need to take power by force in order to build a new social, political and economic order", the summary states.

As the Guatemalan government became increasingly repressive, "sectors of the left, specifically those of Marxist ideology, adopted the Cuban perspective of armed struggle as the only way to ensure the rights of the people and take power." On the other hand, according to the report, the state's response was "totally disproportionate to the military force of the insurgency" and "can only be understood within the framework of the country's profound social, economic and cultural conflicts."

"The United States demonstrated that it was willing to provide support for strong military regimes in its strategic backyard. In the case of Guatemala military assistance was directed toward reinforcing the national intelligence apparatus and for training the officer corps in counterinsurgency techniques, key factors that had significant bearing on human rights violations during the armed confrontation."

While the commission does not diminish the responsibility of the insurgents for inflicting violence on the population, it also concludes that the government "deliberately magnified the military threat of the insurgency." This was done to justify a "concept of the internal enemy", a notion that allowed the state to include anyone within the citizenry as a state enemy.

In its analysis of the conflict, the commission outlines four major periods:

- 1962-1970: Military operations were concentrated in the eastern part of the country, Guatemala City and the south coast. Most of the victims during that period were peasants, members of rural unions, university and secondary school teachers, students and guerrilla sympathizers.

- 1971-1977: "Repressive operations were more selective and geographically dispersed," according to the report. Victims included community and union leaders, catechists and students.

- 1978-1983: The most violent and bloody period of the entire conflict, when military operations were concentrated in Quiche, Huehuetenango, Chimaltenango, Alt and Baja Verapaz, rural areas in the north and northwest heavily populated with Mayans; the south coast, and the capital. Most of the victims during this time were Mayans.

- 1986-1996: The final period, when "repressive actions were selective", affecting the Mayan and Ladino population to a similar extent.

Summary of the report:

The National Security Doctrine fell on fertile ground in Guatemala where anti-communist thinking had already taken root and from the 1930s had merged with the defense of religion, tradition and conservative values, all of which were allegedly threatened by atheistic communism. These views were strongly supported by the Catholic Church until the 1950s, which qualified as communist any position that contradicted its philosophy, thus contributing even further to division and confusion in Guatemalan society.

Only recently in Guatemalan history did the Catholic Church abandon its conservative position in favour of an attitude and practice based on the decisions of the Second Vatican Council (1962-1965) and the Conference of Medellin (1968). The Church prioritized its work with the excluded, the poor and underprivileged sectors, promoting the construction of a more just and equitable society. These doctrinal and pastoral changes clashed with counterinsurgency strategy, which considered Catholics to be allies of the guerrillas, and therefore part of the internal enemy, subject to persecution, death or expulsion. The guerrilla movement saw in the practice of what was known as "liberation theology" common ground on which to extend its social base, and it sought to gain the sympathy of its followers. A large number of catechists, lay activists, priests and missionaries were victims of the violence and gave their lives as a testimony to the cruelty of the armed confrontation.

The Truth Commission Report also states that the state's repressive response was totally disproportionate to the military force of the Guerrilla movement. It shows that broad sectors of society participated in the growing social mobilization and political opposition to the country's long established order (1978-1982), and that some of these movements maintained ties of a varying nature with the guerrillas. Yet at no time during the internal armed confrontation did the insurgents have the military potential necessary to pose any real threat to the state.

The Report concludes that the state deliberately magnified the military threat of the guerrillas, in order to justify the concept of the internal enemy. The including of all opposition under one banner, democratic or otherwise, pacifist or guerrilla, legal or illegal, communist or non-communist, served to justify numerous serious crimes. Faced with widespread political, socio-economic and cultural opposition, the state resorted to military operations directed toward the physical annihilation or absolute intimidation of this opposition, through a plan of repression carried out mainly by the army and national security forces.

One quarter of the direct victims of human rights violations and acts of violence were women. They were killed, tortured and raped, sometimes because of their ideals and political or social participation, sometimes in massacres. Thousands of women lost their husbands, becoming widows left with their children and with no material resources to adequately care for their families.

The Report reveals the degrading elements of the army's training of a special counterinsurgency force known as the Kaibiles. The training included the killing of animals, eating them raw, and drinking their blood, in order to demonstrate courage. This force became a 'killing machine'.

The Report makes special mention of the rampages of the Kaibiles in their operations against the Mayan communities. Their strategy led not only to violations of basic human rights, but also to crimes that were committed with particular cruelty. Acts such as the killing of defenseless children, often by beating them against walls or throwing them alive into pits where the corpses of adults were later thrown, the amputation of limbs, the impaling of victims, the burning of victims by covering them with petrol and setting them ablaze. These and other inhuman savage acts were not only actions against defenseless victims, they also morally degraded the perpetuators, and those who inspired, ordered or tolerated these actions.

The responsibility for a large part of these violations, reached the highest levels of the army and successive governments. (Cover Story, *National Catholic Reporter*, Tom Fox, March 12, 1999.)

During a visit to Guatemala in March of 1999, President Bill Clinton expressed regret over American support of Guatemala's successive right wing governments. He acknowledged that it was wrong and pledged that it would never happen again. President Clinton was the first American President to make such an acknowledgement. "We are determined to remember the past", he said, "but never to repeat it."

The Guatemalan Bishops Conference issued a statement on February 26, 1999 stating that the report should "lay before the eyes of Guatemala and the world, the deep abyss of dehumanization and deterioration of moral values into which our country has fallen."

The Bishops Conference also noted that the Report "corroborated what had already been revealed in the Church's Project for the Recovery of the Historical Memory." The project's findings, entitled

Guatemala: Never Again, were published on April 24, 1998. Two days after the findings were released, Bishop Juan Gerardi, the coordinator of the project, was murdered. His murder has never been solved, but many believe the military was behind it.

Bishop Juan Gerardi had been bishop of El Quiche in the highlands of northwestern Guatemala, that had been the scene of army massacres of Mayan peasants back in 1980, and Gerardi had closed down the diocese. When presenting the Report, the 75 year old Gerardi had stated: "Discovering truth is painful, but it is without a doubt a healthy and liberating action. Forgiving does not mean forgetting." Gerardi's death and the intimidation of Human Rights Activists demonstrate that the 1996 Peace Accord still faces major obstacles in becoming a reality for Guatemalans.

One year later, on April 25, 1999, 80,000 Guatemalans gathered for an anniversary Mass for Gerardi. In his homily Bishop Gerardo Flores called on Catholics to follow the example of the murdered bishop. "He dreamed of building a better country", Flores preached. "I am in no doubt that the seeds he sowed and nourished with his blood will eventually bear fruit."

A sad footnote to this brief history is a recent decision by Guatemala's highest Court allowing General Efrain Rios Montt, to run for the Presidency of the country. The Human Rights Office of the Guatemala City archdiocese has criticized the decision as reported in the *National Catholic Reporter* on August 1, 2003. As noted, Rios Montt, (eulogized by Ronald Reagan as a man of great personal integrity), was President of Guatemala for 17 months during 1982-83. Tom Roberts, in the *National Catholic Reporter*, wrote that his reign of terror oversaw the butchering of thousands. In his artlce he included the following quote from the *New York Times*: "there will be virtually nothing to stop him, and his network of former military officers, of returning Guatemala to the dark ages". (Tom Roberts, *National Catholic Reporter*, August 15, 2003.)

Argentina

One would hardly imagine that the atrocities committed in Guatemala could find their equal. However, in Argentina, with a population of 35 million, 85 percent being of European descent, we see an old-world sophisticated society that regressed to the point of becoming a savage society. The social fabric of the country disintegrated during the country's "dirty war" of 1976-1983. Like her neighbours on the South American continent, Argentina used the ideology of the National Security State to unleash a wave of violence and terror. Many have compared the levels of brutality and terror inflicted on the civil population by the military to Hitler's Germany.

The scope of the terror is revealed in the statistics compiled by Amnesty International, the United Nations, the Catholic Church, and the World Council of Churches.

- 20,000 people detained or disappeared between 1976 and 1978
- 12,000 political prisoners in regular prisons or concentration camps by 1977
- Political killings averaged seven persons a day
- Systematic cleansing of society of all elements who voiced opposition
- The introduction and use of sadistic methods of torture and confinement. Special units of the military, indoctrinated and trained as 'torture' specialists.

The fundamental issue was popular rule. Penny Lernoux points out in her book, *Cry of the People*, that although the causes of violence in Argentina were complex, the source of the violence could be traced to the lingering tensions between the military institution and its allies in the wealthy classes, and the labour movement and its allies within the middle classes.

Argentina in the 1940s had developed a strong trade union movement. Workers were first and second generation immigrants from Italy and Spain, and the country became industrialized very quickly. Juan Peron had organized the labour movement, and used it as his power base when he first took power (1943-1945). Even though Peron was a corrupt, fascist dictator, he adroitly used the labour movement (presenting himself as its saviour), to counter the old alliance of the military and the power elite. Ever the consummate politician and nationalist, by changing this balance of power, he won over the masses. He was a master at the game of divide and conquer.

Though he had been ousted from power and exiled to Spain in 1955, his shadow and the masses in the working and middle classes were a threat to the military and the elite of the country. Even from exile his aura influenced the population. He encouraged the left to organize a guerrilla movement to harass the military. By 1973 he was able to return home, and again took up the Presidency. But once back in power the myth of Peron was exposed and the young turned their back on him. These former Peronistas turned to guerrilla warfare, a movement he himself had encouraged against the military. His disillusioned right wing followers formed paramilitary and death squads.

With the death of Peron, his wife Isabel, became President. But she was inept, with few political skills, and soon handed over power to the Peronistas of the right. Thus a bloody encounter between left and right was inevitable. Although the military had distrusted civilian rule, they had been outfoxed by Peron.

By 1976 the stage was set for a bloodbath with the establishment of the Argentine Anti-Communist Alliance (AAA). The military had themselves added to the instability of the country and the guerrilla revolt that ensued through their brutal repression and constant interference in political life. With the creation of Anti-Communist Alliance a free hand was given to the military and police to torture, murder and blackmail victims. This was total war. The enemies of the state were not only the guerrillas, but also union leaders, students, journalists, politicians and priests, as well as right-wing business people.

As in other Latin American countries, the United States was heavily involved in the unfolding tragedy within Argentina. Between 1950-1976 Argentina received $352.4 million in U.S. military credits. Four thousand military personnel, including the head of the dreaded Secret Service, were trained in the United States and in the Panama Canal Zone.

During the Ongonia dictatorship (1966-70) the CIA in Buenos Aires was well aware of the formation of right-wing paramilitary and death squads, and the growing use of torture. "If you think the Brazilian police torture methods are bad, you should see what goes on in Argentine prisons", was the comment of one CIA agent. The Argentine Federal Police were the CIA's principal liaison in Buenos Aries, assisting the agency in telephone tapping and other operations, according to Philip Agee's *CIA Diary*. There is ample evidence that the AAA death squads were creatures of this same police force.

In May of 1974 the American government agreed to give the Argentine police increased training and funding for narcotics enforcement. Two hundred and sixty Argentine police officers attended seminars in the United States and the Panama Canal Zone under the narcotics program. The United States also funded the acquisition of vehicles, communications and laboratories. The irony of it all was that the Social Welfare Minister Lopez Rega, who controlled the police, was involved with other ranking ministers in the trafficking of cocaine in the country. The Drug Enforcement Agency became a cover for the CIA and the use of funds for fighting drugs were used for fighting the guerrillas.

When Juan Peron returned to power in 1973 anti-Semitism became rampant throughout the country. Communism and the economic situation were blamed on the Jewish community of 400,000. Jews were openly persecuted, and Peron made Argentina a world centre for the publication and distribution of Nazi literature. Official protection was given to Nazi war criminals. Since the death of Peron this anti-Semitic campaign has fostered and been promoted.

There was also a campaign against the progressive sector of the Catholic Church. Propaganda linked the progressive wing of the church with world Judaism and Marxism. By the end of 1977, 17 priests and nuns had been murdered and thirty were in prison. In a fake automobile accident security forces had killed Enrique Angelelli, the bishop of La Rioja. This diocese is located on the impoverished northeast; a territory of huge haciendas and Indian serfs. Angelelli was an outspoken advocate for human rights.

One of the tragic consequences of the "Dirty War" was the successful use of the Catholic hierarchy and the Catholic Church in the military's reign of repression and murder. There is mounting evidence that the church officially condoned the National Security strategy, and willing participated with the military. The enemy of course, was communism.

A book written in 1986 by Emilio Mignone – *Witness to the Truth* – and sub-titled, "The Complicity of the Church and Dictatorship in Argentina 1976-1983", presents evidence that the hierarchy supported the regime and its killings. Mignone was also an early accuser of Pio Laghi, the pro-Nuncio to Argentina at the time (Laghi, now a retired cardinal, was subsequently Nuncio to the United States). Mignone states that Laghi was a friend and tennis partner of Eduardo Massera, Commander-in-Chief of the navy, and must have been aware of what was happening. Massera was a member of the junta that overthrew Isabel Peron.

Mignone charges that Laghi was seen in detention centres, and was consulted as to whether prisoners should be spared or killed. He also accused Laghi of silencing international protests. Mignone, a lawyer and University professor, states that "Laghi knew what was happening, and had knowledge from the beginning of the characteristics of the repressive regime created by the military." Certainly some of Laghi's public statements at the time seem to indicate he favoured the regime and its objectives of ridding the state of undesirables. Laghi has always vehemently denied such accusations.

Emilio Mignone recounts the story of Robert Cox, editor of the *Buenos Aires Herald* 1968-1979. In 1976 three priests and two seminarians were murdered. Cox testified at the trial that he was a neighbour and friendly with Laghi, that Laghi had told him he was convinced the murders were the work of the security forces. Cox also claimed that he could remember the exact words of Laghi, that he had said, "I had to give communion to General Suarez,... imagine what I felt as a priest. I felt like hitting him in the face with my fist." Mignone asks, "How can one justify his elaborate praise for the armed forces, when he was convinced that what they were doing was criminal?"

In 1997, the Mothers of the Plaza da Mayo petitioned the Italian government to prosecute Cardinal Pio Laghi as an accomplice to the brutal regime that terrorized their nation. They charged that they could produce 20 witnesses that would testify against Laghi. These Mothers of the Plaza are a group of women who gathered each week in the Plaza da Mayo to demand answers as to the whereabouts of their "disappeared children." The Vatican daily newspaper, *L'Osservatore Romano*, stated that the charges were unjust, dishonest and historically wrong.

Robert Cox has stated that Argentina has never come to grips with healing the terrible injustices and brutality of the "Dirty War", and that it needs a Truth Commission. "So far the country's leaders have taken the path of evasion of the truth. "The Mothers of the Plaza have almost a sacred role to play as the conscience of democratic Argentina, as a reminder of the time when the nation had no conscience."

A new book by newspaper columnist Horacio Verbitsky entitled *The Flight Confessions of an Argentine Dirty Warrior* (New Press, 1986) written after Adolfo Francisco Scilingo, a former Lieutenant Commander of the notorious Navy School of Mechanics, had approached Verbitsky two years earlier. Scilingo, who had been stripped of his rank on fraud charges, was retaliating against senior officers who were being pardoned of crimes. He related to Verbitsky in detail what had long been suspected. The dumping of drugged, and manacled prisoners into the Atlantic Ocean from a Navy Skyvan each Wednesday. Admiral Ruben Jacinto Chamoro, Commander of the concentration camp, interrogated prisoners. He decided who was to live and who was to die. Between 1,500 to 2,000 prisoners were disposed of in this manner. According to Scilingo he only made two such flights. After the first he was comforted by a chaplain. "He was telling me it was a Christian death, they did not suffer, it was not traumatic, they had to be eliminated, war was war, and even the Bible provided for eliminating the weeds from the wheat field."

Scilingo's chilling account of such military madness, and his personal revelations, illustrates how even trained killers were forever haunted by their cowardly and inhumane acts of cruelty.

As Robert Cox, the former editor of the *Buenos Aires Herald,* has stated, Argentina has never come to grips with its dirty past, and certainly needs a Truth Commission. But the Argentine church as well needs to confront its shameful past. Only one bishop has ever publicly acknowledged any wrongdoing. At Easter in 1997 Bishop Miguel Esteban Hesayne of Patagonia expressed regrets, by stating that the Conference of Bishops "has sat down to eat with those we called torturers. We have received them in the heart of the Conference of Bishops so that they could excuse themselves, or rather so that they could try to deceive us by claiming that these were merely excesses."

While bishops who have stood with the poor and the marginalized have been subjected to church investigation, no one in the hierarchy in Argentina has ever been censured or publicly reprimanded for their stand with the military. Argentina and her leaders, and the Roman Catholic Church, need to beg forgiveness for their crimes and collusion against their people.

Sources

The Tablet, January 11, 1997 (London England)

Michael Farrell, *National Catholic Reporter*, September 20, 1996, and June 20, 1997.

Gary MacEoin, Emilio Mignone, *Witness to the Truth*, Orbis Books, 1986.

Horacio Verbitsky, *The Flight Confessions of an Argentine Dirty Warrior*, New Press, 1996.

Chile

Father Ronaldo Munoz, a Chilean theologian has written: "Some Catholics think of the church as called exclusively to provide spiritual consolation to nourish the elevation of the soul.... The church does this through religious beliefs and norms of personal morality organized mainly around worship, thus orienting the faithful toward eternal life. People who think this way are surprised to hear that the church's most traditional mission is to denounce social injustice, that she is called to be *a voice of those without a voice.*"

"The poor must have the Good News of Jesus Christ announced to them. They must have real opportunities to commit themselves to their own cause, in an authentic community of believers. They must be given a concrete sign of that new order of justice and communion, which Jesus proclaimed, as the Kingdom of God."

The detention and house arrest of General Augusto Pinochet of Chile, in October of 1998 in London, England, made international headlines. It brought to world attention the tragedy of Chile's recent past. A British High Court had ruled in favour of extradition proceedings against Pinochet, which would send him to Spain to stand trial for human rights crimes. While the aged general withered away in a rented mansion on the outskirts of London, and was comforted by Margaret Thatcher, his battery of lawyers had continued their legal manoeuvreing to prevent this extradition.

Pinochet's arrest and the extradition process brought against him by the Spanish Judge Baltasar Garzon, has allowed the world to examine his 17-year bloody dictatorship in Chile. An article in the *Toronto Star* by Linda Diebel, the *Star's* Latin American correspondent (03/04/99) tells the story of Francisco Ruiz, a victim of Pinochet's National Security State strategy back in 1973. Ruiz is quoted as saying, "You would never pick him out in the street as anyone special, just as you would never pick out any of the women and men who stamped burning cigarettes into the flesh of prisoners, applied electric shocks to genitals, jammed live rats up vaginas, broke ribs, smashed skulls, or sliced abdomens so people would sink when tossed out of helicopters into the sea, or dreamed up other ways of inflicting pain."

Francisco Ruiz, now a Canadian, was one of the 6,000 political refugees that Canada rescued from Pinochet's Chile. Fingered by DINA Agents (Chile's Secret Police), Ruiz was incarcerated in Vila Grimaldi, a prison for dissidents. He was subsequently shipped to Puchancavi, a concentration camp on the Pacific coast. Here he was subjected to electric shock treatments, near drowning, penothol, slashings and other instruments of torture. Francisco Ruiz was saved from death and further torture, he believes, through the intervention of Cardinal Raul Silva, the Archbishop of Santiago during Pinochet's military dictatorship in Chile.

The military coup led by General Augusto Pinochet took place on the night of September 11, 1973. Tanks and the military took over Santiago. Chilean airforce Hawker Hunter planes fired rockets into Lan Moneda, the presidential palace. President Salvador Allende, in his second floor offices is said to have committed suicide. As Linda Diebel reports, it has been said that as the bombing and fighting took place, Allende had asked for his trusted General, "where is Augusto?" General Augusto Pinochet had betrayed his President, and was busy engineering a coup against the duly elected President of the country.

Days and weeks of even greater horror followed the night of terror, as Pinochet's brutal military rounded up thousands of so-called dissidents. Santiago's soccer stadium became the holding depot as thousands of men and women who were apprehended, tortured, and sent out to prisons and concentration camps awaited decisions on their fate. These so-called dissidents were considered to be the scum of the earth and had to be eradicated for the sake of National Security.

Chile, a country of 12 million, had long been a nation that prided itself for its democratic and civilized behaviour. In addition to the Christian Democratic Party, Chilean socialists and communists were well established in the political arena. They had had a long history of participation in the country's political life. Their strength came from their popularity amongst the working class.

The Christian Democrat Government of Eduardo Frei was unable to deliver on promised reforms. Like the rest of Latin America, a small elite controlled industry, finance and most of the land. The middle classes identified with the elite. The poorer classes and workers favoured the policies of the socialists and the communists. With the Frei government stalled on much needed reform, the stage was set for a Socialist victory. There was no meeting of minds or compromise between the left and the right.

The Catholic Church was wary of both the socialist and the communists; the hierarchy favoured the Christian Democrats. The United States Government was opposed to Allende and his Socialists. In the months leading up to the election that pitted the Christian Democrats of Eduardo Frei against the Socialist forces of Allende, the CIA was heavily involved in campaigning against Allende. Theirs was an unholy alliance between the conservative church and the CIA.

Many church people were active agents of the CIA both as informers and as activists supported by American money. Roger Vekemans, a well known Belgian Jesuit, and a rabid anti-communist activist, was supported by the CIA and the American Government in his crusade, not just against communism, but any form of socialism. He received millions of dollars to finance projects, and mount a campaign against Allende. An ultra-conservative Catholic group, 'Tradition, Family and Country', founded in Brasil, waged all-out warfare against leftists and any church leaders or groups that were suspected of sympathies for civil reform or rights for the poor.

As well as the American government's grant of $13 million to defeat Allende's Socialists, many American companies with huge financial interests in Chile were active prior to the election trying to influence its outcome. I.T.& T., Anaconda and Kennicott Copper promoted the platform of Frei and his Christian Democrats. They certainly supported the coup when the Allende government attempted to nationalize the copper industry. Noranda Mines of Canada was also out to get rid of Allende.

Allende's attempts at reform for the poor brought furious opposition from the right within the country. The thin veneer of discrimination that was always present in Chilean society became public as the elite revolted against such reforms. With the right staunchly against him, and the Nixon Administration hostile toward him, Allende's days were numbered. The left wing within his government had pushed too hard. Allende had no room to move.

The bloody coup that was initiated on the night of September 11, 1973 brought an unmitigated reign of terror upon people like Francisco Ruiz and thousands of his fellow Chileans. In the first weeks following the coup, Amnesty International estimates that between 5,000 and 30,000 people died. Between the years 1973 and 1986, 151,000 Chileans went to prison, or were detained for political reasons. Chile, like Brazil, was governed by the Doctrine of National Security.

The Vicariate of Solidarity (human rights organization), set up by the Catholic Church under the leadership of Cardinal Raul Silva, dealt with over 300,000 human rights violations in its first ten years. Silva became 'the conscience of Chile' in his open criticism of the harsh repression, the terrible brutality and human rights abuses of Pinochet's culture of death. Thus, the progressive church became the enemy of the state. Four hundred priests were expelled from the country in the first 13 years of the dictatorship. Bishops, priests and lay workers who worked with the families of the 'disappeared' and with the poor, suffered frequent attacks from the military. Ten priests were imprisoned and one killed. By 1986 most of the hierarchy and the clergy, including the conservatives, were opposed to Augusto Pinochet and his military regime.

It is important to note that the Papal Nuncio in Santiago, Archbishop Angelo Sodano opposed Cardinal Raul Silva and voiced opposition to Cardinal Silva's public statements against the Pinochet regime. Sodano was a great defender of Pinochet and his regime. The Vatican, too, came to favour conservative rapprochement with the government. Sodano, now a Cardinal, is the Vatican's Secretary of State, under John Paul II.

Selected Bibliography

Books

Abbott, Walter M. (SJ), editor, *The Documents of Vatican II*, The America Press, New York: 1966.

Bernstein & Politi, *His Holiness, John Paul II*, Doubleday Publishing, New York: 1996.

Boff, Leonardo, *Faith on the Edge*, Orbis Books, New York: 1991

Diedrich, Bernard, *Trujillo: The Death of a Dictator*, Little Brown and Company, New York: 1978.

Dunn, Joseph, *The Rest of Us Catholics*, Templegate Press, Illinois: 1994.

Gutierrez, Gustavo, *The Theology of Liberation*, Orbis Books, New York: 1972.

Gutierrez, Gustavo, *The God of Life*, Orbis Books, New York: 1991.

Lernoux, Penny, *Cry Of the People*, Penguin Books, 1982.

Lernoux, Penny, *People of God*, Penguin Books, 1989.

Levine, Harold, *Central America*, Life World Library, Time Incorporated, New York: 1968.

Mignone, Emilio F., *Witness to the Truth*, Orbis Books, New York: 1988.

Ribeiro, Sylvia de Oliveira, *E Deus visitou o seu Povo*, Edua, Manaus, Amazon: 2003.

Stourton, Edward, *Absolute Truth*, Penguin Books, London: 1998.

Szula, Tad, *John Paul II*, Scribner Books, New York: 1995.

Torres, Camilo, *Revolutionary Writings*, Herder and Herder, NewYork: 1969.

Verbitsky, Horacio, *The Flight Confessions of an Argentine Dirty Warrior*, New Press, 1966.

Articles

National Catholic Reporter
  Peter Hebblethwaite 15/01/91
  Peter Hebblethwaite 15/02/91

    Editorial, 17/06/88
    Francis McDonagh, 02/06/95
    Michael Farrell, 20/09/96
    Gary MacEoin, 20/06/97, 10/09/99, 24/04/99
    Tom Roberts, *Guatemala Report*,12/03/99
    Editorial Report, 19/11/99
    Robert Drinan SJ, *U.S. Foreign Policy*, 09/04/99
    Jose Comblin, *Global Perspectives*, 02/07/003, 09/07/003,
    web site edition

The Tablet, London, 11/01/97

Latin American Press, 16/10/86

Jim Loney, *Catholic New Times*, 28/11/99

Linda Diebel, *Toronto Star*, 07/04/99

John Elson, "John Paul II", *Time Magazine*, 02/01/95

Carl Bernstein, "The Holy Alliance", *Time Magazine,* 24/02/92

Life Magazine, New York, *The Galindez Case*, 1957-58

Acknowledgements

I wish to express my sincere gratitude to all those friends and family members who encouraged me to publish this manuscript.

I acknowledge those who helped me with their objective critique and professional help: Pat Hancock of Toronto; Harry MacNeil and Claude Geougeon, now deceased, of Ottawa; Ken MacAulay and John Walsh of Scarboro Missions; Justice Norman Nadeau of Craighurst; Joanna Manning of Toronto; and Madeline Ritchie of Elmvale.

A special thank you to my nephew James Barry, and to Gerry Hedican, both of whom worked tirelessly on the manuscript.

Thanks to James Barry, and to the *Scarboro Missions* for the use of their photos.

I am grateful to Pat McDermott and Bob Michener of Toronto, for their professional help in marketing, and Jillian Hedican for the cover illustration.

Finally, to my editor and publisher Greg Humbert and Tomiko Publications, I owe a special debt of gratitude for accompanying and working with me on this project.

abracos
Mike